The Psychodynamic Image

The Psychodynamic Image is the first selection of John D. Sutherland's major papers. It provides an overview of the development of his thought on self and society and reveals the extent of his contribution to the field of mental health.

Jill Savege Scharff introduces Sutherland's most important and influential essays. These reflect his range as a theoretician, moving easily from the intrapsychic to the interpersonal level, building bridges between points of view and integrating psychoanalytic and social theories. Sutherland's work calls for changes at the individual level through understanding conflicts and unconscious processes as aspects of parts of the self in interaction. He inspires respect and understanding of the self and its drive toward autonomy.

Sutherland's papers push the boundaries of psychoanalytic thinking and succeed in demonstrating the wide relevance of psychoanalysis. They will be of great interest to psychoanalysts, psychotherapists, counsellors and social workers.

John D. Sutherland served as Director of the Tavistock Centre 1947–1968, was Sloan Professor at the Menninger Clinic, and distinguished guest lecturer at Austen Riggs, the Institute of Contemporary Psychotherapy, and the Washington School of Psychiatry.

Jill Savege Scharff is Co-Director of the International Psychotherapy Institute, Clinical Professor of Psychiatry at Georgetown University, Chair of the International Institute for Psychoanalytic Training, and Teaching Analyst at the Washington Psychoanalytic Institute. She is co-editor of *The Legacy of Fairbairn and Sutherland*, and editor of *The Autonomous Self: The Work of John D. Sutherland.*

The Psychodynamic Image

John D. Sutherland on Self in Society

Edited by Jill Savege Scharff

Routledge
Taylor & Francis Group
LONDON AND NEW YORK

First published 2007 by Routledge
27 Church Road, Hove, East Sussex BN3 2FA

Simultaneously published in the USA and Canada
by Taylor & Francis Inc
270 Madison Avenue, New York, NY 10016

Routledge is an imprint of the Taylor & Francis Group, an informa business

Typeset in Times by Garfield Morgan, Swansea, West Glamorgan
Printed and bound in Great Britain by TJ International Ltd, Padstow, Cornwall
Cover design by Sandra Heath

This publication has been produced with paper manufactured to strict environmental standards and with pulp derived from sustainable forests.

British Library Cataloguing in Publication Data
A catalogue record for this book is available from the British Library

Library of Congress Cataloging-in-Publication Data
The psychodynamic image : John D. Sutherland on self and society /
edited by Jill Savege Scharff.
p. cm.
Includes bibliographical references and index.
ISBN-13: 978-0-415-41183-7 (hbk)
ISBN-10: 0-415-41183-1 (hbk)
ISBN-13: 978-0-415-41184-4 (pbk)
ISBN-10: 0-415-41184-X (pbk)
1. Sutherland, John D. (John Derg) 2. Self. 3. Self-perception
–social aspects. 4. Social psychology. 5. Psychoanalysis.
I. Scharff, Jill Savege.
[DNLM: 1. Sutherland, John D. (John Derg). 2. Psychoanalytic
Theory–Collected Works. 3. Psychoanalysis–Collected Works.
4. Ego–Collected Works. WM460 P97793 2007]
BF697.P759 2007

2006021392

ISBN: 978-0-415-41183-7 (hbk)
ISBN: 978-0-415-41184-4 (pbk)

For David

Contents

Biographies

The author

John D. Sutherland CBE, FRCPsych, FRCPE, PhD served as editor of the *British Journal of Medical Psychology*, the *International Journal of Psycho-Analysis*, and the *International Psycho-Analytic Library* (producing twenty-eight books). Analyzed by Sylvia Payne, he qualified in 1948, became a member of the British Psychoanalytical Society in 1952, and training analyst in 1954, responsible for publications and training including the development of a common basic curriculum for candidates. In London he was Director of the Tavistock Centre from 1947 to 1968. In the United States, he was Sloan Professor at the Menninger Clinic, and distinguished guest lecturer at Austen Riggs, the Institute of Contemporary Psychotherapy, and the Washington School of Psychiatry. In Edinburgh, leading a group of colleagues, he co-founded the Scottish Institute of Human Relations. He was the author of many papers published in the major journals and of *Fairbairn's Journey to the Interior*, his perceptive biography written at the age of 83! For his contributions to mental health he received the Order of Commander of the British Empire, an honour given to only two other analysts, John Bowlby and Anna Freud.

The editor

Jill Savege Scharff MD is Co-Director of the International Psychotherapy Institute and Chair of its International Institute for Psychoanalytic Training in Chevy Chase, Maryland, USA, Clinical Professor of Psychiatry, Georgetown University, and Teaching Analyst, Washington Psychoanalytic Institute, both in Washington DC. She has authored, co-authored, and edited many books, including *The Legacy of Fairbairn and Sutherland*, *The Autonomous Self: The Work of John D. Sutherland*, *Self Hatred in Psychoanalysis*, *The Primer of Object Relations (2nd edition)*, *Object Relations Family Therapy*, *Object Relations Couple Therapy*, *Object Relations*

Individual Therapy, *Projective and Introjective Identification and the Use of the Therapist's Self*, *Foundations of Object Relations Family Therapy*, and *Tuning the Therapeutic Instrument.*

Preface

The year 2005 was the centenary of the birth of John D. Sutherland, a suitable time to celebrate his contribution as a remarkable thinker and man of action for mental health. He devoted his full-time work to managing staff, teaching and supervising trainees, developing programs, and working with the community to build a caring community of mental health service providers, he maintained a full analytic private practice, and he also edited the major psychoanalytic publications. Sutherland was unusual as an analyst in that he shifted easily between levels of scale from the intrapsychic to the interpersonal level, and from self to society, building bridges between points of view, and integrating psychoanalytic and social theories (Kohon 1996). Because of the scope and depth of his vision, Sutherland's work has relevance for psychoanalysis, psychotherapy, social work, community development, and organizational consultation.

In his theory of development across the life cycle, Sutherland viewed individual and society in a process of mutual influence. In his practice, he moved readily from the one to the other as a venue for evoking change. In his teaching he was respectful of all points of view, generous and encouraging of debate and inquiry. In his editing he encouraged original contributions. In his writing, however, he was somewhat blocked, choosing to promote the work of other minds that he regarded as more brilliant and original than his own. He wrote papers, of course, but he did not see their value as a body of work. As editor of the International Psychoanalytic Library, he brought twenty-eight books to completion for others but not for himself. So after his death, it fell to me to put all his papers and some of his keynote speeches together posthumously in a comprehensive collection, *The Autonomous Self: The Work of John D. Sutherland* (1994).

Now one hundred years since his birth, I want to select the pivotal papers that led to his thinking about the self in relation to society, and those written in his retirement that push the boundary of psychoanalytic thinking. How did Sutherland become capable of such original writing after years of editing and expository teaching? Toward the end of his life, while writing a biography of Fairbairn (yet another devotion to the work of others), Sutherland analyzed his negative attitude toward his own productivity and creativity. He found that he had been envious of his parents' union, and attacked it by keeping separate in his own mind the industrious qualities he inherited from his mother, from the more relaxed contemplative nature of his father. This insight allowed him to bring both aspects of himself together in his self, which allowed for the union of male and female elements, thinking and feeling, and resulted in a tremendous flow of creativity late in life. From deep inside his own experience, he realized the value of self analysis and the importance of integration of aspects of the self. This prompted him to conceive of the need for a theory of the self and pursue it much more actively than before. He did this by writing out his ideas and inviting study groups to discuss them in the light of their clinical experience.

As a woman editor, I have taken the liberty of broadening Sutherland's use of "he" as a generic pronoun, a form that was standard in his time, and was no indication of prejudice on his part. He was devoted to his wife and daughter, respected and liked professional women, and supported the training of women mental health professionals, and so I think he would be glad to move with the times. I would have liked to update the title of Chapter 8, "The Psychodynamic Image of Man," so as to include the female of the species: for instance, the psychodynamic image of the human race, of the person, or of man *and* woman. Whatever I chose sounded awkward or inaccurate. "Man" was the only word that captured the individual, the group, and the human race. In addition, "The Psychodynamic Image of Man" is Sutherland's most quoted paper in Scotland. So the title of the chapter remains as it was in the original paper.

It is too bad that Sutherland did not live to complete his project on developing a theory of the self. It is too bad that his concepts have not been widely available, especially in Great Britain where he lived and worked. My goal in this volume is to promote his work (as he did for so many others), and so fuel the development of a psychoanalytically sophisticated generation of trainees and increase interest in psychoanalysis by making it relevant to the wider society.

Acknowledgments

I want to express my thanks to Anne Sutherland, heir of the late John D. Sutherland, and the publishing houses, journals, and training institutions for permission to reprint the following articles. Chapter 1, based on a re-edited lecture "On Becoming and Being a Person" (1990), is printed by permission of the Washington School of Psychiatry, Washington DC. Chapter 2 features the paper "Object-Relations Theory and the Conceptual Model of Psychoanalysis" (1963) from the *British Journal of Medical Psychology* 36: 109–124 and is reprinted by kind permission of the British Psychological Society. Chapter 3, featuring "The British Object Relations Theorists: The Contributions of Balint, Winnicott, Fairbairn, Guntrip" (1980) was originally published in the *Journal of the American Psychoanalytic Association* 28: 829–960 and is reprinted with permission. © 1980 American Psychoanalytic Association. All rights reserved. Chapter 4 is based on "Recent Advances in the Understanding of Small Groups, Their Disorders and Treatment" (1965) and is reprinted from *Psychotherapy and Psychosomatics* 13: 110–125 with permission of S. Karger AG, Basel. Chapter 5 comes from "Psychoanalysis in the Post-industrial Society" (1969) which appeared in the *International Journal of Psycho-Analysis* 50: 673–682 and is reprinted by permission of Anne Sutherland to whom copyright has reverted. Chapter 6, based on "The Self and Object Relations: A Challenge to Psychoanalysis" (1973), was published in the *Bulletin of the Menninger Clinic* 47(6): 525–541 in 1983 and Chapter 9, "The Autonomous Self" (1980), was published in the *Bulletin of the Menninger Clinic* 57(1): 3–32 in 1998. Both articles are reprinted for one time use including world rights in all languages, non-exclusive permission granted by The Guilford Press. Chapter 7 is based on "The Self and Personal (Object) Relations" (1978) which was first published in *The Legacy of Fairbairn and Sutherland*, ed. Jill S. Scharff, pp. 187–201, and is reprinted courtesy of Anne Sutherland and by permission of Routledge. Chapter 8, comprising "The Psychodynamic Image of Man: A Philosophy for the Caring Professions" (1979), was read as The Malcolm Millar Lecture of 1979 at the University of Aberdeen, Scotland and as the Frieda Fromm-Reichmann

Lecture at the Washington School of Psychiatry, Washington DC and is reprinted by permission of both institutions.

I owe many thanks to Kate Hawes for believing in the value of a Sutherland selection, and to the other editors, designers, and promotional staff of Routledge, especially production editor Kathryn Russel and editorial assistant Claire Lipscomb. I am deeply appreciative of the Sutherland Trust's support of my interest in preserving the Sutherland legacy, the administrative help of Jo Hilton, June Nelson, and Jill Prentice, and the collegial encouragement of Molly Ludlam, Colin Kirkwood, and Eileen Francis. I am delighted that the Scottish Institute of Human Relations, of which Sutherland was a co-founder, contributed the cover art for the book jacket design. Ana Granados willingly typed the entire manuscript with amazing accuracy; Anna Innes helped me with everything else, and without them I would have been lost. My children are gone from the home now, so I don't need to apologize for writing paragraphs in my head during dinner, but I want them to know that I am grateful for their forbearance as adults when I have been preoccupied.

Without Anne Sutherland this book could not have happened. I am grateful to her for giving me permission to select these papers, for providing me with family photographs to broaden my understanding of her father, and for generally encouraging my efforts. Last but not least I am grateful to my husband for his love and for his support of my interest in the ideas of Jock Sutherland.

Introduction

Jill Savege Scharff

The man known as Jock

What kind of a thinker, leader, and man was John D. Sutherland? How better to begin my introduction of the man than to paraphrase what his collaborators say about him. On the anniversary of his birth, the Sutherland Trust convened colleagues from the Scottish Institute of Human Relations for a conversation about the man they knew and loved as "Jock." Colin Kirkwood (2005) described Sutherland as a collaborator and a bridge builder, free from orthodoxy and wide-ranging in his reading and academic contacts. Sutherland was able to implement his innovative, comprehensive vision thanks to his personal qualities of warmth, openness, curiosity, sincerity, an intelligent vitality looking toward others, and a well-developed enabling function. He gathered together a disparate collection of highly creative and independent-minded people who evoked from one another a combination of energy and direction and practical action of the highest quality. This is how he was able to transcend the ivory tower of psychoanalysis and use it to reach out to the caring professions, business organizations, and the wider community (Kirkwood 2005).

Molly Ludlam (2005) evoked Sutherland's passion for developing and maintaining the institution he had co-founded as an open learning system. Sutherland would be so pleased to hear from her that his colleagues are taking up the challenge to be continually responsive to the environment and maintain an open learning system, which is increasingly difficult in the atmosphere of adversity stemming from the prevalence of biological treatments, cognitive behavioral methodologies, and so-called "evidence-based" techniques. He had no time for jargon and so he would agree that psychoanalysts today must develop their message in dialogue with the community and refine their message until it is clear and relevant.

In his psychoanalytic theorizing, Sutherland was committed to the object relations perspective and in particular to the idea that affects were the engine of human development, long before access to sophisticated neurobiological research methods. He always admired the work of Colwyn

Trevarthen and would have delighted in Trevarthen's statement that descriptive analysis, aided by television and processing of audio records, of exactly how expressions are exchanged between mother and infant has demonstrated the role of shared rhythms and immediate intuitive transmission of feelings. The motivating processes in single minds, including aesthetic and moral feelings, are shown to be transmitted between brains by immediate sympathy for their conscious and unconscious qualities. The capacity for human sympathy, as described by the philosophers of the Scottish Enlightenment, is a natural brain function. The baby is born with it (Trevarthen 2005).

Sutherland's theory base

Sutherland was always impressed by what the baby is born with. The baby comes ready to relate, create joy, inspire devotion, and elicit care. To him, these were signs of a competent ego. That is why he was so attracted to Fairbairn's theory of object relations and so turned off by instinct theory. Of course, he also admired Fairbairn's systematic, empirical, philosophical argument and appreciated its academic rigor and clinical relevance. Unlike Freud who had analyzed phenomena from the outside looking in, Fairbairn began from the center of the personality (Fairbairn 1952a, Sutherland 1989). Fairbairn thought that the infant was born with a whole ego, and there he caught Sutherland's imagination. According to Fairbairn, over the course of experience dealing with those who relate to and care for the infant, this pristine ego begins to split into parts by a process of dissociating one from another and repressing unacceptable parts while allowing others to remain in consciousness. All this made sense to Sutherland. He had noticed that infants at birth seemed quite purposeful, capable of taking initiative and getting what they wanted. He immediately thought that this infant activity was evidence of an ego functioning from the moment of birth, not merely a set of instinctual responses. Working in psychotherapy and psychoanalysis, he found that his patients revealed various aspects of themselves, some of which functioned collaboratively and others of which remained fragmented. He took this as evidence of the splitting and repression that Fairbairn had described. He also noticed that his patients tended to people their worlds with good and bad objects in reflection of an inner state of mind in which experience has been sorted and stored as good and bad.

Fairbairn emphasized the need to internalize the bad object, to split it off from the ego and repress it actively in order to control the frustrating feelings associated with it, this process of internalization then becoming the basis for the structuring of the self. The self tries to control the bad object so as not to be controlled by it, but what happens if the experience is good? Sutherland supposed that the good object simply infuses the self with its goodness and colors the self in a positive and hopeful tone, instead of having to be controlled inside the self as an object. As he used to put it, the good object suffuses the self, giving it a warm glow. Sutherland was particularly interested in affect as the driving force for the creation of psychic structure. It is affect that connects the ego's perception of an experience; it is the nature of the affect that colors the object as good or bad; and it is the strength of the affect that determines whether the object can be held in consciousness or must be repressed. Affect connects each part of the ego with the corresponding part of the object to which it relates. New research findings on the neurobiological basis for affect regulation show that structure follows the experience of affect in relation to the mother's attunement (Schore 1994).

Sutherland was intellectually sophisticated, yet he spoke simply. Psychologist, physician, psychiatrist, group therapist, industrial consultant, teacher, writer, editor, and psychoanalyst, he had read widely and could argue with behaviorists as well as with ego psychologists from inside their own camps using their terminology. Yet in his own clinical work and teaching he liked to keep it simple, using words closely related to infantile experience, as he called them, "four-letter words like love, hate, milk, bits." He did not speak of persecutory objects: he talked in terms of a part of the self that feels terrible. He did not speak of ambivalence: he spoke of a part that hates and a part that loves. I did not hear him use the terms projective identification or object relations: he talked about making someone feel bad. I cannot imagine him saying to a patient, "You are projecting your feelings of rage into your mother." He might say, "You feel that your mother has a terrible anger at you, because you bring it out in her because of how dreadfully angry you are at her that she wasn't there for you when you longed to be with her and needed her desperately." It is typical of him to use words like dreadful, desperate, terrible, to emphasize the force of the primitive affects.

Sutherland was not concerned about the instincts because, to him, they were subsumed in the internal object relationships unless there had been a breakdown in the creation of the internal object relationships (Padel 1995). Unbridled compulsive sexuality or the aggression of war might seem to validate Freudian theories of pathological psychosexual development and Klein's theory of the death instinct. To Sutherland, these kinds of symptoms are actually the breakdown product of a failed connection between the self and the object. The internal object relationships bind the drives, express the drives, color them, give them meaning, and invest them with interpersonal significance.

Sutherland was respectful of Freud's discovery of psychoanalysis, his essay writing style, his constant revision of his theories, and most of all of his opening the world's eye to the influence of the unconscious and giving analysts a way to work with the underpinnings of neurotic conflict. As I have said, Sutherland did not care for instinct theory at all. Even after Freud arrived at the concept of structural theory, which Sutherland saw as a great advance, it was still built on the drives and was not adequate to explain the wholeness of the person in relationship. That is why Sutherland had to look beyond Freud.

He read Melanie Klein with interest because she too was concerned with the functioning of the ego, but, like Freud, Klein continued with a dual instinct theory. Basically Sutherland could not accept the Kleinian theoretical perspective either, but he did find some practical value in it. Even though he disagreed with Klein's idea that aggression stems from the death instinct, he found her emphasis on aggression, especially hate in the transference, clinically useful. Sutherland has his own ideas on aggression, which go beyond Fairbairn and Klein. More of that later. In general, Sutherland thought that Klein gave too much emphasis to unconscious fantasy and not enough attention to structure.

Looking to the American literature, Sutherland found that, among the Freudians, Hartmann was closest to the object relations theorists in that he focused on the ego, but as something separate from, and in opposition to, the instincts. Sutherland thought that instinct was totally subsumed in ego. He appreciated that Kohut dealt with the self and recommended an empathic stance as a *sine qua non* of therapeutic endeavor but Sutherland thought that Kohut overused his empathy to block aggression. Sutherland thought that Kohut's concept of the bipolar self was a simplification compared to Fairbairn's theory of the ego undergoing multiple splits in response to developmental experiences. Sutherland drew most on Lichtenstein's (1977) view that the self-structure is whole from the start, expects to be treated like a person, and evolves its identity in interactions.

Sutherland took what he could from all sources. He believed strongly that many perspectives were needed to comprehend the complexity of the human personality. But he always resonated most with the work of the British object relations theorists among whom he included Balint, Winnicott, and Guntrip, in addition to his mentor, Fairbairn (Sutherland 1980b). They were beginning to think in terms of the self – by that time no longer regarded as an unscientific term – rather than the ego, a mechanistic concept left over from drive/structural theory, and retained by Fairbairn in respect of Freud even though his theory was a radical revision of Freudian theory. Sutherland liked the deep insights that Balint brought to bear on the basic fault at the center of the self, a fault-line that he discovered in his most narcissistically withdrawn patients. He appreciated Winnicott's concept of the false self, covering, protecting, and expressing the true self in ways acceptable to the environment. With their influence he moved on from the mechanistic term "ego" to the more human "self." But even these theories were disappointing in the end, in that they could not account for growth over time.

Sutherland had concluded that the self is not a linear entity created by the ego out of instincts seeking expression across pre-arranged developmental stages, and eventually having structure imposed on them at the time of the resolution of the Oedipus complex. Instead he saw the self as a gestalt, and he knew that it takes a gestalt to relate to a gestalt. He got the idea of the self as a shape that relates to the shapes that are encountered as the self moves through the life cycle, reconfigures itself in the light of experience with others, is shaped by their shapes, and reshapes them in a mutual interaction. The self is central, but it is made of its relationships. The self is always the agent of action, and it expresses its endopsychic structure in action in its relationships. Sutherland saw the self as "an open system that both molds and is molded by the caretakers" (Averill 1992, p. 427).

Sutherland valued the idea of the self consisting of internal object relationships all in dynamic relation. This view of structure made the most sense to him, but he preferred to think in terms of the many functions and processes of these structures (Padel 1995). He wanted a view of the self as something that continues to grow and develop, not one that is set by resolution of the Oedipal complex, a self that is open to being modified in the light of future experience. His primary concern was always the self in relationship, not the self in isolation. He tried to see how the self develops in the family and in the culture, and how it is sustained in interaction with others throughout the life cycle in work, in play, and in connecting to the institutions of society (Harrow *et al.* 1994). The self must have a central place in the mind of the analyst attempting to understand the patient's conflicts and relationships. Not only that, but Sutherland believed that people who want to be responsive and productive must learn how to think about their own self and become conscious of the various aspects of the expression of the self and its parts.

Sutherland's view of the self is of a structure that engages in various ways at various times for various reasons, changing and unchanging across the life cycle. To develop this line of thinking, Sutherland had to draw on sources outside psychoanalysis. Needing more of a handle on the behavioral change of the human organism as it develops, Sutherland looked to evolution and biology, open systems theory, and holograms to conceptualize the self in a way that was relevant to the late twentieth-century ambience, just as Freud had focused on the force of instincts and their need for control by an equal and opposite force while he was operating in a nineteenth- and early twentieth-century culture of scientific materialism, and psychoanalysts in the twenty-first century working against the backdrop of a rapidly adapting, information-processing global culture frame their concepts in terms of chaos theory (J. Scharff and D. Scharff 1998). Nineteenth-century science, current when Freudian theory was invented, held that all organisms are governed by negative feedback to maintain homeostasis. In that context, the idea of an ego buffeted by the force of the drives, striving to return to the resting state, made sense. In the late twentieth century, however, it was known that the living organism is in a state of non-equilibrium, always interacting with the environment, taking in positive feedback, adapting, changing, growing, and moving forward in an unpredictable, complicated pattern (Prigogine 1976, Jantsch 1980). From there it was a short step to the thinking of Chein (1972) and so to Sutherland's emerging view of the person as the actor in a "continuing set of unending, interacting, interdependent and mutually modifying long-range enterprises" (Chein, 1972, p. 289, quoted in Sutherland 1979, p. 275).

Sutherland's is a process-oriented interpretation of the development of the self. He emphasizes that all parts of the self are in dynamic relation in an open system, the repressed and split-off parts always seeking to rejoin the self, which can then become a whole interacting self. The unconscious parts are always seeking to expand that central ego so as to have it not shorn of the excitement, rage, rejection, abandonment, which had to be repressed. The central ego is not fixed. The self is always in a state of dynamic relationship: its boundaries are shifting, depending on the security of the relationships and the cultural context that it finds itself in. The healthy self with easy access to all its elements has color and vitality. The unhealthy self (which has repressed painful or rejecting elements to avoid being overwhelmed) is relatively empty, bland, neutral, and it operates in a closed system that is hard for the therapist to breach.

Now, what about holograms? A hologram consists of all possible views of a scene collected on a single plane of light-modulating patterns (Negroponte 1995). Sutherland applied the idea of holograms to conceptualize the self as one that develops out of its being viewed from many angles, as various others mirror the self. The self is built from many encounters and relationships, built and rebuilt, modified, and developed over time.

As I said earlier, Sutherland thought of affects as the engine of development. He also described affects as constituting a "monitoring system that could deal with all kinds of stimuli, and could set in motion internally a reactive mechanism" (1994c, p. 419). He thought that the structures of the self are constantly being built on the basis of affect-driven shifts that must actually change the neurological structure of the brain, and show up in specific feelings and behaviors that correspond to structure. In fact, this has now been demonstrated by brainscanning an 8-week-old infant, whose whole brain lit up when looking at a photograph of a woman's face (Trevarthen 2005). Activity was seen not only in the patch of cortex known to be important in recognizing faces, but also in areas of the brain specialized for speech and hearing. The baby's brain shows an innate sympathetic response to the image of the person, and prepares to respond. Even though the baby as yet has no words, receptive and expressive communication begins.

These structures receive and transmit affects that further determine the structure of the self. The structure of the self determines how affect is communicated to the next generation. How each individual baby responds modifies the mother's capacity to transmit and modify affect and also modifies her view of herself as a mother. Human development is a huge feedback loop. We are all in a state of interdependency with the people we care about, engaging with them in processes of self-regulation, self-organization, self-renewal, and self-transformation all the time. This concept of the self that Sutherland brings us is a positive one with plenty of hope for improvement and development.

Here is Sutherland's definition of the self: "The self is a dynamic organization of purposes and commitments whose behavior is governed by conscious and unconscious motives, and whose developments and functioning are inseparably linked to the social environment" (Harrow *et al.* 1994, p. xxv). To be true to this definition, any psychoanalytic endeavor cannot focus only on the individual wishes and fears and conflicts, but must consider the self in society as well.

Sutherland encouraged psychoanalysts to take psychoanalytic knowledge outside the consulting room and share it with those who are responsible for the structures of society – the social workers, family doctors, and clergy dealing with symptoms of social distress, such as high rates of teenage pregnancy, drug addiction, and domestic violence found in disadvantaged communities – as well as with their colleagues who treat the individuals, couples, and families suffering from mental distress. Social ills and mental distress are symptoms of lack of containment of individuals and families by the structures of society, which have become inadequate to the task. The community loses control and effectiveness and then splits up into warring parts in the same way that the individual self disintegrates into a weakened central self pitted against its internal objects battling for recognition (Savege 1973). Sutherland believed that psychoanalysis had a role in helping communities to reflect on their structures, listen to the signs of ill-fare, and understand how that community reflects the wider society. One community may be the repository for troubled and unwanted parts of other communities that are unable or unwilling to deal with them. That is why a comprehensive view of a whole city is needed to understand any one community and what it represents for the whole. That is why the community-based care professionals need to collaborate so as to achieve whole understanding and create healthy environments for human development.

Sutherland's view of the self is both intrapsychic and social: the self is an intrapsychic dynamic system open to feedback from the social group, open to learning from experience and from self-reflection. Sutherland advised all of us to contemplate the functioning of our self. He recommended self analysis: analysis *of* the self *by* the self. He did not intend us to do the kind of self analysis that interprets conflict in the light of infantile fantasies and looks at dreams for evidence of hidden wishes. To do self analysis as he meant it, we must observe how we feel, think, and act at leisure and under stress, in social, family, and work situations, with various people we like and dislike, so as to detect the various aspects of our self in action. We will look at our dream scenarios as "shorts" – film clips of the personality in action – so that we can understand and monitor our self, learn from experience, and make choices and changes.

Here is an example of self analysis from Sutherland's own reminiscences (Sutherland 1994c). Even though he had written plenty of papers and led a productive life as an administrator, Sutherland felt incomplete. He had a block against abstract thinking, a quality he admired and facilitated in others. Even though he had been teaching and writing about Fairbairn's ideas for years, he had not put together a book of his own. He said later that he really had not understood what Fairbairn meant about the self at all until he had a transformative insight in his own self analysis (Sutherland 1994c). At the ripe old age of 83, when writing *Journey to the Interior*, his biography of Fairbairn (again he was promoting the ideas of someone he regarded as more brilliant than himself), Sutherland came across the idea of Fairbairn's splitting of his mother and father figures. Suddenly he realized that all his life he had been identified with his busy and ambitious mother in preference to his father, a productive, but more laid-back man. He realized that he had not let them both inhabit his identifications in order to keep his parents apart, out of envy and hatred for their union. With this insight, he was then able to allow their coming together as a couple in his mind and this opened him to a tremendous upsurge in creative, abstract thinking. At the age of 86, he was still working towards a book on his own ideas about his main interest, the self. He did not live to finish it, but the last four papers in this book, including his final paper "The Autonomous Self," represent his thinking up to the time of his death.

In using the term "autonomous," Sutherland does not imply that the autonomous self operates independently of others. He means to refer to a quality of wholeness and integration toward which the autonomous self is impelled. The autonomous self must do, it must relate, it must reach forward. It must go on being no matter what, and at the same time it is developing, differentiating, becoming, fulfilling its potential, always growing into a shape that lies ahead of it. The autonomous self has to take in feelings and ideas, and put forth feelings and express ideas in language. The autonomous self can conceive, symbolize, communicate, share, plan, and negotiate. The autonomous self keeps the needs of self and other in balance and builds relationships of mature interdependency. At the same time, it is capable of conceiving of itself as a self over time, and contemplating its reality as a system of parts in dynamic relation within the self and its relationships with others.

In his later years, when the Scottish Institute that he had co-founded in the early 1970s experienced the problems of an adolescent institution, Sutherland became more aware of the need to analyze aggression. He could not agree with Klein that aggression was a desperate defense against annihilatory anxiety provoked by the death instinct. He agreed with Bowlby that aggression arises as a protest against loss of security. He agreed with Fairbairn that aggression arises from the frustration of desire for a satisfying relationship. But Sutherland felt that the infant's aggression is not only a protest in response to lack of proximity, security of attachment, and a meaningful relationship, but also an expression of the infant's struggle to pursue autonomy when frustrated by the inevitable dependency of childhood. To quote Sutherland: "Far from being undifferentiated as Freud described it at birth, the self is being formed steadily and only interference with the self determining dynamic elicits intense aggression" (1980a, p. 330). Here lies the crux of the matter: "Where Freud saw sexual and aggressive drives, where Klein saw life and death instincts, Sutherland sees an autonomy drive leading the self to become the self that is inherited and that will be developed in interaction with others" (Scharff 2005, p. 209).

At this point we must make the transition to Chapter 1, the final, informal statement of Sutherland's views.

Sutherland speaks in his easygoing, anecdotal way, covering a vast range of ideas about the development of the self in its social group set in its scientific and philosophical context. This gives an overview of the ideas to follow, ideas which he spells out with the greater precision of the written word, beginning with his early thinking about conceptual models. Chapter 2 is based on a classic paper that brought object relations to the fore as a theory that called for a revision of the conceptual model of psychoanalysis and influenced a generation of psychotherapists. In Chapter 3 Sutherland gives another overview, this time bringing the work of the four major British object relations theorists, Balint, Winnicott, Fairbairn, and Guntrip, to the American audience. Sutherland worked not only with individuals in psychoanalysis. He was active in group therapy and community development. In Chapter 4 he shares his understanding of group dynamics and in Chapter 5 he gives his insights on the provision of mental health care that is appropriate to the needs of our society after the industrial revolution. Sutherland, who loved to challenge the status quo, opens Chapter 6 with a clinical illustration to confront us with the need to recognize that instinct theory cannot account for complex phenomena, cannot achieve integration of a fragmented person, and that nothing less will do than a thorough understanding of the self.

Chapter 6 is the segue to the four major papers of Sutherland's most creative years. Chapter 7 is an essay on the self and its object relations in which, by this time in the development of his thinking, he prefers the term personal relations. Chapter 8 gives the text of his best known, highly influential paper on the psychodynamic image of man. Sutherland prescribes coordinated intervention by the caring professions in response to society's ill-fare and yet zeroes in on the need for change at the individual level through understanding conflicts and unconscious processes as aspects of parts of the self in interaction.

Having traced the maturation of his views in chapters based on his major papers on psychoanalysis, self, and society, we conclude our journey with Chapter 9, the culmination of Sutherland's thinking on the development of the self and its drive toward autonomy, the autonomous self.

Chapter 1

Becoming and being a person

Editor's introduction

In this lively discursive piece, adapted from a lecture, Sutherland shows the breadth and depth of his thinking but the weight of what he is saying is lightened by his easy delivery, his personal sense of conviction, and his typical Scottish humor. He admits to his total preoccupation with developing a theory of the self, and looks beyond the pluralism of psychoanalytic theories emphasizing instinctual energy and individual psychic structure, to consider the impact of society on the developing mind. He thinks of instinct as an obvious necessity, and attachment as a precondition, for the development of the loving relationships that are essential to the creation of the self. Drawing from ethology, evolutionary biology, and holograms, Sutherland makes the case that this self operates in an open system, responding to feedback within the social context, adapting in the light of experience, and looking to find its shape and maintain its wholeness. The self is separate from others but communicates with them to express will, find identity, make choices, share values, and commit to long-range goals for the common good.

In recent years, I have got rather obsessed with the problem of the self because of what I feel to be the clamorous need for a new paradigm in psychoanalytic theory. So I've chosen as the title for my theme: On Becoming and Being a Person. The agency of human motivation and conduct is the self, and we've got to understand more and more about its nature, its origin, and its functioning.

One of the unfortunate features of psychoanalysis is the awful subservience to the tablets the master brought down from the mountain. Nobody dares say anything that would criticize Freud – he was regarded as the last word. I think it's terribly unfortunate that there isn't more openness. I believe, and many have remarked, that classical metapsychology has failed to do justice to the essential personal quality of the individual in its account of human nature. Moreover, I believe that it is the failure to give an acceptable theoretical basis for the personal level of behavior that has created the most prominent feature of the current psychotherapeutic scene, namely, a pluralism in theory and practice, with consequent confusion and uncertainty in those trying to appraise its various claims. This development has been of concern to analysts in recent years. They've become concerned lest their work and its importance for society become discredited.

Some years ago the president of the International Psychoanalytic Association, Dr. Robert Wallerstein (1988), entitled his presidential address "One Psychoanalysis or Many?" – in which he provided a masterly survey of this aspect of the current scene. There, Wallerstein considers the anomaly of very different theoretical ideas being associated with comparable practice by analysts remaining within one professional body, the International Psychoanalytic Association. So they must feel that there is something common that keeps them and holds them together, and that can be recognized and evaluated. The anomaly of this situation, with different theoretical ideas associated with comparable practice, led him to put forward some ideas based on thoughts from Joseph and Ann-Marie Sandler. In the early history of analysis, challenges to his theoretical principles led Freud to exclude the prominent dissidents from the psychoanalytic movement, because their views were associated with clinical work that abandoned what he deemed to be the essential core of psychoanalysis. Yet, in Freud's view, any line of investigation that recognized the two facets of psychoanalysis, namely transference and resistance, and took them as the starting point of its work, even though it arrived at results other than his own, had a right to call itself psychoanalysis.

That was fair enough. Proceeding from his own metapsychological principles, Freud formulated his structural theory of the personality, which brought a period of outstandingly productive cohesion. As in all scientific work, developments inevitably exposed theoretical limitations, and in psychoanalysis these were plainly in the understanding of the ego. Anna Freud, followed by Hoffman and his colleagues, in a surge of fresh thinking, filled out a conspicuous gap in the structural theory with her creation of the psychology of the ego and so, in some measure, introduced a more holistic view of the person. Preserving much of Freud's metapsychology nevertheless, this line of thought was widely adopted as part of what has become known, certainly in the United States, as the mainstream development of Freud's work.

A different fate befell the work of Melanie Klein, despite her repeated emphasis that it, too, was evolved directly from Freud's theory of the instincts, especially his later concept of the death instinct. Her findings proved so disturbing that there were early reactions to them as not falling within the scope of psychoanalysis. Thus, the suspicion arose that inclusion within the analytic field was to be determined by theoretical conformity to Freud, rather than by the careful appraisal of new data, even though these were gleaned by the psychoanalytic method.

Now, the impact of Fairbairn's papers, published during and immediately after the War, was minimal, and this disregard has continued increasingly in the United Kingdom, though progressively less so in the United States. It's particularly striking that it was Fairbairn who introduced the term *object-relations theory* to describe views that challenged Freud's theory of the instincts radically. Many factors contributed to the neglect of his contribution, despite the fact that he was a devoted and highly sophisticated adherent to psychoanalysis as Freud had wished it to be. Indeed, it was soon after his first paper appeared that the term he introduced for his views – namely, an object-relations theory – was being used widely, for example, to cover the work of Balint and Winnicott as well. The views of Klein, who in her earlier writings stressed the importance of the influence of relationship, were also regarded as coming within the object-relations theory category. For myself, I believe the neglect of Fairbairn has been a serious loss in the development of psychoanalysis because of overlooking the closer links his views made with the person, links that he felt strongly were required.

Let me return to Wallerstein's address. He suggested that the anomaly of these different views being associated with acceptable practice could be resolved in large measure by the adoption of the Sandlers' suggestion that we distinguish a present unconscious from a past unconscious (Sandler and Sandler 1984). The present unconscious includes the derivatives of the past unconscious that are closer to experience, for example, the mechanism of defense. We deal with the past unconscious when we deal with the infant that is hidden by the infantile amnesia within the person. The nature of the past unconscious is inferred from its perpetual intrusion in fantasy and transference in the analytic situation. The Sandlers point out that the understanding we gain about this part of the personality rests on creative acts of reconstruction. They make the further suggestion that in fashioning a general theory of infantile development, the different accounts are couched in metaphors, rather than in the real realities. When a metaphor captures enough realities, then dynamically similar factors can follow from very different metaphors.

Wallerstein is somewhat pessimistic about achieving a widely acceptable general theory of development because the true factors lie too far beyond the realm of empirical study and scientific progress. He grants that this position will change, but he is not optimistic about achievement in the near future. The use of metaphors, Wallerstein reminds us, is common in all scientific endeavor at certain states, when they are virtually indispensable, but the great danger they introduce, especially in the human sciences, is that the metaphorical factors all too readily become regarded as realities. When they're felt to fit aptly and closely with the phenomena, they gain a powerful grip, both from their heuristic value and from unconscious sources.

Now, when confronted with the growing mass of new clinical data, along with the fact that modern evolutionary biology has advanced understanding to a point where the Newtonian principles of the science of Freud's day can no longer be regarded as a tenable foundation for comprehending the phenomena of living organisms, then Freud's metaphoric base for the understanding of human nature and motivation must be reappraised, despite the extraordinary tenacity with which the id metaphor has persisted. In his last contribution, "An Outline of Psychoanalysis," Freud (1937) opens his chapter on the instincts with the statement that the power of the id expresses the true purpose of the individual organism's life, namely, to satisfy its innate needs arising from the force of the instincts.

The Congress of the International Psychoanalytic Association in 1987 started from Freud's paper, "Analysis Terminable and Interminable" (1937). Exemplifying the tenacity of the id metaphor, André Green (1987), the French analyst, in his paper at this conference, expresses the view that it is Freud's concept of the instinctual nature of the unconscious that has given rise to significant reservations, both in regard to the specific instincts postulated and their mode of functioning. Yet there is a great reluctance to face up to this issue. When he lists some of the alternatives proposed, he selects, first, those who radically reject the concept of instinct in favor of the theory based on object relations. He then names primarily Fairbairn and Guntrip.

It seems to me that Green's way of putting things is totally misleading. Fairbairn regards instinctive endowment as an obvious necessity in accounting for development. What Fairbairn rejects is Freud's concept of *the instincts as somatic energies* that, in his phrase, give the ego a kick in the pants to get on with some activity, as a means of arousing action to discharge tension, rather than as an innate potential motivating an organism to seek relations. The subsequent proactive transactions between organism and environment – that is, between the infant and mother primarily – give rise to the dynamic structures required for the organization of experience. They, thus, constitute the embryonic ego; for no learning can take place without such structures being involved from the very start. The arguments of nature versus nurture, of instinct theory versus object relations, to me are thus largely irrelevant, as is also the adversarial relationship between society and the individual stressed by Freud. Instinctive endowment only becomes identifiable through its realization in the object relations it meets and seeks.

The viewpoint of modern evolutionary biology is radically different from the science available to Freud. In his day in the nineteenth and early twentieth centuries, the organism was described from a paradigm taken from mechanistic engineering in which the preservation of the structure is of foremost concern. The primary concern is how it maintains its equilibrium as a basic condition for achieving this, and the answer is found in homeostasis as the cybernetic mechanism. In the mid-twentieth century, in the theory of open systems for conceptualizing every living organism, the dynamic phenomena of development and maintenance of life are conceived as permanent processes in which *positive feedback* is characteristic – not negative feedback, but positive feedback – that is, not coming back to the previous equilibrium, but breaking out of the boundaries of that to evolve new structures. From the original state of wholeness and order within the innate components that initiate the appropriate transactions with the environment, the organism undergoes self-adaptation in a self-organizing whole, which preserves its identity, despite constant transformation. Such living systems cannot be built up from the aggregation of parts, but start from their living progenitors. Each organism contains an organizing principle that determines the potential shape of the adult organism.

I found myself many years ago using the idea that the organism's innate potential has some shape and characteristic activity. Activity, which is the constant motivation of the organism, ensures that it reaches outward until it meets in the environment something that fits the shape. Two sources support my view of the organism reaching toward a shape: Tustin's book on autistic children and the theory of holograms. Frances Tustin (1972) describes the dreadful, tragic situation of children who have failed to make a relationship with the mother or caring figures, and so fail to develop a self. It's very striking that these autistic children have an intense interest in shapes, and circles appeal to them greatly, perhaps because a circle signifies a mother figure. Holograms within the central nervous system demonstrate that shapes of the holistic form of the organ and of the structure can be contained in a potential form that permeates the whole structure. So my old idea of the potential having shape is not such a fanciful notion after all. Indeed the whole mind/body problem has changed radically since the days when Freud tied his theory to the prevailing science of chemistry and physiology.

Evolutionary biology

Development within an organism, which is an open system necessarily, demands an autonomous urge to maintain this wholeness of the shape; otherwise, the organism dies. A threat to the autonomy of the organism is tantamount to a threat from a lethal predator. To survive it has to assert itself autonomously at all times with varying degrees of force, up to the point of maximum ferocity. Paradoxically, its resources for doing so, however, have to be developed – and to an increasing extent as we ascend the evolutionary scale – from its relatedness with the adults. The organism's life becomes the dynamic process of preserving its autonomy within the heteronomy of relatedness with its social group and the psychical environment.

In summary, the first principle to start with and grasp firmly is that the living organism has this inherent shape and that it is an open system. It grows with organizing principles forming its interactions with the environment and transforming these into the shapes needed so that the adult form of the organism is reached. Resources for achieving this potential have to be developed.

It's characteristic that, as we go up the evolutionary scale, the innate potential has more and more plasticity, more of a potential, rather than an inherited specific pattern. And the potential to reach adult development has to be realized within the framework of relationships with adults. The lower down the evolutionary scale we go, the more the behavioral patterns that mediate survival are ready-made. The tadpole can get off, swim away, and feed itself, and so on. It doesn't need a great deal of support from the adults. Dinosaurs are said to have done something similar, and recent evidence rather suggests that adult dinosaurs did do more than just protect the young. They could communicate to the young how to anticipate dangerous situations of a non-manifest kind.

Based on the findings of human evolution, I conclude that the innate potential has to be highly complex and plastic because the human organism has become a social animal and its survival takes place only within social groups. In the lower levels of the evolutionary scale, the cohesion in the group is fairly largely concerned with protection, and so the group is tied together by attachment to the dominant male. In the human group things are very different. It seems here that to provide for the plasticity the human race requires to exploit the environment – and, indeed, as evolution has gone on, the capacity to *make* our environment – we need very different resources.

The evolutionary value of a social approach to human development is evident; for a human group, a social group that got established in a certain environment, naturally needs its young to grow up with knowledge of and familiarity with the features of that environment. There is an immense need for communication, and so capacities for thought develop, with the associated requirement for language. The relatedness of the individual is increasing in depth, as well as extent, all the time.

Freud's method of reaching his views about the instincts was to make inferences from the neuroses of individuals; and, hence, sex and aggression were taken to be the dominant drives in man. But human nature was thus conceived as derived from forces internal to the organism, rather than through creative structuring from the interaction of a plastic potential with the environment. From experience of encounters with the environment, the ego was created on the surface of the id, as Freud originally put it, although he later saw that id and ego could not be differentiated in the earliest stages of development. With greater importance attached to the role of the environment and to the importance of aggression, investigators find that the instincts appear to be much more complex and holistic – not so much a matter of ethologically proscribed behavior, but striving towards and reaching an end state, rather than following specific behaviors. I doubt whether any valid generalizations about instincts can be made from clinical data, simply because the history of the environmental influence upon individuals is completely unknown.

All embryologists, when starting their work, prepare themselves with a thorough knowledge of the adult or the mature organism to which development is headed. So if, rather than looking at the individual as Freud did, we take the view of ethologists looking at what happens in species, then we ask what are the behavioral characteristics that large groups of animals have in common. If these can be shown to be relatively free from environmental influence, then they are not the products of training, and presumably we are dealing with innate potentials that underwrite those broad clustered features of behavior. It's only when you've got a population to study that you can eliminate the specific features of individual experience.

Yankelovich and Barrett, two notable philosophers, one a social scientist as well, in their book *Ego and Instinct* (1970), a remarkable critique of the basic principles of psychoanalysis, took such social studies as were available – namely, those of Cantril (1955), the social psychologist – of more than a dozen utterly different cultures, and they asked what were the common features of people in the groups. Rather than seeing individuals whose motivation is founded on instinctive forces of a totally impersonal kind driving the organism to seek pleasure, they found from the study of the social group quite a different collection of patterns that lead to a different theory of human motivation. What Yankelovich and Barrett found in all thirteen cultures were characteristically human features that go beyond individual requirements, as follows: the quest for satisfying the needs for food, shelter, territorial security and for an individual security, and the procreation security for the future; a need for order, certainty and form to give assurance that experience could be repeated; a need beyond adaptation to the environment by a search for new experiences and a hunger for knowledge; the capacity to make choices, the freedom to do so, and the responsibility for acting upon the decision made.

Yankelovich and Barrett go on to enumerate other characteristic features of humans: a need to feel their own security and identity, and to have it maintained within the culture – that is, to be valued by others; the hope that the future of society will fulfill their aspirations; to have a system of values and beliefs to which they can commit and for which they may even sacrifice. And then to facilitate all of these, humans have the need for language. The characteristic that is new in the evolutionary scale is sharing, and individuals cannot share unless they can communicate what they are feeling and thinking. Language becomes a prerequisite for development of that kind (Yankelovich and Barrett 1970, p. 400).

From this list we can also infer the need to conceive a central organizing system of self, which not only mediates its internal organization, but which can communicate its thoughts and other mental activity freely, so that sharing with others can be carried out. The self is also facilitated in its functioning by the unique property in the animal world of being able to transcend itself to appraise its function. It can look at itself. When motives are conflicting, the self considers the conflict.

Now, the conception of a human nature that seeks to meet these needs is a very different one from the manifestation of instincts in the traditional form. As Isadore Chein (1972), the distinguished philosophical psychologist, puts it, the essential psychological human quality is one of commitment to developing a continuing set of unending, interacting, interdependent, and mutually modified long-range purposes. The development of such commitment starts from the innate potential in the infant in constant transactions with the carers, chiefly the mother and family, transactions that are determined in the earliest phases by the innate factors in the organism, and also by the parallel evolutionary development in the mother, which equips the mother to make the right moves toward the needs of the infant at the right time.

I equate the human person with having a self. The development starts from an innate potential that finds its shape within constant transactions determined in the earliest phases by the innate factors in mother and child, and later with the carers in the family and in that particular culture, all of which, therefore, play an increasing part in our evolution. The full development of this commitment to human group goals or end-states is what characterizes a mature person. Failure to achieve such development means that the person is not fully realized, though the potentiality to become so may well be there. But this realization needs an appropriately responsive environment from society to give the growing organism the care and concern that it needs for its evolution.

The function of the self, or the person, is to integrate a developing series of differentiated substructures within what has been an integrated whole to cope with various specific needs, but a structure that retains its holistic quality. I postulate an autonomous self.

You might object and ask how I can talk about a self before experience starts. Well, you get into a rather vicious circle about the cart and horse there. It doesn't seem to me that it's a problem nowadays, because if we conceive of the organizing principle, not as a content of behavior, but as an affective tone that informs the organism that this or that experience is right or not, then we can see a monitoring system for development. If infants are getting the right input of food, fine. If they aren't they protest in various specific ways. But the same is true in regard to psychological needs: if not being treated as a self, the infant protests. And that, indeed, may be the strongest argument for the existence of some innate holistic structure.

The developmental psychological work in recent years confirms this view that the infant behaves as a whole, and behaves as a person, and adults respond to the infant as a whole person. The infant has the inherent quality that it is going to become an adult human being, and that quality is responded to and fostered by the community. This ability to transcend itself, to look at itself and appraise its existential situation, is unique to humans in the animal world.

Our development is dependent on a certain affective tone: a sense that we're doing all right, that our self feels all right, that we don't feel deprived, and we don't feel we're doing the wrong thing. That affective tone is a plastic monitor for a wide range of different activities. The baby is given the innate impulse to grope for the breast. The baby doesn't know what will be found there. All the baby has is this innate groping activity. When the mother puts the breast in front of the baby's mouth, the baby's feeling right away is, "this is what I've been looking for all my life, and here it is." So then you get experience beginning to be structured; but you can't learn without some previous structuring of the search, the groping, and the experience.

Freud and Melanie Klein introduced the ego and the self, but mostly referred to the ego, because "self" was regarded as a kind of nonword in scientific discussion, it was so subjective. But it's rather striking how both of them say "the ego does this" or "the self does that." In other words, the self's value as the agent of behavior is assumed, referred to, but never studied as such. It never becomes separated as a concept in the earlier stages of development.

In contrast, it was on the central place of the self that Fairbairn's work started; and this, I sometimes think, is not referred to enough. You cannot have an object-relations theory without a self. It's only a self that relates to other selves. As one of the philosophical biologists has said, it takes a gestalt to relate to a gestalt. An aggregate of parts cannot produce this holistic quality of responding to what is essentially the quality of the whole in the organism, so that you have to have these holistic gestalts – that is, the self – developing in this way.

Now we know that from the structural potential the self grows rapidly, and we have a fair idea of what takes place there nowadays. When we see the work of the child development researchers like Daniel Stern linking up with the clinical studies of the analyst then we see a bipolar situation. The infant developers are starting from day one, working forward. The analyst starts from the adult end, working backwards. It's going to be like the Channel tunnel – hopefully, the two ends will meet! The two areas of study are absolutely complementary, and we need both. The infant developmentalists cannot, without knowing the features of the adult self, appreciate what is going on completely. Whereas, if we study only the adult self, we're apt to make theories about fantasy possibilities or to deny possibilities that are there.

There is no question, when you review classical analytic theory and psychological theory, that the whole potential of the infant is grossly underrated. The capacity of infants to smile knowingly, to recognize a human face, and to play is quite amazing. When you see videotapes of the early development of infants just a matter of a week or two old, it's astounding to see just how personalized they are.

Fairbairn started from the particular group of patients he was concerned with, schizoid individuals whose difficulties were that they couldn't make relationships. His conclusion about the common factor was that these people had never had their self developed because they were never loved for their own sake. Now to understand him when he states that the infant has a unique self that grows only when it is loved for its own sake, we've got to have some idea of what is the innate self and what we mean by love. And besides, it's only in the human animal, you could say, that the particular quality and duration of nurturance establishes what we call love and care. We don't get socially related comprehensive love until we reach the human level. There is something like love in animals' protection of their young, but it does not extend to their injured. I suppose it is too dangerous to stay back with a sick one, because of the risk of predators. Only humans deal with the injured of the species and show care and concern for the survival of the person, the self.

This conception of human nature, then, is very different from the classical one, in that it holds that instinctual satisfaction, the quick-fix, is not adequate as the sole feature of motivation. Motivation has to keep the animal directed toward concern for the total community, for its survival, for the building up of experience and knowledge, and for its transmission. These are all part of the instinctive potential. Most philosophers agree that freedom of will, the capacity to make a freely determined decision, is a characteristic feature of human beings preferable to their being compelled by instinctive patterns all the time. Sexuality, for instance, is far from primitive. This was known quite early on. Malinowski (1927, 1929), the anthropologist, pointed out that the Western idea of primitive sexuality amongst savages was completely misleading. Sexuality was part of a highly social, organized behavioral complex to ensure the preservation of the group. The more we seek to exploit the environment, to control the environment, and to be self-actualized, the more we need learning, organization, and experience.

Freud's concept of id postulates that while we appear to be one way in reality, really we are a mass of all these powerful instincts below the surface. There's increasing feeling, certainly amongst philosophers, that we're kidding ourselves here. This so-called real reality is a fantasy construct, simply because we have believed sufficiently in the fact that the higher levels of organization always produce a new repertoire of power in action, a new set of properties, which do not belong to any lower level and which are unpredictable. It doesn't matter how much we know about hydrogen and oxygen: no one can predict that the resultant product is the best additive to

Scotch! These qualities are unique and emergent. The same thing is going on in the organism: properties are emergent all the time.

The more you think of the self, the more you realize that object-relations theory has acquired a misnomer that has given it a misleading status. It's really a theory of the self. The self makes the relationships, and the self is made by the relationships; the two interact, and the self is the agent of action. Now we all know clinically that neurosis is constructed by the person. It doesn't just happen. Symptoms don't just happen. They are created by the person as a whole. For instance, when we study projection tests like the Rorschach, we can see that it is a total self that governs the perception because, while the self organizes a holistic precept, at the same time the substructures perceive details and interpret them in some other way. But the important point I think is that the total self is always in action. What we call the ego, I am suggesting, is that bit of the self that is most developed around experience with the real world.

Although Wallerstein has difficulty with metaphors in analytic theory, I don't think we have that difficulty when we deal with the self. Is there anything more real than saying "I feel this" or "I think that"? In other words, what the self does is synchronous with reality in human contact.

A common difficulty has been the theory that the infant at the start can't possibly have a separate self, as if it were inevitably merged with the mother's self as a kind of extension of the mother's self. Now, that is not what behavioral observation suggests. Watching nursing couples, we note that, right from the start, babies are highly determined little creatures that know what they want and get it, and make the mother adapt. In his self-object theory, Kohut describes the need for a close, mirroring figure to maintain the sense of self. Without that, there's a nonfunctioning structure in the infant. But, to me, the self is not a passive extension to the mother's self. There's an autonomous, competent self there in the infant. In our theorizing, we've got to postulate this highly autonomous urge. The frustration of this highly autonomous quality sets the ground for most psychopathology.

Perhaps the autonomy of the self has been obscured because of the physical dependency of the infant and need for closeness to the mother much of the time. Bowlby's work on attachment has given a widespread idea that "attachment is the thing." I cannot see that attachment is anything other than a precondition for the development of the self. It's the first step. The baby has to become attached to the mother, to cling to, to hold onto the mother, and to find security there; and it's out of all the constant experience of being in attachment that the infant builds the self. Bowlby himself speaks of the self being evolved from the attachment situation by increasing modeling. Certainly it needs to be developed by the input of loving models; but it also has its own capacity for fantasy, for play by which it can try out modes of behavior and build up possible self attitudes. The infant self is already a highly dynamic whole self with a powerful sense of autonomy.

Psychoanalytic experience certainly suggests – and behavioral researchers would agree – that the inner security to do this, to set up an active, exploratory attitude to the world at large, comes from the experience of being loved. The plain fact seems to be that the infant has a powerful urge to get to the right experience, provided it's made reasonably available. So by denying the ordinary caring attention, we create intense situations of frustration that lead to splitting of the object and the self.

All I want to stress is that we've simply got to take as the basic feature in metapsychology the autonomous struggle of the self. Rather than the vicissitudes of instinct, let's think of the vicissitudes of the self in the relationships it finds.

Two case illustrations

Now I'll quickly give you two cases, the first from a British Independent point of view and the second from the Kleinian perspective, both of which bring out the kind of problems that have haunted us. I've also used these cases and two other cases of Fairbairn and Betty Joseph to elaborate upon my argument (Sutherland 1989), but here I'll confine myself to two cases by Patrick Casement (1990) and Terrtu Eskelinen de Folch (1988). First, I'll quote a case from Patrick Casement's book *On Learning from the Patient* (1990). It's always a good thing to quote from somebody else, because then I can't be accused of quoting evidence I've created.

A young woman, Miss K, was referred for help with compulsive eating of several years' duration. She described her mother as manipulative and intrusive, preventing her from having any real independence. The mother had a flamboyant enjoyment of breast feeding, which could well have fostered an oral fixation. When 2 years old, a sister was born, and her mother withdrew to the pleasures of the nursing relationship, leaving the patient for several weeks with a nanny. Miss K then developed a highly seductive relationship with her father, which ended with his death when she was 17. Feeling bereft and empty, she dealt with her grief and depression by overeating. The intensity of her attachment to her father led her to feel that her sexuality was bad. Young men said she was devouring. Her mother's sexual orientation and her unusually seductive behavior with both her and Miss K's sister confused Miss K.

Miss K's overeating also derived from her mother's ambition to make her slim and beautiful, which was so possessive and overpowering that Miss K ceased to feel herself to be a separate person. Eating asserted an independence from the mother's control, yet she clung to her mother, despite the feeling that the mother was like a permanent cancer inside herself. The guilt she felt about her sexual contacts with men also added to her eating, which she thought would chase the men away.

Miss K had had a previous therapist before she had come from abroad to England, and he had fostered her dependence on him by offering extra sessions and physical comfort. Casement's attentions in the form of interpretations were taken by her as an attempt to control her. It became clear that her experience had led her to feel that all relationships were manipulative. When Casement resisted her demands for more and more of this and that, she reacted aggressively by having other treatments, outside of analysis, especially with her brother-in-law, who was a family doctor. These posed a serious problem at times. For instance, she got antidepressants secretly, and later had her jaws wired, despite which contraption she managed to feed herself with triumph. These measures intensified the hatred of her mother, which emerged as biting sarcasm to those who angered her. A behavioral therapist then repeated the physical acting out she had with her first therapist, until her sexual excitement frightened her away from him.

Casement interpreted these other treatments as enactments of the relationship she wished to make with him, but had to keep apart from him to maintain him in the image of the nonintrusive mother and the nonsexual father. Intense ambivalence evoked Miss K's wish to protect her mother against her murderous feelings. That, of course, is the primary reaction to frustration of the self: intense rage with murderous ferocity.

Some confrontations with the mother about her attitudes on a visit that the mother made to England improved the relationship. After a year in analysis, she began to free herself from her mother, but remained overweight, lest her mother and her brother-in-law could think they had been responsible for her progress. In the patient's last session before leaving London, after about eighteen months, Casement was impressed by her statement, "I am becoming my own version of myself."

Casement describes often being made to feel helpless and destroyed. He believed it to be essential that he had let Miss K come to her own realization of her unconscious need to experience the freedom to be destructive with no intrusion from him. The essential dynamics of the treatment, therefore, he took to be the opportunity to survive her intensely destructive efforts to wreck the treatment and him. As Winnicott put it, when the assertive strivings of the baby are repeated in analysis, the critical thing is that the analyst should accept all these and survive, because that's what the ordinary mother does, thereby, of course, giving the deep physical instinctive proof that mother can take it. The very substantial change in becoming her own person was seen a few years later when Miss K wrote, telling him of how she had discovered her creative abilities with a newfound confidence.

Using a classical formulation, her behavior would have been reduced to an oral fixation under the influence of oedipal guilt, while the Kleinian perspective might be that she had regressed due to preoedipal factors such as intense oral sadism from the death instinct. Casement, however, adopts another way of looking at Miss K's conflicts. We cannot but agree with him that Miss K's symptoms are pressing because of other, more complex purposes of the self than drive satisfaction.

The value of that case for my purpose is that it has all the drive manifestations from which Freud made his classical theories – oral, anal, and the next thing. But what seems to be the best explanation, the most plausible one, the one that is the best fit for the total situation, is simply that she felt that her mother had deprived her of a feeling that she was doing her own thing in her own way.

The other case that I would like to quote from was described by a Kleinian analyst, Eskelinen de Folch (1988). She notes – and, I thought, very sharply – that if the unresolved clinical problems prompting Freud to write "Analysis, Terminable and Interminable" are still with us, then our present-day explanatory capacity is not sufficient to resolve them. She then focuses on the analyzability of certain concealed nuclei of the personality that appear to be remote from the analytical relationship. Such patients, even after long analysis, have great difficulty acknowledging destructive impulses, such as hatred and envy, as belonging to them. They are terrified of disintegration, a dread that Klein described as aroused by primitive terrifying objects that are deeply repressed. Eskelinen de Folch believes that it is not necessary for these patients to be in a crisis for these primitive objects to appear, as she illustrates from a clinical case.

The patient, a brilliant academic man held in very high regard, had come seeking treatment because he felt something lacking in his relationship with his wife and in life generally. He was burned with a sense of impending disaster. In analysis, he began to have dreams of terrorists who set fire to bookshops: sometimes he is the terrorist, yet he maintains he has nothing to do with it. Early in analysis, he dreamed of a small boy in danger of falling from a balcony. He then saw himself in a diver's suit, taking a shower and becoming excited. In the third part of the dream, he was carrying his own dead body to the little boy's mother, asking her for a death certificate, the cause of death being something like "death by annihilation."

He kept impersonalizing his relationship with the analyst, which made her think that his terrifying object had come actively into their relationship and had to be defended against. In a subsequent session, he was intensely anxious, and said, quite unusually for him, that he felt some intense rage against her when he realized they might speak of important things. On the way to the session, he had seen one door of the lift labeled "exit," while the other opened into the void; and this idea related to his silences after moments of some true contact. He was horrified that the image of himself as warm and understanding, the goody-goody, was not at all accurate. He then had a silent period, after which he was surprised by how indifferent he felt. Just as the session was about to end, he revealed he had forgotten to tell the analyst that he and his wife had decided to have a child.

In discussing such material, Kleinians see the dangers of hate, but they account for that, as Freud did, by postulating an instinct of destruction within the organism, whereas people interested in relationships, like Fairbairn, see the hate and the aggressive phenomena as a violent reaction for the survival of the autonomy of the self. In Winnicottian terms, I might say that the patient had become an academic through a false self forced upon him by his mother. In his dreams of the arsonist who came in and set fire to bookshops, I might see a tremendous resentment that began to come out about his mother not allowing him a spontaneous self.

In response to that dream and the theme of death by annihilation, Eskelinen de Folch applies Kleinian ideas. With regard to instincts, ego structure, and object relations, she notes that highly destructive defense mechanisms are fueled by the death instinct; that impulses to split are related to objects internal and external and to the analyst in the analysis. She adds that the patient may acknowledge these impulses after prolonged analytic work as his own but he may then find himself caught in a painful repetitive experience from which he may derive a sadomasochistic satisfaction that seems to have a life of its own and which he strongly resists giving up.

Eskelinen de Folch then brings in some of Bion's ideas about a particular form of repetition compulsion, namely the fragmentation of objects that leads to intense anxiety of being persecuted by the objects into which the fragments have been projected. The person makes a pact with these objects, which, while lessening the persecution, leads to compulsive acting out. The objects terrify the person while another part of the personality establishes other normal relations. Eskelinen de Folch thinks that this part of the personality that is struggling with psychotic anxiety is shaped not by love but by the strength of the death instinct. The possibility of changing these object relations is limited by the violence of the splitting process and by the amount of satisfaction derived from the situation.

Quoting work on this type of problem by Betty Joseph and Elizabeth Spillius, Eskelinen de Folch refers to serious countertransference problems. Through the exploration of countertransference, the underlying internal object relationships can be recovered. Eskelinen de Folch concludes that the concepts of the death instinct and the repetition compulsion can help us build our theory. The death instinct implements the splits while the integrative character of the life instinct acts as a counterpoint. The concealed nuclei of the personality appear as a sinister result of the action of the death drive. According to Eskelinen de Folch the repetition compulsion, however, may represent attempts to deal with the primary trauma in a less catastrophic way. This primary trauma arose because the death instinct was not mitigated by an appropriate external object – the good breast or the good mother.

I am impressed by Eskelinen de Folch's penetration into the primitive self levels, based on a highly developed sensitivity to the expression of early relationships in the transference created by a correspondingly sensitive use of the countertransference. It seems to me that this is where the advances made by Klein and her students lie.

Wallerstein notes comparable work with the present unconscious among analysts of different persuasions, but I do not want to underestimate differences among the various schools of thought in psychoanalysis. The identification of what is going on in the present unconscious in Eskelinen de Folch's case is to me of a different order than occurs in non-Kleinian analyses. She attributes her work to recognition of the impersonal death instinct along with mechanisms operating at a personal level, mainly projective identification and envy. For Eskelinen de Folch, the concealed nuclei of the personality are intensely repressed object relationships, as a non-Kleinian might think. But the Kleinian concept of internal object relationships is based in instinct theory.

Early in analysis, Eskelinen de Folch's patient dreamed of a little boy falling from a balcony, then being excited by the prospect of engaging in deep diving, and then demanding from his mother a certificate of the cause of his death by annihilation. From my own object-relations perspective, I would conclude that he felt that his mother had annihilated his self. His manifest self was one of great academic success and popularity, but with failure in his close relationships. This suggests to me that his success came from a self adopted under his mother's pressure, a *false* self in Winnicott's terms. This self is inevitably identified with the mother that he wishes to destroy because of what she has done to an essential part of his self, namely the part that could have permitted him to make close relations with others. From his dreams of terrorists who set fire to bookshops, I suspect a denied, enraged self that attacks what his mother has made him into. To admit this, he would have to overcome the terrifying anxiety of a vengeful destruction of his mother who has given him what he lives by. More important than any guilt over this action, however, is his fear of disintegration if he carried out this murderous attack – a fear of falling into space with nothing to support him. I suggest that this rage burst out against the analyst when he thought that she might expose his secret intentions and he was shaken to feel that this might now destroy her.

To account for this patient's personality and his difficulties, I need a structural theory founded on the self and its needs, a theory that recognizes that failure to meet these needs in the earliest stages of development evokes intense aggression from the very beginning. A crucial feature of our working with the self as the agent in its presenting difficulties is that we deal very little in metaphors. The self's experience is an ultimate factor, the thing in itself, and not requiring hypothetical realities other than itself. Admittedly the immense contribution of the Kleinians has been that their understanding of early phenomena has given them a capacity to use these manifestations in the analytic situation, working with transference, countertransference, projection, and projective identification; and that's been an enormous gift for psychoanalysis. But I don't think the theory is a help here. I don't think we need Klein's death instinct. What we need is a protesting organism.

Summary

The complex issue of the self is a widely ramifying theme. For me it's such a critically important one. I think that the future of psychoanalytic theory will certainly rest on getting the self properly conceptualized. What I've tried to do is to give an evolutionary biological background to where the self is needed in the evolutionary scheme, to share my ideas as to how it could have evolved in that way, and to describe some of its properties and its necessity for us as social animals that are self-organizing and able not only to adapt to, but to make our own environment. These, I think, are possible only through the development of this highly integrative structure, which can permit us to internalize the world, play with it inside, and make innovating possibilities: the autonomous self.

Chapter 2

The conceptual model

Editor's introduction

Sutherland compares the classical ego psychological model following Freud with the object relations model of psychoanalysis based on Fairbairn in which the ego is a central system guiding and monitoring primitive need/control systems (superego and repressed internal object relations). Sutherland applies Fairbairn's model and elaborates on it to arrive at his own view of the aims of psychoanalysis, the psychoanalytic method, the psychoanalytic relationship, and the development of transference. He concludes that his model is flexible, comprehensive, and relevant to understanding human interaction and conflict in personal and social situations throughout the life cycle.

In recent years there have been two prominent areas of development in psychoanalytic theory:

1 The advances in ego psychology, in which Hartmann, Kris and Loewenstein (1946), and Rapaport (1960) in the United States and Anna Freud (1946) in the United Kingdom have played a leading part.
2 The work on the role of object relations from what has been called loosely the English school. Although deriving in large part from Melanie Klein (1935, 1946), these views have had major contributions from British analysts other than Klein's associates, for example, Fairbairn (1952a) and Winnicott (1958a, 1965).

To British analysts it is striking how far apart these two areas of work have remained. (For some years it seemed that the work of Klein had been declared an un-American activity!) There are now signs that this situation is changing. I believe this trend is due to a growing realization that some of the apparent differences do not represent incompatible lines of work, but, on the contrary, can be seen in substantial measure as complementary. In what follows I propose to make use of the conceptual models that have been developed as a result of the theoretical work in these two areas to focus attention on where some of the differences lie and so help to promote a fruitful interchange of viewpoints.

In his book, *Energy and Structure in Psychoanalysis*, Colby (1955, p. 79) prefaces his description of his model of the psychic apparatus with some observations on the status and function of models. Models represent one method of describing the parts of a whole and their organization. They are "visual aids, but they picture only imaginative constructions of organization." Further notes of caution are sounded when he points out that, although they do not constitute a theory but merely help to illustrate it, they are often mistaken for the realities of which they are representations.

The complexities of the massive body of observations and constructs that now characterize psychoanalysis make it most unlikely that any one model would cover other than limited aspects of its theories, and this is probably one of the reasons that have led psychoanalysts to prefer verbal descriptions of their theories. Nevertheless, the *fons et origo* of psychoanalytic theories, the psychoanalytic process, has universally accepted features which readily suggest the use of models. Karl Menninger (1958), in one of the recent books on this theme, *Theory of Psychoanalytic Technique*, finds a working model of the way in which psychoanalytic therapy operates as a helpful device. The position may be put more strongly. Psychoanalysis is a long-term process that is set in motion deliberately by the analyst. Analysts assume that only through psychoanalysis do patients get the necessary conditions for achieving certain changes in their personality functioning. Moreover, analysts expect to control this process in substantial measure by their activities. A statement in the form of a model, or quasimodel, of the concepts used in the theory and practice that underlie their activities is a necessity if assumptions are to be adequately scrutinized and checked, and hence greater power and precision achieved.

The requirements Colby (1955) lists for a model of the psychic apparatus can be taken as a starting point. For him a model should:

1 distinguish the variables of primary importance from others that are secondary or derivative;
2 show how internal biological conditions are integrated with the external environment;
3 allow for maturation and experiential development;
4 provide for individual uniqueness and societal variations;
5 indicate how it works.

Of this list, the first one contains the crux of the matter. What are the *variables of primary importance*? I believe it is the failure to get these right, rather than the complexity of the data, that has led to the neglect of conceptual models. Most psychoanalysts have found the models put forward so far to have only limited relevance to their practice; and for those with more theoretical interests, the awareness of this gap between theory and practice has confirmed their lack of enthusiasm for them.

In considering the applications of Hartmann's (1958) development of psychoanalytic thought, Rapaport (1960) notes that the essential task of studying a relationship between an explanatory theory and the method of observation by which the data are obtained is rarely pursued. We need to know, for instance, "to what extent does psychoanalytic theory reflect human nature, and to what extent does it reflect Freud's methods of studying human nature?" (p. 79). He then goes on to state that the psychoanalytic relationship . . . may well require a distinction to be made between ". . . a *general* psychoanalytic theory and a *specific* psychoanalytic theory which is greatly dependent on them" (p. 79).

It is abundantly clear that in Rapaport's writings, as he himself states, he focuses on those aspects of the theory that are not obviously dependent on the clinical method and tries to avoid concepts that obviously are tied to it, like transference, interpretation, and so forth. A noteworthy instance of this divorce from the clinical findings occurs in Rapaport's earlier paper (1951) "The Conceptual Model of Psychoanalysis," ". . . for reasons that lie beyond the scope of this paper – I will not deal here with the relevance or irrelevance of this model to phenomena which are variously referred to as those of conscience, ego ideal, superego, etc." (p. 232).

I believe that some of the differences in the two areas of work may be related to this apparent greater distance between clinical data and theory in the ego-psychology group as compared with the British workers. To quote Rapaport again (1960), "When the rules of thumb of clinical psychoanalysis are equated with the theory of psychoanalysis, the observations and concepts which bridge the gap between the basic concepts and the initial observations are inevitably overlooked" (p. 84). What to my mind is the most important part of this observation is the phrase "the rules of thumb" because it indicates that the psychoanalytic method for him is a rather haphazard one from the scientific point of view. Rapaport further notes that: "The psychoanalytic writer and practitioner is inclined to speak of psychoanalytic concepts and theories in terms of 'content.'" He then adds that ". . . Content is an important '*guide*' to the practitioner," but the

> majority of contributions to the literature tend to dwell on content to the neglect of other guides. . . . What is lost sight of – and the practitioner need not necessarily keep this in focus or even in sight, but those interested in theory must – is the functional (and thus also conceptual) relationship *to which* the content is a guide. . . . No content yields its full meaning unless its formal characteristics, and those of the

> time, place and context of its appearance, are taken into consideration, that is to say, abstracted. . . . The stress on content seems to be one of the main causes for overlooking the relationship between concepts and observables.
>
> (pp. 84–85)

Much of this stricture is arresting to psychoanalysts brought up in the tradition of the British School. For them the distinction that is being made between the content and the formal relationships would not exist, because the focus of attention all the time is the study of the relationships going on between the analysts and their patients, and to the nature of these relationships content is only one guide. For them, too, clinical data are the foundations on which psychoanalytic theory rests. They therefore view theories not closely related to the data with reserve; and with regard to the method, they would not accept its status as at the "rule of thumb" level.

The classical conceptual model of psychoanalysis and ego psychology

The classical model of psychoanalysis appeared many years ago when Freud (1923) formulated his structural concepts. The ego was the part of the personality concerned with organizing the adaptation of the person to the external environment, regulating the means by which he or she sought satisfaction for their drives (the id) and reconciling these with a more primitive control system (the superego), which operated unconsciously within the ego. These structures were finally shaped by the experience of the Oedipus conflict according to the first formulations. This theory permitted a considerable advance in psychoanalytic understanding and consequently produced a fresh mass of observations from the widened range of conditions it enabled the psychoanalyst to treat more comprehensively. It seemed to give a foundation for so much that had been obscure, especially the unconscious sources of resistance and guilt. It led to an interest in the structural parts of the personality, the ego and the superego, and to an understanding of how the ego was patterned by its defensive needs. The development of the ego in its earliest phases became increasingly important, a trend related to the fact that data from the neuroses gained in width and depth and also to the new findings of child analysis.

Freud's view of the id as a reservoir of unorganized drive energies with the structured ego and superego trying to regulate their discharge was gradually perceived as an oversimplification. Hartmann began to publish his well-known series of papers, many his own and others with associates, on a new concept of early development according to which the ego and the id were differentiated from the first undifferentiated phase. The ego was structured not only by the experiences of the infant and young child in the satisfaction and frustration of its drives, but also by the maturation of autonomous ego capacities, for example, motility, perception, and so forth. As part of these developments Hartmann took psychoanalysis to be no longer a theory restricted to conflict or to unconscious processes but a general psychological theory. His additions, however, to the theory of ego development and the concept of autonomous ego do not alter basically Freud's model. For him, the id still derives from libidinal and aggressive energies.

The value of Freud's model in relation to the clinical phenomena is obvious enough and so it should be since the component parts were postulated to account for clinical phenomena. On the other hand, the ego-psychology group has tended to regard some of the conceptual usages and developments from these theories, for instance, the superego, as anthropomorphic notions. To quote from Rapaport again,

> In the clinical parlance (and even in the theoretical writings) of psychoanalysis, the explanatory concepts are anthropomorphized, reified, or at best presented in existential terms, giving the impression that they refer to entities or at least that each of them refers to a specific behaviour. But this is not consistent with the theory. The tendency to anthropomorphize and reify, and the preference for hypothetical constructs, probably derives from clinical practice, where there is a premium on the "plausibility" and "uncomplicated everyday application" of concepts.
>
> (1960, p. 40)

There has certainly been a massive move here from what Brierley (1951) has described as the personological level of description to the terms of process theory. Guntrip (1961) in his recent book has dealt with some of the implications of this move at length and I shall not devote any attention to it other than to summarize by saying that herein lies the critical issue. In Rapaport's model he combines three primary models designed to explain action or conation, ideation, and affect, each of which was formulated early on by Freud. He then has to outline secondary models, which are concerned with the development of derivative drives.

> In contrast to the primary models, all the secondary models involve structuralized delay, that is to say, progressive, hierarchically layered structure development. The structures in question are: defense and control structures, structures which segregate affect charges, and the means structures which subserve secondary action – and thought-processes. A parallel development takes place in the hierarchy of

> motivations; each step in structure development results in a delay imposed on motivations which in turn gives rise to new derivative motivations and affects. The multifaceted hierarchic development is the development of the ego . . . and involves the differentiation of the ego from the id, and the super-ego from the ego. The id–ego–super-ego trichotomy is the broadest structural articulation of the mental organization and, as such, a crucial conception of the clinical theory of psychoanalysis. Since it can be derived from the models discussed, it is not an independent model and we shall not dwell on it here.
>
> (1960, p. 33)

The critical issue, as Guntrip (1961) brings out in his discussion, may be put this way. While it is true that the eventual organizations that are at the top of the hierarchy can be derived from previous processes, in what sense are we to accept the earlier processes as the primary variables that Colby stipulated as the first requirement in a model? Here we are up against a familiar problem in biological thinking, of the extent to which one may lose sight of essential qualitative differences that supervene at the highest levels of organization by relating these complex phenomena to variables appropriate to lower levels. It is not of course that Rapaport is ignoring this problem. For instance, after noting the steps in psychoanalytic theory in a discussion of the structure of the psychic system from the adaptive point of view he goes on to say that

> the fifth conception of reality, foreshadowed by both Freud's third conception and Hartmann's, is the psychosocial one developed by Erikson. . . . Man is potentially pre-adapted, not only to one average expectable environment, but to a whole evolving series of such environments. These environments to which man adapts are not "objective," but rather social environments which meet his maturation and development halfway: social *modalities* (e.g., the socially accepted forms of "getting") foster, select and harness his developing *models* (e.g., the incorporative oral mode) of behavior (Erikson 1950). This is the genetic counterpart of Hartmann's systematic formulation; it is thus far the only attempt to conceptualize the phases of epigenesis . . . through which pre-adaptedness becomes effective, and in which processes of adaptation inseparably unite behavior epigenesis and environmental conditions.
>
> (p. 61)

For Rapaport, however, the inclusion of the psychosocial point of view is "a mark of systematic weakness, since it is merely a specific aspect of the adaptive point of view" (p. 65). He states that "Hartmann's and Erikson's theories are too new, their implications too little understood, and their relationship to each other too little explored . . . to permit a statement disregarding all but systematic considerations" (p. 66).

In short, therefore, the main theoretical trend deriving from the work on ego psychology has thus far led to a concentration on rather limited concepts for the functioning of the personality. Although the relatedness of the ego to the other parts of the personality is constantly acknowledged amongst the ego-psychology group, the failure to do justice to the structuring in the other parts, especially in that area covered by the term *the id*, has led to the development of concepts that perpetuate, or even increase, a divorce between theory and clinical practice that many analysts have recognized in recent years. One of the main features in ego psychology seems to be a need to formulate theories in terms that are thought to be more appropriate to science, or more accurately, to other scientists. For analysts, however, as for others, theories must be closely linked to their practice, and the data of psychoanalysis do not lend themselves to too much depersonalization.

The object-relations model

The most radical statements of object-relations theory in Great Britain, those of Fairbairn, and the detailed expositions of Fairbairn's theories, together with his own contributions, by Guntrip, adopt a completely opposed standpoint in trying to create a model that operates in a way that can be directly related to clinical data and social interaction. This move in the direction of adopting more anthropomorphized structures, that is, structures that do justice to the phenomena of interpersonal relations, would also appear to be a direct development of the last major trend in Freud's work: the structural theories and the introduction of the superego. It is not, as I suggested earlier, a development incompatible with the ego-psychology work, but a development on a more comprehensive front and one into which the ego-psychology work can, I believe, be fitted.

Several developmental trends in Great Britain have contributed to a particular interest in the structuring of the personality from the very start in terms of the relationships between the infant and its environment. Balint (1952), stimulated by Ferenczi (1955), was one of the first psychoanalysts to make a definite pronouncement on the primacy of the object relations. Using observational data from the feeding interaction between mothers and young babies, he linked his inferences from these with the findings from child analysis, the study of psychotics, and the greatly enriched data coming from the psychoanalysis of the neuroses following developments in the use of the transference consequent on Freud's structural theory. The work of Susan Isaacs (1948), Middlemore (1941) and Winnicott, and others reinforced this trend.

It was Klein's work, however, that eventually impinged more widely, more profoundly, perhaps because she was the first analyst to make full use of the extraordinary richness and complexity of the phantasy lives of young children. Moreover, whatever reactions her theories may have aroused, there was no question of her data being too much the product of her method because children's phantasies can be studied in considerable detail without analytic intervention provided the observer is prepared to spend time with a young child. Such manifestations required the postulation of a relatively high degree of structural development at early states.

Klein and her co-workers suggested that from the start of extrauterine existence the painful affects of frustration and the intense aggression associated with these feelings led to the creation within the psyche of developing *imagos* of the early objects. At first the breast was predominant, but the internal objects rapidly extended to the whole of the mother's body and her person. These structures evoked within the child the same feelings of persecutory relationships as had the external object. Alongside these persecutory imagos, there are also being laid down imagos of the good breast-mother.

According to Klein, these inner objects are very real and concrete in the experience of the child. The ego grows in active relationship with them and its successful development is governed by the intensity of the affects in these internal relationships. Much controversy has been engendered on the nature of these internal objects and their role. Because of the concrete qualities she attributed to them, many analysts have felt there was a strong anthropomorphic tinge about Klein's theorizing. Nevertheless, it does not seem that there is anything improbable or unpsychological about such internal imagos developing from the earliest stages, or that these imagos should play a dynamic role. As Brierley (1951), one of the most careful and objective writers amongst British psychoanalysts, puts it, there is no real difficulty in conceiving of an embryonic imago of the object from the start because of the different feelings that must be present when the object, in this case the nipple, is actually present (p. 50). What is of fundamental importance is the function of this inner imago or object. As a built-in part of the relationship between the infant and the object, it appears that it can be used as the object itself – Freud's hallucinated object – or as part of an object-seeking system in which it patterns the perceptual organization. This latter role is what Klein describes as the projection–introjection system of object-relations development. That is to say, outer objects tend to be perceived and responded to in terms of inner ones. Normally, however, the outer objects do not behave as badly as the inner ones. When the former are introjected again they are therefore less persecuting; social learning occurs.

When the affect within the relationship system is too disturbing, the inner objects become too frightening to be used in this projection–introjection system. Relations with the outer world can become seriously restricted.

Such systems are then split off within the psyche from the central one in which the transactions with the outer world are proceeding apace. The systems which get segregated retain their bad objects and because of the latter being relatively unmodified by the transactions with the real objects, the frightening qualities of these inner objects remain governed by the primitive affects and phantasies. The internal bad objects for Klein are the precursors of the superego and the severity of superego persecution in many patients, adults and children, supports her view that these structures must have been laid down in very early states.

The full implications of Klein's observations and formulations for some of the classical theories of psychoanalysis were not followed through by her, and it remained for Fairbairn (1943) to point these out in a series of papers beginning in 1940. Although expressing his indebtedness to Klein's views on the importance of inner objects, Fairbairn developed his own ideas in complete independence. The starting point of his thinking was the nature of the difficulties presented by schizoid patients. It has long been known that these patients have pronounced difficulties in their social relations, but what had not been recognized, according to Fairbairn, was the extent to which their inability to make satisfying personal relationships appeared to be the root of their troubles. Moreover, he asserted on the basis of his clinical experience that underneath the symptomatic differences between the various psychoneurotic conditions, there was a severe schizoid problem.

To account for the phenomena of the schizoid disorders, Fairbairn was led to the view that it is the relationship with the object and not gratification of impulse that is the ultimate aim of libidinal striving. The *cri de coeur* of all his patients, he concluded, was for a loving mother or father, and not for the quenching of more limited tensions. In keeping with this longing, the main features of the schizoid patient are defenses against the painful affects of not being loved by a parent figure with full acceptance. The conflicts within the primary relationship of the infant and its mother lead to a splitting off or segregation within the originally unitary ego of the intolerable aspects of the relationship. Such a split involves a division of the pristine ego into structures each of which contains (a) a part of the ego, (b) the object that characterizes the related relationship, and (c) the affects of the latter. Fairbairn therefore proposed that the libido theory in its classical form and the concept of unorganized id should be replaced by concepts of dynamic structures derived from a psychology of object relations.

Revisionists of Freud's theories have often been castigated for their failure to give systematic form to their views, and to state how their revisions affect psychoanalytic theory as a whole. It is also commonly said of them that they do not grasp psychoanalytic theory fully. A careful appraisal of Fairbairn's writings removes the grounds for any such criticism being applied to him. He writes with admirable lucidity and reveals the close relationship of his own views to those of Freud. Thus in his paper on "The Repression and the

Return of Bad Objects" (1943, p. 61) he shows in Freud's own writings how the nature of the repressed can be related to objects. Freud had noted that as well as the internalized relations between the superego and the ego (the relationship of the ego to its "good" internalized objects), the superego also represented an energetic reaction formation against the earliest object choices of the id. The significance of this statement, as Fairbairn points out, is surely to imply that the repressed will be concerned with the relationship of the ego to "bad" internalized objects.

Fairbairn has given an outline of the development of object relations from the dependence of infancy to the mature relationships of later stages. The fact that he has not filled in this development in detail is of little consequence, for the conceptual model of adult behavior which he developed readily permits Colby's requirements to be met. Guntrip has described Fairbairn's final model (1961) and here it is only appropriate to note its main features. These are:

1 a central ego in relation to an ideal object directly repressing the following structures:
2 an antilibidinal ego related to the rejecting object (sadistic primitive superego); and
3 a libidinal ego related to the exciting object.

The repression of this latter structure is further reinforced by (2).

These structures are conceived as interrelated dynamic psychological systems, constantly in active relationship with each other and with the outer world. Each structure has a great complexity in depth into which is built its history. The particular experiences of the person will contribute many subsystems that could, for instance, be precipitates of repressed relations at the oral, anal, or phallic phases of classical theory; but there is a tendency for these constituent subsystems to group or to assume a hierarchical order around the image of one person, even if only loosely. The first manifestations of a bad object relationship in the course of analysis may therefore center around one or other of these subsystems, but as the analysis proceeds all the components come to the surface.

Fairbairn has retained the adjective *libidinal* to describe the object-seeking tendency of the person. I think his libidinal ego might be more accurately described as the repressed or rejected libidinal relationships, for while it is true that the repressed needs are libidinal in character, not all libidinal relationships are "outside" the central ego.

To minimize the intrusion of possibly confusing theoretical stereotypes I propose to put what I take to be the essence of Fairbairn's conceptual model into a series of statements and propositions. Many of these are about behavior or are at a first level of abstraction from the kind of phenomena met with in human relations in general and in psychoanalytic relationships in particular. Where they contain inferences about the nature of underlying process I believe these inferences can be clearly recognized.

(1) The person is related to his social environment by means of a number of dynamic psychic structures or systems, which vary greatly in the degree to which they are in open transaction with the social environment.

(2) The word *systems* indicates that these structures are organized and seek to effect certain kinds of relationships. By the term *transaction* is meant an ongoing relationship in which there is a *reciprocal interaction*. Each person is involved in such relationships in an active way with his or her needs constantly affecting the behavior of the other and vice versa.

(3) Systems vary in their mode of activity and in their topological position within the personality as a whole. They fall into two important groups:

a Those that are felt to belong to that part of the self the individual wants to be. These come within a central organizing structure (the ego).
b Those that are split off or repressed from this self or central system. (The words split, repressed, dissociated, or segregated are used interchangeably in this context.)

The central system, or ego

(4) This system has assimilated and organized much of the experience with significant people in the early environment and hence much of the cultural pattern in which the individual is reared. This central organization (the ego) is characterized by its relatively much greater capacity to learn and by its unique feature, namely that its integrative functions appear closely connected with consciousness.

In the healthy adult, the main needs are sufficiently egosyntonic and of such a character that a manifold set of personal relationships is sought and maintained. The relatively free transactions between the need systems themselves (greater communication) in the healthy person also mean that he or she responds more as a whole, is more integrated in assessing inner and outer reality. The central ego in such a person is therefore being enriched throughout life and this *constant enrichment provides a motivational growth and support.*

Typical of the healthy or strong ego are this freedom of communication between different need systems and the consonance of the main needs over time.

The whole question of the scale and the maturational phases of developments in the human personality is something which only Erikson (1950) has attempted to encompass. Although Fairbairn discounts instincts in the sense in which they have been commonly used in psychology and psychoanalysis, the work of the ethologists has shown that a more flexible and illuminating approach to the instinctive roots of behavior can be made, particularly in regard to social behavior and object relations. Bowlby has made a major contribution in this direction concerning the nature and development of the attachment of the child to his mother. The tie between the reproductive pair is almost certainly mediated by a number of response and need systems that allow for the rearing of the family over time. It is this kind of approach that could lay a biological foundation more in keeping with the need for sustained object relations than is the primary model of drives and their tensions conceived so often in hydrodynamic terms and requiring so many derivative structures for the social behavior that is basic to human survival.

The development of the relationship of the person with himself, his identity, as consolidated by Erikson's epigenetic phases, might well be illuminated by future studies incorporating an ethological approach, particularly in revealing the factors contributing to the development of the need for whole person relationships from the point of view of rearing the family. The survival unit of the human being is the family. The interplay of the manner in which the dependent status of the child contributes to the building up of the need for whole person relationships and the extent to which these are reinforced by future needs stemming from the reproductive constellation within the family, and of the position of the latter within the social group, provides endless scope for further work.

(5) The capacity of the central ego to tolerate conflicting needs and to organize them appears to be largely an acquired property. Certain kinds of early experience make or mar this capacity in a profound way. What starts off the ego as an adequate independent organizer, in other words, what lays the foundations for an organizing ego, independent of the mother who has been the first organizer, is particularly important.

Fairbairn's inferences about what seems to have gone wrong in his schizoid patients are in line with the work of many psychoanalysts. The importance for the future functional power of the central ego of critical phases in the early mother–child relationship is now very familiar in phases that have become bywords in analytic writings – Balint's primary love, Erikson's basic trust, Winnicott's true self, and so forth.

(6) In the relationships fashioned predominantly by the central ego the identity and reality of the other is fully accepted, that is, the overall acceptance of the person raises the threshold of toleration for unfulfilled expectancies so that the relationship is maintained. If the frustrations in the relationship are too great despite mutual adaptation attempts, it can be ended without destructive behavior. The concern for the other in adult relationships stems from many sources, one being the patterning of the central ego's actions by the tendency, even though this be very much a latent process, to make the real relationships approximate to that of the ideal ego with its ideal object.

Repressed needs and primitive control systems

(7) These systems comprise:

- a certain need systems, which may be designated *repressed aspects of object relations*, and
- b *primitive control systems* (the superego) derived from early inhibition of certain need systems.

In contrast with those of the central ego, the relationships sought by the repressed need systems are relatively closed, in other words, the objects sought are not individuals with mature independence but are realizations of the inner figures. In extreme cases, it can be clearly perceived that the individual has a relation with an inner object with whom he or she is virtually completely identified, that is, who is a part of the self. This is particularly striking in the self-gratifying perversions – the transvestist who has the sexually exciting relation with the woman with a penis by finding her in the mirror image when he is dressed up. More often the inner object acts as a scanning apparatus, which seeks a potential object in the outer world. The subego of this system then coerces these people into the role of the inner object. Such objects are not permitted to have any real independence or individuality; they have to fit the inner imago. Sadomasochistic perversions illustrate this activity, and the ease with which the individual can change roles in these perversions indicates the switch from the identification with one end of the system to the other.

(8) The goals sought by these subsystems represent *aspects of the total relationship* with the significant figures of infancy and childhood and range from relationships characteristic of early infantile dependent states of development (for example, "oral" needs) to genital behavior.

(9) These subsystems have been split off because their aims were incompatible with the preservation of the egosyntonic relationship with the needed person. The conflict gives rise to "pain" (fear, anxiety, guilt, depression, and so forth) associated with their activity.

(10) They are excluded from the conscious self by forces of varying resistance. Their dissociation from consciousness means that little or no adaptation or learning occurs within them.

(11) The original frustration apparently leads to many of them containing, in addition to the affect associated with their own aims, for example, genital gratification, intense anger, and destructiveness towards the person sought; in other words they are largely sadistic in character.

(12) They are constantly seeking outlet in ordinary relationship and/or in phantasy and thought, that is, they have the compulsion to repeat.

(13) Their activity is particularly evocative of the superego systems, that is, they are accompanied by varying degrees of anxiety and guilt.

(14) The resistance some of them show to being brought back into consciousness becomes increased:

a by their finding hidden satisfactions within the self (in which case a part of the self is treated as the object to be loved and/or hated in the forbidden way). For Fairbairn, it is the secret tie to the repressed exciting object which is the explanation of much of the resistance to giving it up. Or

b when their objects are projected into other people – especially in close relationships.

(15) A particularly important feature of these needs is that, though there is a defensive tendency for people to take them to other people than those with whom they wish to maintain their close good relationships, nevertheless, there is an even more powerful trend for them to come back into a close relationship with one person. That is to say, *the repressed not only returns, but it tends to return to the representative of the more comprehensive relationship from which it was originally split off.*

(16) All of the psychic systems are interrelated functionally and their relative strengths and capacities for securing satisfaction must be conceived as stemming from a continuous process of interrelated development. The boundaries between the systems vary greatly in their "permeability."

These statements, based on Fairbairn's model, describe the functioning of a person in his or her social relationships. They provide at least the outline of a model for human interaction, particularly for conflict in social behavior. They are intended primarily to meet Colby's first requirement, that variables should be at the right level, and his other requirements can be readily fulfilled also.

The study of the central ego, its functions, and development, provides ample scope for ego psychology. The interrelatedness of ego function and the intrusive effects of unconscious object-relationship needs suggests that a comprehensive statement of object-relations theory will provide a suitable framework for the development of psychoanalytic theory. I am dubious, however, about the extension of psychoanalysis to be a general psychology. Psychology requires many methods of study of which the psychoanalytic method is one. Psychology is hollow without psychoanalysis, but it has to draw on many methods and data other than those of psychoanalysis.

Some uses of the model

The aims of psychoanalysis

The *general aims* of psychoanalysis can be stated in terms of an object-relations model as initiating and maintaining a process whereby repressed relationship-systems are brought back within the organizing system of the ego so that they can be subjected to learning and adaptation. Psychoanalysts secure this process by:

1 Providing a specially designed situation in which there can be freer communication between the parts of the self and between the repressed systems and a special external object, the analyst. The analyst facilitates these changes by interpreting the hidden aims of the dissociated relationships as these emerge in the spontaneous behavioral and verbal expressions of the individual toward the analyst.
2 Offering a personal relationship in which the patient eventually uses the analyst as the object toward whom dissociated systems can be expressed, brought into awareness with sufficient affect, and tested against the continuing reality of the analyst's interest. This bringing of the dissociated need systems into the requisite kind of awareness allows "extinction" of some needs and learning of new objects for others to take place again.

A greater degree of integration is sought through a twofold process, namely:

a Increasing the integrative capacity of the central ego system through the overall relationship with the analyst by establishing a capacity to transact with people more freely.
b Bringing back the dissociated systems for new solutions.

A certain intensity of treatment and its special setting are required for this process to be adequately maintained and regulated.

I shall not do other here than to refer to the "setting" of the patient's total life situation as creating obstacles to the analytic relationship. Certain alterations of this may be required for the analyst's aims to be possible. For instance, parents may maintain with a child – or one marital partner may exert on the other – a pressure to keep a sub-relationship in being, thereby requiring the relationship to be altered for the analysis to proceed.

Transference and the psychoanalytic relationship

Transference phenomena enter into all human relationships so that their existence within the psychoanalytic relationship is in no way characteristic. All kinds of people are made the pegs on which the objects of repressed relationships are hung. What is it that is specific to the transference in the analytic relationship? I believe the answer to this question is that the analytic process permits a unique setting for the reintegration of the split relationships in the self. The affects and aims of repressed relationships tend to be acted out by all human beings in some of their personal relationships without the discharge of these affects having other than a minimal or negligible effect on their compulsion to repeat. But the analyst, starting as a good object, usually an ideal one, creates the essential feature of the analytic process in that the split relationships are reexperienced with this *one person* who does not reject them intolerantly. This is, of course, no new statement. It is universally agreed that it is the transference experiences within the analytic setting that lead to change. Karl Menninger's (1958) model of the analytic contract describes this process. I believe, nevertheless, that its implications for our structural concepts have not been fully realized. Can we account for this *crucial aspect of the transference relationship* unless it is postulated that what is repressed, as Fairbairn has described them, are bad aspects of an original unitary relationship of one ego with another whole person, the mother? In other words, can we explain why the analytic relationship is sought and maintained by the patient unless there is an original supraordinate structure that is trying to reunite within itself parts that originally belonged to it, and whose segregation is sustained only by constant strain within it?

Rapaport asks if the analytic method does justice to the phenomena of human relationships or whether instead it creates artifacts. It would appear that this inner compulsive striving to unite the original splits in the ego and its object within one relationship is not a product of the analytic process but a general tendency of human personality. The literature of the world points to Fairbairn's conception of the splitting within an original unitary structure as a universal truth; in short, it is the human tragedy that "each man kills the thing he loves" – or, at least, tries it the uttermost. But what Wilde did not know, and what object relations theory emphasizes, is that the killing is not to destroy but is to make an infantile protest from which the good relationship will reemerge magically.

A source of evidence with which I have had a good deal of experience in recent years, and which is very telling in this connection, is that which stems from work with marital conflicts. The commonest presenting pattern of these is as follows. In the early phases there is an idealized relationship, or at least what is felt to be a good relationship. This phase may last over years and often includes sexual relationships that are satisfying to both partners. There then begins an insidious process, frequently starting with more initiative from one partner, but sooner or later colluded in by both, through which the repressed relationships with the original significant parent figures are brought in. The particular pattern follows, of course, the specific content of the individual's history and it is remarkable at times how closely the settings and *patterns of original relationships* are reproduced. With these cases, there are many complications, but the common characteristic keeps reappearing, namely, of the bringing into the good relationship the repressed bad aspects of the relationships with the parents. In marriage, processes of this kind are universal but they are ordinarily contained by the balance in favor of the good relationship and its enrichment. Where the difficulties become of such an intensity that help is sought, then a further feature emerges. Despite the tensions and often fairly prolonged periods of hostility and mutual recrimination, there remains a strong desire to get the relationship right. Often this is reinforced by external considerations, for example, for children, but this need is usually present without these factors. In view of the frustrations and sufferings of so many of these spouses before marriage, it would be expected that desperate measures would be put into action to preserve in the relationship the goodness of the early phases. What then determines the entry into the good relationship of the repressed bad relationships? The most plausible theory to my mind is that the spouses are trying to undo the experiences of an early relationship in which the bad aspects belonged with the good. Unfortunately when, as so frequently happens, both partners collude in a process of this kind the relationship becomes one in which both are living with their bad objects projected into the other and they remain stuck in this position. Psychotherapy directed towards these collusive forces in the relationship often produces good effects in persons who separately would be regarded as much more difficult prospects for individual psychotherapy.

The psychoanalytic method

Under the stimulus of the object-relations concepts as these are expressed in the writings of Bion (1961), Rickman (1957), Fairbairn (1952a), and Ezriel (1951) put forward a statement of major importance concerning the study of the psychoanalytic method. Ezriel concluded that most doubts about psychoanalytic theories center on the validity of the psychoanalytic method. Using tripartite object-relation structures as described by Fairbairn, he assumed that the psychoanalytic situation would be dominated at any one time by three forces corresponding to the three systems. Thus, the central ego would seek one relationship with the therapist, the repressed needs would drive the individual to express another, and the inhibiting superego would create a feeling of impending threat, disapproval, or catastrophe. He proposed to conduct therapy without making any historical reconstructions and to confine his comments to how he saw these three relationships determining the behavior of the patient. In other words, the psychoanalytic session could be treated as an experimental situation provided the therapist stuck to the here-and-now forces operating in the setting.

Not only was this a way of investigating the psychoanalytic method, but in Ezriel's view it provided the much needed theoretical framework on which all interpretations should be based. The verbalizations made by most analysts during sessions can be very different in status and complexity, ranging from simple affirmations, requests to give more material, and so on. His thesis, however, was that the interpretation – the crucial aspect of the analyst's verbalizations – must consist of bringing to the patient's notice the three types of relationship in the situation. Fairbairn (1952b) also wrote a short paper subsequent to Ezriel in which he expressed very similar ideas. That is to say, the analyst must account for what the patient is expressing to him by a response in which three components are discernible, namely: (1) When you say (or communicate by behavior) *x*, you are striving to maintain relationship *a* with me, (2) but *x* also indicates that you want to express another relationship *b* with me, which you must not admit to *because* you fear (3) relationship *c* in which I shall do something disastrous to you (reject, punish, attack, be sexual with, and so on). Thus the unconsciously sought relationship, the defense against it, and the reason for the defense are incorporated in these three parts.

Social relations and group psychotherapy

Freud's (1921) study on group psychology was a remarkable contribution to our understanding of group processes. Here was one of the early examples of theory in object-relations terms because the group members became related through their common introjection of the leader as their ideal object. Kleinian theory with its multiplicity of internal objects suggested that the social relations created by the individual would reflect situations comparable to those between the ego and his inner objects. Bion (1961), Jaques (1955), Menzies (1960) and others developed these ideas. In a number of contributions they showed how illuminating these primitive object relations of the inner world could be in understanding and handling both intragroup tensions and those between groups.

Summary

I have outlined some features of the object-relations theory of the personality that started in the work of Klein and the advantages of which have been formulated so penetratingly by Fairbairn. Its main aim is to formulate a theory closely related to the phenomena of human conflict and of personal relationships. There is a danger to psychoanalytic theory and practice in trying to reduce the phenomena to components that have the appearance of being more scientific because they avoid errors of anthropomorphism. An object-relations model can be flexible and comprehensive with regard to the understanding of behavior at any one time in terms of the here-and-now manifestations and of how these are the product of historical layerings. It has the added advantage of giving a more rigorous basis for the study of the psychoanalytic method.

Fairbairn's formulations try to do justice to the phenomena of human interaction. I have suggested that the way the personality seeks to undo its splits within one relationship is only explicable by a theory of the kind that Fairbairn has stated, namely that these splits occurred within an originally unitary structure that mediated the relationship between the infant and his first object, the mother.

Chapter 3

British object relations: Balint, Winnicott, Fairbairn, Guntrip

Editor's introduction

Sutherland highlights the contributions of four of the most prominent and influential analysts working independently and contemporaneously in Britain in the mid-1900s. He describes their background and the intellectual and social context of their views. He summarizes their ideas: Balint on the basic fault and therapeutic regression; Winnicott on transitional objects in the development of the true self as the baby goes on being and doing in the context of the mother/baby relationship; Fairbairn on the personality as motivated by the drive to be in a meaningful, satisfying relationship and evolving a dynamic ego structure by dissociation and repression in response to frustration of that drive; and Guntrip on the deepest, most primal anxieties leading to distortion of the structures of the self observable in withdrawn states.

From the requests to give talks on the work of these analysts, I assume that the growing interest in it is not simply historical. On the contrary, I believe that the issues that they struggled with have become questions of widespread concern today for the advancement of psychoanalytic theory and practice. The reasons for taking this quartet as a group do not stem from any joint work they did. They did not constitute a group in that sense at all. Guntrip's work is closely derived from, and related to, Fairbairn's; but Balint and Winnicott pursued their paths independently of each other and of the others, and both were rather superficial in their comments on Fairbairn's writings, as were most analysts for many years. What gives point to their being bracketed together is the extent to which their contributions eventually embodied a common development. Even in this respect, however, they preserved their individuality, for while Fairbairn stated clearly that his clinical findings required a recasting of some of Freud's central formulations, Balint and Winnicott did not take this step. Indeed, Winnicott shared with Masud Khan (Winnicott and Khan 1953) the view of Fairbairn's book (1952a) that "if one could escape this claim" by Fairbairn that his theory supplants that of Freud, "one could enjoy the writings of an analyst who challenges everything, and who puts clinical evidence before accepted theory" (p. 329). As Guntrip (1961) tersely observes, this is no way to advance any science!

The independence with which their work progressed adds, of course, to the weight of their similar conclusions. It is remarkable, too, that all were contemporaries, born approximately in the last decade of last century and all dying in their early seventies. Personally, they liked and respected each other, though disagreeing about their theories. I should add here that in using the adjective "British," I am not prompted by the Scottish Nationalist spirit that has become prominent in recent years. It is true that Fairbairn carried out all his work in his native Scotland, but I have used the more comprehensive adjective to distinguish this group from what has been referred to as the English School, a term commonly denoting Melanie Klein and her co-workers.

While restricting this group to these four contributors, I do not imply in any way that they were the only ones who have developed object-relations theories. Many others have done so. However, I think these four have been more fundamentally concerned with this theme and have written more explicitly on it. The most notable of my exclusions is obviously Melanie Klein. There is no doubt that her work was highly influential on all of our quartet, though perhaps least on Balint. Guntrip, possibly because of his position outside the formal analytic groups and his interest in the historical development of psychodynamic thought, never ceased to emphasize that in his view it was Melanie Klein who made the first major challenge to the foundations on which Freud's metapsychology rests. Her work with the inner worlds of young children established the need to postulate the structuring of object relations from a much earlier stage than had been thought. Although a remarkably gifted and courageously dedicated research worker in this field of the earliest stages of development, Melanie Klein lacked the kind of intellectual rigor that enabled her to follow through the theoretical implications of her work. Her views therefore remained largely as brilliant presentations of some of the phenomena we have to take into account, phenomena which she failed to systematize convincingly, largely through her adherence to the theoretical use of the death instinct. In this way she seems to most analysts to minimize the role of the external object almost to that of confirming the fantasies produced from within by the activity of the instincts. She thus appears at times to create a kind of biological solipsism rather than a conceptual framework for the evolution, from the earliest stages, of structures based on experience with objects.

Winnicott (1958b) certainly acknowledges his debt to Melanie Klein at various points, albeit mainly in relation to specific concepts such as the depressive position. With Fairbairn, however, her influence was more fundamental. It was her use of the concepts of multiple internal objects along with her object-related views of the paranoid and depressive positions that led him to break away from the classical position, in which the theory of psychic development was based on the unstructured energies of the id, in order to account for his clinical findings with schizoid patients.

The independent way in which our theorists developed their work allows us the more readily to look at the contribution of Balint and Winnicott separately and then to consider Fairbairn and Guntrip as creating successive phases of the same line of thought.

I shall be relatively brief about Balint and Winnicott, whose work has always been better known since both were prominent members of the analytic movement, locally and internationally. By contrast, Fairbairn worked alone from his isolated position in Scotland and so had few opportunities to discuss his work with a wide range of colleagues. Recognition, especially from international sources, came to him relatively late in life. Guntrip was even more isolated from the analytic scene in that he was not a member of the British Psychoanalytic Society. A much more prolific writer than Fairbairn, his books, however, brought him into a wide range of contacts with analysts and analytical psychotherapists.

Michael Balint

Theoretical preferences and styles are very much influenced by the personalities and backgrounds of the individuals. It might therefore be of interest to make a few remarks about each of our subjects. Balint completed his analytic training with Ferenczi in 1926 and along with his first wife, Alice, concentrated entirely on the early development of the ego. Their backgrounds comprised biology, medicine, anthropology, and education, and their work was intensely mutual. Unable to accept the theory of primary narcissism with its implication that the infant only gradually becomes related to objects, they advanced the quite opposite view of the infant's growth as absolutely dependent on an intense relatedness, biologically and libidinally, with its environment. Alice Balint died soon after their emigration to England in 1939, and Michael continued to develop their early theories. From his analytic work with patients who regressed deeply, he was led to describe a condition that he termed *The Basic Fault* (1968). The patients said they felt a "fault" or "something missing" inside themselves, rather than a feeling of something dammed up and needing to be released; and Balint added "basic" because its effects permeated the whole functioning of the person. He assumed that this fault, which in some measure is universal, is caused by a failure of fit between the needs of the child and the response of the mother; but beyond his description of it as a fault or an "area of the mind," he did not really conceptualize it.

It is from this area that the Oedipus complex develops in response to the increasing experience with parents as maturation occurs. Alongside the oedipal phenomena, however, he postulated an "area of creation" in the mind in which the individual creates objects or artistic products in a private internal way to try to make something more satisfying than the real objects. The basic fault is also a precursor to the emergence of two types of object relations: *ocnophilia* in which objects are cathected with great intensity and so clung to for security, and *philobatism* in which the inner world is cathected to provide a degree of independence from the precariousness of objects. These object relations are thus for Balint a defense against the effects of the failure of the environment.

In the treatment of individuals who manifest the basic fault regression to a marked degree, Balint concluded that the standard analytic method of giving only verbal interpretations was unable to alter the stalemate produced in the regression. The patient's state was not one that could be analyzed away, so to speak. What the patient needed from the analyst was the opportunity to make good a deficiency. The analyst had therefore to be the kind of object or environment with which the patient could discover his or her own way in the world of objects. With all basic fault states, analysts had to convey through the relationship with the patients that they understood the patient's needs and that in doing so they recognized each patient's own inner life and valued his or her unique individuality.

What Balint described by way of theory and practice in these regressions is well known, and my purpose in sketching it again is to draw attention to the main position he reached. From his clinical data, Balint suggests that a critical primary developmental phase has to be surmounted for the individual to emerge with a general capacity to relate to objects and to himself in a reasonably effective and satisfying way. Although Balint eschews any attempt at making an adequate theory, it is clear that the individual who escapes major trouble at this basic fault stage must have achieved a very important *structural change*, a fundamental epigenetic development. As Morse (1972) has put it, Balint appears to have refused "to become a psychoanalytic heretic by attempting to formulate the revised structural theory he needs to explain his data" (p. 498), and because he stopped short, he gives us a metaphorical description instead of an explanatory theory. The new structure must function as a very basic organization for all subsequent development if, as Balint (1968) says, its influence extends probably "over the whole psychobiological structure of the individual, involving in varying degrees both his mind and body" (p. 22). It allows us

> to understand not only the various neuroses (perhaps also psychoses), character disorders, psychosomatic illnesses etc., as symptoms of the same etiological entity, but also – as the experiences of our research into general medical practice have shown – a great number of ordinary "clinical" illnesses as well.
>
> (p. 22)

Balint accepts that analysts have worked out an adequate theory and practice to encompass the oedipal conflicts, which arise from the parental triangular situation, as opposed to the problems of the basic fault, which occur in the earlier dyadic relationship. Nevertheless, he does not attempt to show in what way, for instance, the earlier developments might correlate with the oedipal phenomena. Again, while the basic fault failure leads to either a clinging to objects, which are then introjected for support, or creative activities, we are not really taken much beyond that for we are not offered any views about the structural changes that must underlie the development of persistent patterns of behavior such as ocnophilia or philobatism. Also, while hate for Balint is located in the struggle to overcome the oppressive dependence on the primary object and the giving up of primitive omnipotent wishes – and it is the struggle that makes for the intense positive and negative feelings in the "new beginning" phase of the analysis when the basic fault is reached – he makes no reference to related structural concepts, for example, of internal objects.

Benign regression, which leads to a "new beginning," is contrasted with malignant states. Characteristic of the former is the patient's need to feel he is being recognized and responded to as an individual, an outcome that commonly needs some minimal action from the analyst, for instance, touching hands. The patient does not wish for instinctual gratification, and for this reason Balint implies that the need is of a holistic "personal" nature. In contrast to the benign regression, the patient in a malignant condition moves to insatiable demands for orgiastic gratification and so drives the analysis to a "tragic or heroic finale." Balint does not suggest that these different outcomes arise from different structural features. Instead, he thinks that some malignant regressions may be the result of inadequate experience and skill in the analyst with a recreation of the lack of fit between the infant in the patient and the mother in the analyst.

D. W. Winnicott

Winnicott's work (1958b, 1965, 1971) is even more familiar than Balint's, so again I shall merely put what would seem to be the essence of his position as he left it. His approach to the earliest stages of development draws on the unusually rich material available to him from the fact that he combined the role of practicing pediatrician with that of psychoanalyst throughout most of his professional life. He was, too, a great individualist who brought a characteristic poetic and imaginative quality to his theoretical and practical work.

His experience with seriously regressed patients and the correlation of his clinical data with his extensive knowledge of mothers and young children led him to the same kind of problems that preoccupied Balint, namely, those around the earliest structuring of the psyche. As did Balint, he concludes that there is a very early split, which has profound significance for future development. Balint's basic fault is paralleled by Winnicott in his concept of a true and false self, a split that originates in a failed relationship between mother and infant in the earliest stages. Winnicott believes that the innate growth potential of the infant expresses itself in various spontaneous manifestations. When the ordinary good mother responds naturally to these – and she is especially equipped to do so by a specific development around the time of the baby's birth, what he termed her "primary maternal preoccupation" – the fit between her response and the baby's experience gives to the latter an "omnipotent" creative quality. Repeated experiences of this kind establish in the infant a sense of wholeness, of conviction about the goodness of reality, and a "belief in" the world as a rewarding place. This core of feeling gives rise to a "true self" because the full maturational potential, as this emerges in its increasing repertoire of activity, can be actualized in joyful relations. The confidence in the mother also permits the gradual giving up of omnipotence, with the disillusionment this involves and its swings between intense love and hate. For Winnicott this true self brings with its growth a feeling that its core has to be intensely private, "incommunicado" (1965, p. 187), as he put it later. There is an obscurity about this notion in that the core feeling of having a self appears to depend on its being given to the infant by the input from the good mothering, and so the separation of an absolutely private part is difficult to understand. It could relate to the essence of the growing sense of the thrust of autonomy, the sensing of an "I" as apart from the objects, an embryonic affect for the later "I am real, I am going to do my own thing and not someone else's," and a fear of this being interfered with, but Winnicott seems to imply some other factors of a more primary nature.

Frustration beyond a certain level cannot be contained within the affective cohesion of the experiences of the true self, especially when the mother is felt as forcing herself on the infant, as impinging thereon, with her own responses out of fit with the spontaneous needs of the child. This kind of negative experience gradually becomes organized to form a "false self," that is, one that complies with the mother's attributes; and as the mismatch between the latter and the infant's responses increases, so does the distortion or stunting of development, with the true-self potential receding more and more from its inherent capacity for relatedness.

Like Balint, Winnicott concluded that the experiences structured into the true and false selves are not those of instinctual gratification. Good experiences of the latter reinforce the true self, but its structuring is founded on the quality of the relatedness between the infant and its mother. The relationship between these structures and Freud's tripartite division remains ambiguous. It is again as if Winnicott, like Balint, stopped short of any radical confrontation between the theories he needed and those so well established. Thus although he refers to this early structuring as very close to the id, he continues to emphasize its complete dependence on the quality of the object relations. Guntrip notes his reverting to *ego relatedness* as the critical contributing factor instead of continuing with his almost complete adoption of the term self. Guntrip suggests that Winnicott may have introduced the ego to denote the part of the self involved in relations, but concluded that this idea could not be maintained. It is more likely that it represents a certain inconsistency in Winnicott's theorizing; and in this connection there are various examples of that. Thus Winnicott notes (1963, p. 83) that his account of the growth from dependence to independence makes no reference to the libido theory. He then adds that we can take all that for granted and his scheme for these early structural developments does not in any way invalidate any statement he might have made in terms of erotogenic zones. In all his later papers, however, there can be no doubt that he has moved from the classical frame of reference to an approach of a general systems theory type, for it is the self that operates as the organizing principle for all future differentiation. The critical property of the self is the creativity that takes place within it through play. Winnicott doubts whether we can explain this creative process, although we can study the very important processes through which creative living can be lost and hence lead to the feeling of life as unreal or without meaning. With his descriptions of the functions of play and creativity (1971) he gives more specific suggestions on the development of the self.

The concept of the transitional object was his first stressing of an activity that occurred in this creative "area" between the subjective and the objectively perceived. Later he widened this area as the one in which play, artistic creativity, religion, and culture were developed, as also were the contents of psychopathological conditions. Again, too, it is in this area of playing, as in the formation of the core self, that the process is spoiled by the intrusion of instinctual excitement, for example, masturbation. Playing is a form of doing, but of a special kind in which there is an interplay of personal psychic reality and the experience of control of actual objects. The appropriate responsiveness of the mother allows her to become a subjective object and, with further good interaction, an objectively perceived object; and the self differentiates as a result of the essential role of play. The capacity for play is very much dependent on the mother's love or her object-relating, at first on her active input and later on her reliable availability, as he described in his paper "The Capacity to be Alone" (1958a). It is, in other words, founded on trust. Playing is thus the universal facilitator for growth and social relationships and, indeed, for Winnicott, mutual playing is the essence of the psychotherapeutic relationship. It is only in playing that the individual – child or adult – uses his whole personality in creative activity, and it is only in being creative that he discovers this self. The way in which the self is sensed, in other words, its security or otherwise, has to be mirrored back to the trusted parent. A conviction of one's creativity as "fun" that can be shared is the essence of the self that can enjoy living. It is here that theory must again take the object relatedness of the child into account because the emergence of play and creativity is dependent upon the environmental provision, the quality of the mother's love, from the start.

A further elaboration of Winnicott's views of the first stage of development consists in what he terms the phase of *being* as a necessary precursor to a phase of *doing* for healthy development (1971). In the phase of *being*, the first weeks, the infant acquires from its experience of ordinary good mothering what is apparently a positive affective content to its overall self-feeling. The prototype of this good experience is the relationship with the empathic mother and her breast, and, because the infant is in a relatively passive absorptive state most of the time and because only the mother can give this experience, he terms it, for want of a better, the *female element* in the self. This phase moves on to one of *doing*, which he correspondingly calls the *male element*, wherein the object relatedness proceeds to the differentiation of the self and object. Although the terms may not be satisfactory, he has clearly separated two phases in the course of development of the self toward its becoming a subject in relationship with objects.

While Winnicott, like Balint, leaves a great deal of theoretical work to be done, they have both reached a closely similar general position.

I have already referred to Morse's critique (1972) of Balint; he is equally critical of Winnicott, considering his scheme too inconsistent and even contradictory. The importance of both, however, seems to lie in the role they accord to certain basic developmental achievements. If successfully attained, then individuals are established with the capacity to relate effectively to others and to themselves, whereas failure means restricted or distorted development. A fundamental organizer has been fashioned, not from instinctual satisfactions by themselves, but from these along with the experience of a general fit between the infant's overall psychological needs and the mother's spontaneous acceptance of these. The implications of such a structuring being a template for the future development of the person are profound, and since the same questions arise with our other theorists we shall hold off on answering them until later.

W. R. D. Fairbairn

When we turn to Fairbairn and Guntrip we soon sense a different quality pervading their thinking. Freud's approach was profoundly rooted in the scientific materialism of the nineteenth century, and though his findings drove him persistently toward the recognition of the psychological level of the organism's activity as an irreducible domain, he never reached the point of feeling it had as much reality as the physiological. Balint and Winnicott also tended to retain this influence, though to a lesser degree. While they could both think of love as a human response at a personal level, not reducible to instinctual gratifications, they kept this "area" of their minds largely separated from the area which the classical libido theory had created. Even with Winnicott's increasing preoccupation in his later work with the phenomena for which he used "the self" rather than the less personal terms of Freud's structural theory, he did not pursue the wider theoretical changes his work was inexorably foreshadowing.

The intellectual backgrounds of Fairbairn and Guntrip were very different from the others. Fairbairn's first academic training was in philosophy, from which he went to Hellenic studies and then to theology. He intended to enter the Church until the First World War interrupted this plan, and by the time he finished his four years as a combatant soldier he had decided to take a medical training with a view to becoming a psychotherapist. Freud linked his dislike of philosophers to their speculative *Weltanschauungen*. Perhaps there was sufficient change in the teachings of philosophy by the time Fairbairn came to it, for certainly to him, and even more so to Guntrip, the importance of this influence was the discipline it imposed upon the theorist to criticize rigorously his concepts. Thus Fairbairn always viewed the libido theory and the pleasure principle with the uneasiness that the philosophical criticisms of any hedonistic theory engendered. Also, from his role as teacher in the Psychology Department in the University of Edinburgh, he was influenced by the views on *Instinct in Man* which had been published by Drever (1917), the Professor there. Although armchair in origin, these views had quite a dynamic system nature, for example, any structured propensity that instinct was based on engendered a specific emotional coloring according to whether its aim was being achieved or not. Another influence was gestalt psychology, which did a great deal to reinforce the need to think of the unique properties of the relevant wholes in psychological processes in contrast to the atomistic approach to these fostered by scientific materialism. Guntrip was especially influenced by the philosopher John MacMurray (1961) who expounded the need to conceptualize the personal level and who stressed that one of the most pressing problems for philosophy was a satisfactory conceptualization of the self because for him the self was the essential agent in human behavior.

The papers produced by Fairbairn during the first decade of his psychoanalytic work show that he had carefully assimilated Freud's theories. It was from the treatment of a series of markedly schizoid patients after this period that the primary importance of object relationships struck him. Their impact coincided with another powerful influence, namely, Melanie Klein's writings on the inner object relations of children and adults, and especially her 1935 paper, "A Contribution to the Psychogenesis of Manic-Depressive States." Fairbairn's geographical isolation, with its reinforcement of the independence of his thinking, led him to stress, however, the primacy of the phase earlier than Klein's depressive position. Indeed, he came to think that depression had played too great a part in psychoanalytic theory. It was not, after all, a very common clinical condition, and moreover, much happened in the developmental period that preceded Klein's critical phase.

The clinical manifestations of his schizoid patients convinced Fairbairn that their etiology consisted in the mother's failure to give the infant an adequate experience of "being loved for himself." This condensed phrase is clearly a very complex package, one that essentially connotes the view that the foundation for subsequent healthy development is not laid in the satisfaction of instincts but in imparting to each infant that he or she is "a person," valued and enjoyed as such by the mother. When deprived of this experience, the most serious consequences can occur. Individuals, despite their innate longing for object relations, become too frightened to make them lest their love be rejected, and so they build up a compensatory inner world of relationships. There thus develops massive structural splitting within the unitary ego, which is present from the start. At the time of writing his new formulations, Fairbairn was clearly reluctant to alienate other analysts by introducing too many new terms and so he retained the word ego for this pristine unity. Just as Winnicott and Guntrip found they had to adopt *the self* as a more appropriate term, so Fairbairn found it best to restrict *ego* to the part of the self that is adapted to outer reality, thus leaving *the self* for the more comprehensive *psyche* or *person*. He also reverted at times to the entitative *the libido* when, as he later pointed out, it would have been more consistent had he said that it is the individual in his or her libidinal capacity that seeks objects.

Fairbairn's explicit statement that the development of the person from the very start had to be conceived in terms of dynamic structures based on experience with objects instead of these being derived from unstructured energies was a major challenge to the libido theory. It was one of those changes of standpoint that is simple in principle and yet is soon felt by many as extremely disconcerting. The complexities of psychological phenomena are certainly daunting, and it was Freud's incredible achievement to have provided future investigators with an exploratory instrument. The peculiar feature of the analytic method, however, is that the instrument is the personality of the investigator, informed and supported by his experience, the latter being enlarged through training. Psychoanalytic theory and practice are thus uniquely interdependent, and what Freud's theories had given us were our only anchor points in the uncharted seas that every patient presents. As a result, to challenge Freud's theories has usually been responded to with anxiety, as if a sacrilegious outrage were being perpetrated. Of course we do not change theoretical views lightly, especially when they come from someone of Freud's stature. Nevertheless, his theories, as Freud himself remarked, are the upper stories of the edifice and not the foundations; and Fairbairn certainly had a thorough knowledge of the foundations, which were never in question for him.

The reception accorded to his challenge, which was argued in an impressively compact and tightly logical way, was at first somewhat patronizing, and some of this attitude has persisted. Thus Modell (1968), while acknowledging the value of his clinical findings, regrets that "Fairbairn's theory was not intended to supplement Freud's but to *supplant it*" and so has won very few supporters. Again,

> men like Fairbairn, when faced with these problems, would wish to rip out the entire fabric of psychoanalytic thinking and start anew. . . . It would take a man of Freud's genius to rival Freud, and the history of science shows that such men do not appear to every generation; they scarcely appear in every century.
>
> (pp. 4–5, 6)

When he was writing his papers, Fairbairn in fact would often say that as he kept going back to Freud's writings he was repeatedly astounded to find Freud constantly on the brink of taking a step that would have cast his formulations into the more appropriate one of keeping strictly to psychological structure. Anyone with less sense of rivalry or of "sacrilegious intent" than Fairbairn would be hard to find. He was one of the most conservative of men, a man of great dignity and integrity. He was, moreover, very strongly against people attributing a new school to himself. For him, psychoanalysis and its development were what mattered; but he did not shrink from suggesting a theory that he considered did more justice to the facts, nor did he feel apologetic in doing so. To him it was more of a sin against Freud's legacy to cling to any part that might be improved than to recast it in the light of further knowledge; and intellectually he was well equipped to appraise the status of the concepts needed to fit the data. Within the past decade, Fairbairn has become more widely recognized in the United States, particularly through the writings of Kernberg, who has appreciated the value of his contribution though not agreeing with some of its tenets (1976, 1980).

The essentials of Fairbairn's views on psychopathology are briefly given with slight modifications of his original terms – for instance, he accepted Guntrip's use of the *self* as appropriate for the early ego (Fairbairn 1963).

1. The human infant is object-seeking from the start.
2. This activity is mediated by a unitary ego or self, and the reality principle is operative from the beginning. Impulses cannot exist except through activation of the ego or self, and they cannot be viewed as sources of energy existing apart from structures.

3 Pleasure is an accompaniment of relationships with objects, that is, it has a guiding and selective function and is not the primary aim of activity.
4 Aggression is a reaction to frustration and is intense in the earliest experiences.
5 The original anxiety is separation from the mother and can readily be experienced as of terrifying intensity, for example, when a satisfying object is unavailable.
6 To cope with the unsatisfying original object (breast-mother), this object is internalized by a distinct psychological process and established as a structure within the psyche.
7 This unsatisfying object arouses excitement because it is needed, and frustration because it rejects. With the intensification of these experiences, the exciting and rejecting aspects of the object are split off, along with the part of the self related to them, into subselves, each of which contains the object and the part of the self related to it.
8 The main core of the internalized object then becomes an ideal object or ego ideal, and the part of the ego related to it is termed the central ego (self).
9 There are thus three dynamic systems, each of which acts like a partial self: (a) The central self, related to the ego ideal, which represses both (b) the needy libidinal self in relation to the exciting object and (c) the antilibidinal self linked to the rejecting object. Because the antilibidinal self is attached to the rejecting object, it attacks the libidinal self and so reinforces the repression of the latter.
10 The superego covers the complex of (a) the ego ideal, (b) the antilibidinal self, and (c) the rejecting or antilibidinal object. These structures are interrelated dynamic psychological systems, subselves within the person, and it was important to Fairbairn that psychoanalytic theories should be couched in purely psychological terms at the level of personal functioning. To introduce etiological factors at lower levels of the organism's functioning was to abandon the data specific to the analytic situation as well as to depart from the proper level.

In place of the classical developmental scheme of object relations related to erotogenic zones, Fairbairn puts this progression into one governed by the quality of dependence. The infantile dependence at the start is characterized by its incorporative attitudes and by primary identification. The gradual separation from the object throughout childhood and adolescence constitutes a transitional period from which the healthy individual emerges with the capacity for mature dependence, in which giving is as important as taking and the differentiation of the object as a separate person with an independent identity characterizes the desired object.

The abandonment of the libido theory as a basis for the development of object relations inevitably means a reconsideration of the nuclear position of the Oedipus complex. For Fairbairn, the origin of psychopathology lies in the extent to which the pristine self is split. By the time oedipal fantasies are being stimulated by psychosexual development, the individual has a divided self, and it is the extent to which these divisions are present, along with the intensity of their activity, that determines the outcome of the oedipal conflicts. The three dynamic structures are each modified by later experiences, and indeed Fairbairn states that the unsatisfying relationships have to continue into the later years of childhood for the separate systems to become established with the kind of rigidity that makes for the serious psychopathological disorders. The existence of the needy libidinal self leads, under the pressure of the oedipal conflicts, to one parent being put into the position of the exciting object with the other parent as the attacking, rejecting one. Normally, the parent of the opposite sex becomes the exciting object, but lack of acceptance by either or both parents in the early stages readily leads to pathogenic patterns in the antilibidinal figure and so to the establishment of the various psychosexual distortions and inhibitions in both the boy and the girl.

Fairbairn's dynamic structures with their internal objects make good a defect of Balint's and Winnicott's theories in that they give a structural basis for the development of the different psychopathological patterns from the earliest phase. As dynamic systems, they are constantly active. A degree of splitting of the kind he describes is universal, though in ordinary healthy development the central self remains dominant as a learning adaptive system, which can integrate in large measure the activity of the other systems into a more or less coherent scheme of motivation for the self. In such development the self is then largely coterminous with the ego. When the antilibidinal system is overdeveloped, then a wide range of inhibited behavior is the result. Severe splitting initially, with the associated intensely frustrated relationship needs made aggressive and sadistic by the pressure to satisfy them, gives a good explanatory scheme for the schizoid conditions, while the main pathological modes of relating – the hysterical, paranoid, obsessional, and phobic – are also accounted for in terms of the particular pattern of relationship with the internal objects that becomes dominant at any one time. Not only is each of the main neurotic patterns accounted for, but the scheme also explains the common finding that so many patients can exhibit more than one of the patterns at different times.

The structuring of the relationship systems also makes clear why resistance to therapy can be such a difficult, and even intractable, problem. In his theory of repressed impulses, Freud took resistance to emanate mainly from unconscious guilt, with the lessening of which the impulses could be brought under the influence of the ego and given a different aim or at least made controllable. In Fairbairn's theory, what is repressed is not a forbidden impulse but an attachment of a subself to a forbidden object and of another subself to a rejecting object which can be frighteningly primitive if this system becomes active. This attachment to bad objects seems at first sight puzzling until it is realized that the infant and child has no choice in his attachments. Bowlby, in his use of ethological concepts to give a developmental scheme for relationships, has brought out this feature in the higher mammals as well as in man, that is, clinging to the mother becomes intensified the less secure the relationship is. In other words, a bad object is infinitely better than no object, the latter state being that of disintegrative anxiety. Bowlby's published work (1969, 1973) gives considerable support to the general line of the British object-relations theorists, especially to Fairbairn's views.

For Fairbairn, then, the baby begins with a self system that seeks relationships as a primary need. Within this unitary system there differentiate two subselves in coping with the frustrations of the environment. These two subselves are really not independent in origin since they are both the complementary aspects of the frustrating situation. In other words, the creating of a rejecting inhibiting self goes in parallel with the forbidden relationship needs of the libidinal self. The subselves are maintained as a relatively closed system since in this way individuals seek to have some control over their needed objects. The more they remain absorbed in these relationships with inner objects, the less are they involved with the outer world in a mature way. Such relations with external objects as they do try to make in these circumstances are predominantly externalizations of their inner world, that is, other people are not individuals in their own right and valued as such, but are figures to be coerced into the mold of the inner object.

The overall self system is thus a reactive matrix dominated at different times by one or another of the self divisions. The central self or reality ego ordinarily tries to preserve consistent adaptive relationships with people in the outer world; and when one of the subselves takes over, neurotic patterns appear. The self as a whole thus has what Kohut (1971) has termed *vertical* splits. But it also has horizontal divisions from the fact that experience can be organized in successive layers as well as fused. In this way each of the self systems can expose its structure as it was at earlier stages, though alteration in one cannot occur without all being involved. The tendency is for each system to acquire a characteristic pattern by the time adulthood is reached. Thus the libidinal ego may have created as its exciting object a perversion which remains relatively stable. In treatment, however, it is usually not long before the earlier object needs can be discerned; and, as Fairbairn further suggested, seeking gratification of impulse tension through part-objects develops from the failure and deterioration of object relations.

Harry Guntrip

Guntrip was drawn into a close relationship with Fairbairn's work especially after its appeal led him to undergo analysis with him. The stimulus of this experience was to start him on a very careful study (1961) of Fairbairn's theories in relation to the general analytic scene and particularly of their relationship to Freud and Klein. Guntrip, like Fairbairn, had had a philosophical training as part of his preparation to become a clergyman, and his clinical work, too, had focused on notably schizoid individuals. Perhaps from what he had learned from Fairbairn, his therapeutic experience confronted him with serious regression in several patients. As a result, he began to realize that Fairbairn's picture of the endopsychic structuring of the person failed to do justice to the nature of regressed states. These are characterized by a massive withdrawal from relationships and a deadness that cannot be accounted for by Fairbairn's subselves. In the libidinal self, there is commonly, in contrast to apathy and withdrawal, an active seeking of libidinal relations typically sadistic and primitive but nevertheless actively sought, while the antilibidinal self is correspondingly activated. In those threatened with the withdrawn states, there is in part a desperate struggle to keep these subself activities going as a countermeasure against the great dread of sinking into a total apathetic futility equated with dying. For these phenomena, Guntrip postulated – and Fairbairn approved – a split in the libidinal self by which one part takes flight from all object relations, which seemed to him to be like an attempt to go back to the safety of the intrauterine condition. Besides the powerful regressive flight with its aim of this ultimate security, these patients also experience in analysis terrifying anxiety at the loss of their self, a terror based on a fear of total isolation, in which state there is nobody to hold the self together. He thus adds force to Fairbairn's view that relations with internal objects constitute a desperately needed world in which these are figures to relate to, even though they are not external ones. Guntrip gives clinical material to support his view that not only the neuroses but manic-depressive states as well have a primarily defensive function against this basic terror – a desperate attempt through compulsively active internal object relations to keep the self in being. Helping the patient to cope with this anxiety becomes for Guntrip the ultimate psychotherapeutic problem; and the intense anxieties and resistances surrounding it explain the extremely difficult task that psychotherapy can encounter.

In consolidating his views on these primal experiences, Guntrip makes increasing use of Winnicott, with whom he had a period of analysis, which he has described (1975). He brings Winnicott's concepts of the origin of the self into a comprehensive outline of the development of the self from its beginnings with being and doing up to maturity. His scheme gave him a strong sense of a comprehensive psychodynamic image of the man, one that illumines anxieties and fears as the origins of manifold evasions in regard to self-knowledge. This scheme also conveyed to him a confidence about the scientific status of psychodynamic knowledge, and his paper on this subject (1978) is of particular value to the analyst today when there is not only the challenge to this status but the danger of the right to pursue our research tasks being denied.

Fairbairn's, and much more Guntrip's, accounts of development and its pathology have been thought to have dispensed too drastically with instincts. It is rather, however, that they do not see instincts as the basic determinants of structure in the self. Structures derive from the quality of the relationship experience, and instinctual activity is merely one mode of the activity of structures. Given distortion of the structures, then pathological expression of instinctual activity occurs. Their position in this respect is akin to that of roles for those sociologists who stress these as the structural elements in the person. Roles are universally prescribed, but each individual fills them in a manner determined by his self, in other words, by the way that structures created out of very early experience function.

What emerges, then, as common to this group? In the first place, they all derived their theories from long and testing work with very difficult patients – patients of the kind whose analyses so often end in stalemate or worse. In recent years there have been many critiques of theory and many contributions to its advancement. Some of these have been the work of analysts who have devoted a substantial part of their time to academic study. These critiques and contributions are valuable and always needed. Our four theorists, however, all remained deeply rooted in clinical work. What their theories may lack in academic precision has thus to be balanced against the importance of the data they have exposed and the questions these have raised. Their immersion in clinical work helps to explain another aspect of their approach: they all placed the therapeutic task as paramount. They refused to adhere rigidly to the method when they felt that this might lose the patient. Any parameters introduced were not such as would preclude further understanding. To many, their work would be described as analytical psychotherapy rather than analysis – an issue which, as recent discussions have shown (see Wallerstein 1969, 1975), may well prove to be a relatively unimportant one if our goal is deeper understanding. Analytical psychotherapy does not necessarily mean the unconscious is no longer being explored.

Balint's description of the basic fault highlighted a critical developmental phase. From the way patients related to him while they struggled with the state, he concluded that it reflected a failure in the earliest mothering, one in which there had not been adequate input of what can appropriately be described as love, that is, interest, affection, and enjoyment at the "personal" level. Physical care can be of a high order, instinctual gratification can be experienced, but without this holistic response from the mother the infant does not prosper. Indeed, as the studies of Spitz, Mahler, Bowlby, and many others have demonstrated, without this maternal love, future development is greatly endangered. Balint, however, while giving us clinical data on the existence of the phase and how it manifested itself plus its damaging ramifications, did not take its conceptualization further nor did he suggest how it linked with future conflict.

Fairbairn also concluded that the seeds of all future psychopathology were sown in this early failure in the mother–baby relationship. He then followed up with a theoretical outline of the subsequent differentiation of dynamic structures within the primary self system and so related later psychopathology to the early phase with a unified framework. His multiplicity of subselves has been criticized, yet the criticisms often appear as resistance to their challenge to traditional theory rather than founded on a careful appraisal of their nature and of the phenomena for whose explanation they were evolved. Here it is noteworthy that Kernberg (1976, 1980), who has devoted so much study to patients with marked splits in their personalities, found Fairbairn's approach of considerable value in ordering the manifestations of borderline patients. Fairbairn did not have Hartmann's work available when he produced his theories, and it is striking that two such different endeavors were proceeding almost simultaneously with the common feature of dealing with the inadequacy of the concept of the id as Freud left it. Hartmann retained the notion of energies without structure, a quite untenable concept for Fairbairn and, moreover, one which hampered psychoanalytic development. General systems theory, as it later developed in modern biology, was of course unknown to Fairbairn, though he was familiar with some of its precursors, for example, gestalt psychology. Fairbairn's structures as he described them in his theory of the basic endopsychic situation represent end products. Thus, when he relates the different neuroses to the different patterns of relationships with the internal objects, his references to the latter, for example, as the accepted or rejecting objects, imply the form taken by these objects as they occur nearest to the central self or ego. The complex layering and fusion of the different states of experience that have produced their final form constitute much of the analyst's task. This endopsychic picture of the self as an overall matrix in which there are these internal "dramatis personae" is a conception that is sometimes thought to be anthropomorphic and so to take analytic theory out of the natural sciences. Guntrip has dealt with that issue, and we can note that one gain of abandoning scientific reductionism and placing conflict on the personal level is that the mutual understanding of the writer and psychoanalyst is greatly facilitated. Whereas Winnicott stressed the importance of creativity as bridging the individual to his object relationships, Fairbairn can be said to describe the specific structures this creativity is driven to make according to the particular relationships the individual is situated in.

Taking Winnicott and Fairbairn together, it would appear that the next step they implicitly point to is the study of the self, the conceptualization of its origin and development – a topic that has become central and controversial for psychoanalysis. When Erikson began to discuss the meaning of identity, it was sometimes thought he was leaving the field of psychoanalysis. Why the center of the person should have been so long in becoming the center of our theoretical concern is itself a fascinating question. Lichtenstein (1977), Weisman (1965), and many others have remarked on the barriers that our Cartesian inheritance has created for us, and even today the self is commonly taken to be too vague a concept to be a profitable line of research. A major difficulty in the past was how this subjective matrix could be linked to its brain; and energy ideas, however metaphorical they were claimed to be, have had an insidiously persistent habit of intruding in a reified way into our thinking. Analysts have tended to lag behind in the assimilation of new developments, although Bowlby (1973), Peterfreund (1971), and Rosenblatt and Thickstun (1977) have made efforts to reformulate theory. Insofar as their work has gone, however, we do not yet have the theoretical basis for the integrative organizing center, thus raising the question whether we shall merely get a kind of psychoanalytic behaviorism.

Ernest Jones in his brief foreword to Fairbairn's (1954b) book showed his characteristic percipience into the vital issue by noting that Fairbairn started at the center of the personality and described its strivings and difficulties in its endeavor to reach an object where it may find support – in contrast to Freud who began with the stimulation of the nervous system and proceeded from the erogenous zones and internal tension from genetic activity. As Jones concluded, "This constitutes a fresh approach in psychoanalysis which should lead to much fruitful discussion" (p. v).

The study of biological systems tells us that development occurs by differentiation and every system has to have an organizing principle in order to keep emerging subsystems in the required relation with each other and with the whole. And with biological systems we have to include the environment as integral to the system. As Winnicott remarked many years ago, there is no such thing as a baby – there are only babies with mothers (1960, p. 39n).

Development in an adaptive learning system is inevitably morphogenic, that is, new structures have to embody new adaptive capacities (see Buckley 1967). Without a structural basis it is difficult to understand how these changes are made. Thus Jacobson (1964), who gives an excellent account of the later development of the self and its object relations, nevertheless explains the earliest developments in terms of energic changes. But statements, for example, about libido or aggression being turned from object to self are meaningless without some notion of what does the turning. Perhaps Jacobson's reluctance to structure experience of object relations from the start is reinforced by her view that threats to identity are not predominant in the neuroses, a view that is not shared by our theorists nor, I believe, would it be by a growing number of analysts. Angyal (1965) was one of the first psychotherapists to give a conception of personal development based on the systematic organization of experience. For him the *autonomy* of the individual, a powerful inherent impetus from the start, relates to this central organizing principle, while the constant necessity for the interaction with the social environment, if the organism is to survive, he termed its *homonomy*. No consideration of the person made sense without these two being taken together; no autonomy is possible without homonomy. It is the organizing principle, however, we want to know more about. We have learned a great deal about the mature organism, and, as Angyal says, we have to know its structure before we can understand the embryo.

Mischel (1977) comments that the task of understanding what it is for a person to be an agent is a conceptual rather than empirical one. I doubt if we can make this separation, though there is clearly a formidable conceptual task. We know the stimulus–response views of the behaviorist cannot do justice to the way the person is activated by meanings, purposes, and goals. It is the latter that play the main part in determining what makes a stimulus, and they are developed as the person internalizes a map or model of his or her environment. What Fairbairn's endopsychic situation tries to do is to represent this environment as it is structured internally by the subject. Psychoanalysis has gathered an enormous amount of knowledge on how this inner world gets built up, but what was missing was a more holistic dimension. Fairbairn suggests how this inner world is created to make good the deficiencies of the outer one, while Guntrip has taken this further in his view of the ultimate analytic problem as the nature of the unbearable threat to existence when the person cannot achieve enough homonomy, enough psychic metabolism with the social environment. In connection with this theme, Guntrip (1969) makes the intriguing suggestion that humankind has clung to the belief in a frighteningly powerful impersonal nature within us, the death instinct, for example, or at least an aggressive energy, because of the fear of facing up to the feelings of intolerable helplessness and weakness that characterize the infant, especially in an experience of deprivation.

To imagine an organizing principle at work in the self does not necessarily take us into innate forms or Aristotelian entelechies. What our theorists have brought out is that the future growth of the person in terms of creativity and use of particular talents, and so forth, entails unpredictable emergents from the experiences and opportunities met with in life, nevertheless, the potential for growth is not created without a "personalized" input. The infant at the start presumably fashions from the good enough input an affective field that predisposes the infant to pursue exploring the world with interest and enthusiasm. This is what Winnicott

(1971) seems to be saying with his concept of the female element. Yet, however ill-defined the content of this central experience is, it seems to have a quality that we can appropriately describe as a beginning toward being personified. One recalls here Sullivan's (1953) personification of the self system, and there are clearly affinities. The full nature of the dynamic properties of the system, however, is missing from Sullivan's account, especially as the development of the self-object awareness proceeds, for it is at this stage that, all our theorists agree, the roots of intensely aggressive and violent feelings are laid down.

It is when the self system becomes patterned by its dominant relationship modes that the term identity comes to the fore. Lichtenstein (1977) suggests that an identity theme gets *imprinted* on the self at this stage, a pattern determined largely by the unconscious wishes the mother has for her infant's future, and that this remains as a virtually unchangeable template, an invariant for future development, though naturally the particular clothing put onto the skeletal pattern will vary with experience. But whether Lichtenstein's view of the virtual irreversibility of this pattern is akin to imprinting is probably an open question. Fairbairn's view, and this would be reinforced by Guntrip's conceptions, would be that a pattern for the self would be carried by the internal object structures and, though the task of change can be formidable, it may not be irreversible as our knowledge is enlarged. As in most fields of knowledge, a certain stage is reached when new concepts are proposed. The problem of the self has become emergent and already many responses have been appearing independently, with Kohut's (1971, 1977) work perhaps best known.

Our four theorists have found, as analysts have done under the stimulus of Freud's work, that developments in our theoretical understanding must inevitably be reflected in technique. For all, the parallel between therapeutic requirements and the needs of the infant in its relationship with its mother was more and more forced upon their attention. The gap between theory and practice may well underlie some of our therapeutic limitations and failures, and especially our diagnostic appraisals.

The position of the self for Hartmann and ego psychology has been rather in the background, with the ego given all the prominence, albeit restricted to an impersonal group of functions. Nevertheless, if we take the important consideration of who or what is the agent in our actions, the self appears as the most likely candidate. Chein (1972) in a careful discussion of this issue considers the claims of Freud's three structural entities along with the self and the body. The essential psychological human quality for him is "the commitment to a developing and continuing set of unending, interacting, interdependent and mutually modifying long-range enterprises" (p. 289). In such a commitment, all the entities constitute one system, "the person," and so he takes the person to be the actor or active agent at the personal level (compare also Schafer 1968). Although he chooses the person rather than the self, his decision appears to be based upon his difficulty in envisaging a structural basis for the self. In the ordinary way we use the self it would seem to cover just that overall integrated system he takes as the person – and certainly it is this integrate that our object-relations theorists are speaking about and for which they all envisage or imply a dynamic structure. As a supraordinate structure (Saperstein and Gaines 1973) of great flexibility and perhaps in the nature of a "field force," its primary function is to contain and organize motives from all the subsystems that have differentiated from it. The higher-level organizations we might call the subegos and their related internal objects all fall within its influence.

The ego or central self is that part of the total system that is most related to *realistic* action, that is, to the recognition of others as independent persons with their own characteristics. The course of ordinary development is such that this system has a high overlap with the supraordinate one. The value of the self conceptualized as the overall dynamic structural matrix is that we can give underpinning to the personal level of action as "I" and yet allow for the self to be dominated at different times and in different situations by any of its subsystems, such as the superego.

What all of our theorists have come to is the view that the innate developmental potential has to be activated by an input of loving empathic care from the mother for it to become the proactive matrix with the positive enjoyment that developmental activity requires. To be able to love and enjoy, the baby has to be loved and enjoyed. It is as if a "positive field of force" is patterned as the core of the self system by the effects of the positive self feeling at one pole and the expectation from a supporting figure at the other, at first external, then internalized. The environment continues to add to the structural differentiations, and a degree of correction of early deficiency may be attained. But as Bowlby mentions (1973, p. 336), drawing upon the biologist Waddington (Waddington and Jantsch 1976) who introduced the theory of epigenesis, there is a general organismic tendency for the individual to maintain whatever developmental pathway he or she is already on, partly because the internal structural features influence the selection of the environment and partly because the environment, especially within the family, also tends to remain unchanged.

Summary

What I believe to be the essential contribution of this group of analysts may be summarized as follows. The role of object relations has always been a prominent theme in analytic thought and has become much more so in recent years. Instead of grafting the implications of relations onto a theory that started from a different standpoint, what the British group has done is to show that the development of the person has to be conceived as the progressive differentiation of a structure from a unitary matrix that itself interacts at a holistic personal level from the start. While Balint noted clinical data that required this step, he did not put forward a theoretical scheme. Winnicott, who suggested more specifically how the infant's relationships at the earliest states patterned its whole subsequent personal development, also refrained from following through the theoretical logic of his observations. Fairbairn was the first analyst to expose the questionable logic of a developmental scheme based upon the energic concepts that Freud retained as his theoretical base. Fairbairn's scheme, however, did not account adequately for the earliest developmental states as these were inferred from the study of regressive states. Guntrip, making full use of Winnicott's views, has sought to make good this limitation.

The British group does not presume to have made anything like an adequate conceptual map for the development of the psyche. The theoretical problems are far too complex for that. They have, however, shown a fruitful direction and have influenced many areas of contemporary psychoanalytic thought.

Chapter 4

Advances in understanding small groups

Editor's introduction

Sutherland summarizes object relations theory and shows how the structures of the self are displayed in social interactions, group dynamics, and institutional life. Referring to Bion, he describes intra- and interpersonal dynamics in small groups, and compares them to those that occur in larger groups. He defines the group as a sociotechnical system that organizes around the task to which the group is assigned, and shows how problems with authority and needs for affiliation and affective expression can get in the way of the task. He deals with the value of the group in group therapy, family therapy, and organizational consultation. The idea comes full circle as he concludes with the idea of the personality being structured from its involvement in various groups over the life cycle.

Introduction

The rapid spread of interest in recent years in the small group is perhaps due to the development of new methods of studying it rather than to a new awareness of its contribution to the growth and maintenance of the person. Each approach has produced an enormous volume of research, for example, the field theoretical studies of Lewin (1951) and his pupils, the large number of researches stimulated by Moreno's (1956) sociometric, psychodramatic, and sociodramatic methods, the interaction studies of Bales and his colleagues (1950); and alongside these are the great many descriptive observations from the group therapists.

Faced with this vast volume of research, it seemed to me that the best thing I could do for people like ourselves who have to help individuals in groups was to explore the emergence of unifying concepts – those ideas that make sense of the interrelatedness of the individual being shaped within the family group and then maintaining growth through subsequent group memberships. For the purpose I shall consider first the individual in the group, next the group and its task, and then the process of therapy and change in the group.

The individual and the group

The dynamics of the interaction between the individual and the group present us with the problem for whose solution the lack of an adequate theoretical framework is most apparent. On the one hand we have to account for the fundamental needs of the person for belongingness with others in significant ways. People need their identity, their achievements, and their value to themselves and others to be affirmed by the members of the groups with which they are most related. On the other hand, there are also to be understood the various conflicting attitudes and relationships, at times intensely emotional and irrational, between members, and between members and the group leader or leaders.

Perhaps many of our difficulties in finding a set of concepts we can use to bring order into this complexity stem from the way in which we perseverate in our view of the individual as the unit from which we start, isolating each individual one from another and building up their future social modes from inferred instinctive endowments and other properties of organisms. If we conceive of individuals as having built into them from the start the properties of the social system in which they are reared, our task of relating them subsequently to the groups in which they function is greatly simplified.

It is, of course, nothing new to draw attention to the roles of the family in the growth of the person. Nevertheless, the implications of the way in which the family structures the person have not been systematically considered in our theories of the personality, its development, and its mode of functioning socially. The most helpful concepts are those emerging in what is known as the object-relations theory of the person. This theory develops the view of dynamic structures inside the personality built on representations of parental figures on whom the child is dependent. Although the superego, the best known of such internal structures, has proved an indispensable concept in psychoanalytic thinking, it has often been regarded as a theoretical weakness that such an "anthropomorphic" notion has to be imported. The phenomena it relates to, however, are usually admitted to be the most aptly described by a highly "personalized" structure of this kind, which operates as an inner parent. For the understanding of the individual's social interactions I believe, as Fairbairn has suggested, that we must surmount our tendency to cling to speculative neurophysiologic notions and postulate more boldly the kinds of dynamic psychic structures our theory needs. Theories of this kind have been developed by several sociologists, notably G. H. Mead (1952), and they have had their most thoroughgoing and rigorous expression in the recent writings of Parsons and Bales (1955). It is of particular interest that this latter group of some of the most eminent sociologists of today, starting from their need to account for the phenomena of family and social interaction, are developing concepts that are of the same kind as those being formulated by some psychoanalysts to give meaning to the phenomena of the individual's relations with him- or herself and with others as these are seen in the consulting room.

Because the most far-reaching object-relations theories of the personality have been developed in Great Britain, especially by Klein and by Fairbairn, I shall draw on their formulations. It is not the work of any particular individual or group I wish to present for your consideration but rather to take from this work what seem to be its common essentials. I propose to outline its form in a way that indicates the comprehensive effects of these in-built relationships in all social behavior.

The object-relations theory of the personality

From the moment of leaving the mother's body, the emotional experiences of the infant lead to the segregation of their associated imprints in such a way that constellations grow around "good" and "bad" feelings. The earliest good experiences make an idealized good object or imago of the mother who supplies care and satisfaction of needs unconditionally. (The dominance of the infant's experiences with the breast lead in some workers, especially Klein and her school, to the concept of the earliest imagos being more related to part-objects such as the breast, rather than to the mother as a whole.) Correspondingly, painful frustrations and the intensely aggressive feelings associated with violent attempts to get rid of these pains begin to build an inner object, which appears to threaten the developing self with devastating disintegration and destruction. Between these two poles of idealized blissful fusion with the good mother and the dread of loss of self, associated with an attacking mother imago, there grows what can be termed the *central self* in which the more reality-based differentiation between self and the mother takes place.

Whatever the mechanisms are which contribute to their attachments, infants by the second half of the first year exhibit differentiated relationships with their mothers. Ethological research may well add new insights here to be considered alongside the inferences the psychoanalyst makes from the study of fantasy and behavior within the psychoanalytic setting (see Bowlby 1960). For the present it is sufficient to appreciate this first crucial qualitative change, namely that an interrelated internal and external social system has been established, and that there is a high degree of interdependence between the relations going on in this inner world and those that are made with the outer world. Infants' resources for tolerating frustration grow because they can now use their inner world in which the inner good mother is part of the self. They can feel that they are playing the part of their own desired mother and so fulfill their longings in fantasy or in play with their own body or their rudimentary toys. It is the satisfactions from the real mother, of course, that consolidate the inner imago. Should their tensions become painful, infants tend to feel that they are the object of a fantasy attack, which can be terrifying at times, from the internal persecuting mother. Ordinarily, the experiences with the real mother, especially in times of stress, will keep the effects of the threatening experiences within manageable limits. A preponderance of painful tensions, however, will induce too frequent evocation of this frightening inner figure with desperate attempts to defend against what are felt as its attacks. By projecting it outside the infant can secure a fantasy safety, perhaps reinforced by a clinging to the idealized internal object as well as by the development of the defense of avoiding the objects onto which the frightening figures have been projected. But the price of this phobic defense is that the outer world becomes the place where dreaded objects are located and so interaction with reality becomes restricted. Again, in managing their interactions, infants may tend to assume the role of the attacking imago and turn their anger on themselves and their belongings.

An immense range of possibilities exists for variation in the pattern that may get consolidated according to the different properties of a particular infant interacting with his or her particular mother. It would appear that although relations with the mother may be centered around a variety of activities and bodily contacts, the common pleasurable affective and erotic experiences create the generalized image of her as a whole person. Similarly, the common affective elements in painful experiences seem to fuse these so that what may be termed a generalized "bad" mother imago develops.

With the movement from complete dependence to increasing autonomy, a process in which weaning and development of locomotor abilities and speech play central parts, the father begins to play a second major role. A similar development takes place leading to the creation in the inner world of structures mediating the relationships with the good powerful father who readily becomes the prototype of independence achievement. And, as before, an idealized father along with a more threatening one are also differentiated in the inner world. The addition of these father imagos permits of a great range of inner relationships and identifications and the appearance of sexual interests and fantasies makes for the most intense use of these systems. Sibling relations and identifications with other figures in later childhood, often from stories as well as from objects in the real world, also add to the population of the inner world.

The inner world and social relationships

The multiplicity of these inner object relations and the variety of needs which go into them do not require elaboration here. Of the most importance to us are the ways in which adults seem to function in their social relations as a result of the creation of internal objects. The following summary account puts in condensed fashion some of the main concepts.

1 The individual personality is patterned by its growth within the family into a number of dynamic object-relations systems which seek to effect certain kinds of interaction with others (that is, they are personal need-systems). Each of these systems represents a part of the self related to an inner object which defines in varying degrees the "other" in the sought relationship. The presence of the internal object within the system has two consequences. First, it can be taken as an object for part of the self so that the person can in fantasy play the dual roles of self and object thereby dispensing with the uncertainties of the real external object. Second, the internal object can be used as a mold for selecting people who will fit into it, or for coercing others into it by various manipulations. Thus, the husband who unconsciously wants to settle old scores in regard to his sexually rejecting mother will pursue a course of conduct with his wife that will lead her to frustrate him even though she is a tolerant and sympathetic partner, that is, he will fit her into this unconsciously needed role. Again, in the therapeutic group, a number of passive dependent members will often collude actively to get one member to monopolize the therapist's interest before they make resentful complaints about being put into the rejected position.
2 These systems vary in their mode of activity and in their degree of consciousness according to their position within the hierarchical organization of the person.
3 Those which are felt to belong to that part of the self the individual wants to be come within a central organizing structure of the self, the part we usually refer to as the ego. This overall system leads to a range of relationships being sought and maintained and it is characteristic of these relationships that they are largely reality based, that is, the different identity and reality of others is accepted and mutual adaptation and learning takes place within these relations. The internal objects of this central system appear to be very plastic in keeping with the acceptance of the differentiated identity of the other person.
4 Two sets of relationships are separated from this central part of the self: (a) those containing certain repressed needs and (b) those concerned with primitive control.
5 Repressed relationships contain drives to satisfactions that were sought within the original comprehensive relations with parent figures but which were incompatible with the preservation of these relationships. Because they brought threats of parental loss or retaliation, of varying severity and hence associated with different intensities of anxiety, these relations are segregated by different degrees of "psychic distance" from

> the central part of the self. They also tend because of the original rejection of their aims to have angry and destructive components. Their separation from consciousness means that little or no learning occurs through their activity. They are, however, constantly ready to go into action. Normally their aims are realized in hidden substitute ways but more direct expression tends to emerge in close ongoing relationships with individuals or in groups.

A particularly important way of realizing their aims is by the mechanism of projective identification. That is to say, the others who are in ongoing relationships are used not only as potential objects of repressed needs, but they can also be manipulated to play the part of the self that wants the forbidden relationship. For example, an aggressive individual in a group may be apparently unwittingly provoked and encouraged by the others in order to express their hostility to the leader; or a dependent person may similarly be unconsciously pressed into the role of the "sick one" to give vicarious satisfaction to the dependent needs of members. The boundaries of "the person" at these times have to include "the other."

The personality can therefore be regarded as an overall system that maintains its continuity and consistency, its identity, through social interactions. (The results of the sensory deprivation experiments show how readily the organization of the personality can be disturbed and acute anxiety experienced when the normal constellating inputs are removed. Those exceptional individuals who can withstand prolonged isolation appear to do so because they maintain a relation with an inner object, or substitute object such as a social or religious ideal. Even in these cases, there are at least transient periods when the fight to keep sane is nearly lost or abandoned.)

The central ego in the person is normally engaged in a process of unceasing growth. Concepts of homeostasis in regard to the individual are apt to lose sight of the fact that the person embodies the need to progress through a life cycle with changing achievement goals. In other words, the future is a constant reference point affecting behavior.

The fundamental structures of our being represent needs for attachment and for achievement, and for defining ourself in cooperative relations with others. These needs require membership of different groups for their satisfaction and also that the social climate of the groups permit their satisfaction.

The integrity and value systems of the central self for most people are achieved only by some degree of splitting off of the inevitably conflicting aims of repressed needs. The common range of defense mechanisms does not succeed as a rule in extinguishing these needs and there is an unconscious compulsion to re-create social relationships in which they can be satisfied. This leads almost universally to the selection of others in groups for appropriate partial identifications. Each person tends to choose a number of members to whom he or she is attached in this way and these choices reflect Moreno's concept of the social atom that each individual patterns for him- or herself in affiliative groups.

Repressed relationships are to be seen particularly clearly in therapeutic groups. When a need in several members combines around one individual who is detected as prone to realize it, this individual is perceived as willing to take the lead in this respect. This member is then cast in the appropriate role, for example, the antileader or "the sick one." If the expression of the need arouses too much guilt or anxiety, then the member being used can be attacked or ejected as a scapegoat.

Whatever the mechanisms involved, group situations appear to release at times less inhibited ways of relating, which can have both positive and negative effects. Most investigators are against postulating any hypothetical "herd instincts" and this parsimony would appear to be justified on the grounds that innate social response mechanisms would have been released and structured within the person during the early stages of his development within the family.

Relations with the leader

The most striking group relationships are those evoked towards the leader, and many speculations have been made as to why this should be so. Here again the situation in the group seems to tend towards the reactivation of some of the patterns in the family when the immature individual is uncertain of acceptance, status, and powers of control. In this connection it is of considerable interest that Bales's (1950) work has shown, and sociometric studies tend to confirm, that many groups function best with two leaders, the instrumental leader who maintains the efforts of the group to meet the demands of its task and the emotional-expressive leader who accepts the emotional needs of members while at the same time supporting the instrumental leader.

Bion (1961), whose brilliant descriptions of phenomena observable when the group has no conventional "external" task to perform, postulated certain primitive patterns which he called *basic assumptions*. At first he implied that these ways of responding derived from a specific primitive mental system brought into action in the group situation. Theories which try to relate such phenomena as Bion described by his basic assumptions to innate mental systems or mechanisms would certainly have to consider evidence from group behavior in cultures widely different from Western societies. Later Bion suggested that basic assumption behavior was related to the earliest object relationships made by the individual, that is, with the prototypes of the leader. The theories used by Foulkes (1964) and Ezriel (1950) to account for phenomena in therapeutic groups also support the primary role of unconscious object relations with the leader.

These concepts of the intra- and interpersonal dynamics in the group clearly apply only to the small group which is continuing with its structure and culture over time. The small group is usually thought of as comprising approximately five to fifteen members and it may be that the term face-to-face group provides a link with object-relations concepts in regard to these numbers. Below a certain number there may not be enough differences amongst the members to provide for the projective identifications each individual needs. It really does take all kinds to make a world for the individual's needs. Above the limit quoted, the projections may get so diffused that their connections with the self get lost. The term *face-to-face* certainly has an implication of one identity in relation to another, and only when the identity of others can be perceived does it seem that the individual feels his or her identity affirmed. Some exploratory studies by Rice (1965) and Turquet (1975) in larger groups (thirty to fifty) suggest that individual behavior in these groups becomes more disorganized than in the small group, as though individual response were made anonymously. Apparently to counteract this tendency to loss of identity, the large group tends to break up into small groups with fluctuating boundaries.

The group and its task

The performance of the work group has been the object of an enormous amount of research in which a sociological approach is used, that is, the behavioral manifestations are studied without reference to what is going on inside each member. Various effects on members' behavior and attitudes through their group attachment and group role have been established, but most writers surveying these contributions have noted that these effects have not been related to the dynamics in the group by any coherent set of concepts.

Much work has centered around the contribution of the leader and the effects of different ways of filling this role. Older approaches in terms of the leader's personality, usually implying an authoritarian relationship between the leader and the group, have tended to be superseded by functional considerations. Thus, although a formal leader may be designated, many studies show that the most effective work is maintained when the leader can allow his function to be shared at times by members so that the latter feel that their needs for status as mature autonomous persons with creative potential are recognized and valued.

A most important line of thought in this area is to be found in the attempts being made by Trist (1963) on the basis of a deeper understanding of the group process to link the structure and organization of work groups with the member's emotional needs. This development is of particular interest in industry because these studies were initiated to deal with the high incidence of stress manifestations in the groups concerned.

A brief example of this work shows how an organization based on technological considerations may not match the personal needs of the group members. Traditionally, the task of coal getting had been carried out by a self-selected group which had a high degree of responsible autonomy in carrying out their difficult and often dangerous job. Under the new methods, these groups were divided so that each group had only a limited section of the total task with coordination supplied by an external management. One result was the creation of harmful tensions between and within these groups. After prolonged explorations, a different social organization was evolved which, while retaining the new technical methods, retrieved some of the "self-regulating" features of the traditional group. That is to say, it permitted the psychological tensions thrown up by the human interactions around the carrying out of this particular job to be handled in an effective way. The members were allowed once more to be responsible people planning their own contribution and relating it to what other groups did. Careful comparisons showed that the new social structure led to a fall in the total absence rates, mainly due to sickness and accidents, from 20 percent to 8.2 percent, and also to a substantial increase in productivity.

The concept of the sociotechnical system

To provide a conceptual framework for understanding and handling these situations in which the pattern of group functioning required by the technical procedures for the task must be related to the personal and emotional needs, Trist introduced the term *sociotechnical system*. Every group organized or existing for a job or task can be regarded as such a system and I think this notion can illumine much of our work with groups other than those we are accustomed to think of as work groups. In particular, I believe it to be a valuable notion in dealing with the tensions raised in the family group, faced with its ever-changing tasks as it proceeds with its developmental schedule over the years.

As an example I should like to refer to a family described by some of my colleagues in one of their recent publications (see Pincus 1960).

In a middle-aged couple the marital relationship had become the vehicle of primitive projections rather than a collaborative endeavor. This change had become unbearable when the elder child, a daughter, reached adolescence and began to show manifestations of sexual interest. It could be said that this family had "worked" while dealing with young, and in the parents' view sexless, children and failure developed with the appearance of the new task of coping with sexuality in the children. Unable to meet the new task, there was an upsurge of primitive anxieties, which led to mutual projections, especially by the wife, of their intolerable feelings about sexuality. From being a collaborative group concerned with the natural development of the children, the primary task in the family, mainly under the wife's leadership, became the banishment of sexuality. In the few years before they were seen, the wife had increasingly withdrawn from her husband in proportion as she felt he was little more than "dirty sexual needs." In response the husband had reacted by resorting to evenings in the pub with men friends. The daughter in an outburst of resentment with the mother's repressive attitudes over her going out with boys left home.

This kind of situation, of course, can be described in many ways, and the value to my mind of putting it into the framework of the sociotechnical system concept is that by so doing we see how similar disturbances can be created by a wide range of new tasks. The family moving to a new environment, should one or more of its members fail to adapt, can begin to show the same kind of change, namely, a stirring up within the family relationships of primitive feelings and anxieties when the previous equilibrium state is upset. Effective help requires the elucidation and linking of the "external" and the "internal" factors before new solutions can be achieved, a process which can be painful and protracted.

Therapy and organizational change in groups

The questions all psychotherapists must ask when pondering particular developments in understanding groups will naturally focus on how these help us with our tasks.

Group therapy

As with the study of small groups in general, the enormous literature on group therapy contains relatively few of what Berne (1963) describes as "creative ideas," the kind of illuminating framework that comes from "creative meditation about nature." Such ideas do exist, though, as he notes, they tend to be ignored by professional researchers because of their "informal character." The significant contributions which he selects, those from Moreno, Burrow (1927), Bion, Foulkes, and Ezriel, reassured me because I found I had made almost identical evaluations. It seems to me that in their formulations of the group process, these writers have in common much of what I have described by the term the object-relations theory of the personality.

The particular value I attach to this view is that it can help us formulate the essential task of psychotherapy, whether this is carried out within the *dyadic* relation with the therapist, in the analytic therapeutic *group*, or in a *psychodrama*. The essence of this task consists in the provision of a setting in which the repressed relationship need systems can be brought back within the organizing system of the ego where they can then be used for new learning and adaptation. Many analysts have asserted that what is done in therapeutic groups is not to be identified with the therapeutic process in psychoanalysis. I cannot accept this view when we restrict our attention to essentials. Some of our concepts have perhaps contributed to our inability to see the common core of our task, particularly such concepts as "aggressive energy" and transference. Psychotherapists frequently write of transference interpretations when they point out emotions, for example, angry feelings in the patient. Is this, however, enough? Object-relations theory tries to do justice to the crucial aspect of transference phenomena, namely, the need to bring the repressed *relationship* back to the one person relationship from which it was split off. In this way the individual is able to repeat in the here and now of the therapeutic relationship the pattern of the original "there and then" situation and hence has the possibility of making a new solution. As Ezriel (1950) has put it, object-relations theory requires that interpretations should present to the individual three components in the following form: (1) When you say (or communicate by behavior) "x", you are striving to maintain relationship "a" with me, (2) but "x" also indicates that you want to express another relationship "b" with me, which you must not admit to *because* you fear (3) relationship "c" in which I shall do something disastrous to you (reject, punish, attack, be sexual with, and so forth). Thus the unconsciously sought relationship, the defense against it, and the reason for the defense are incorporated in these three parts.

In the group situation, the way in which the unconscious relationships are expressed is naturally different. The therapist is, nevertheless, the central figure to whom these unconscious relationships are directed and any therapeutic work that ignores the constant reference of the group toward the therapist is in danger of missing the important dynamics. As a rule, the relationships sought by each member at any one time can be inferred from the common theme occupying the group's interest. The defenses adopted by members are different in the group setting, especially through the use of projective identification into other members. The manifold roles, which group members fulfill at different times for each other, may make the interpretation work difficult for their group therapists; nevertheless, when therapists are alerted by these considerations their work is facilitated.

The therapy of natural or primary groups such as the marital relationship or the family has become more popular in recent years perhaps as a consequence of our growing appreciation of the embeddedness of the person in close social relationships. Here again, various degrees of help can be given by the mere fact of a therapist making a relationship with the family and through which there is some facilitation of communication. More intractable difficulties, however, can often be helped only when the unconscious collusions and projective identifications can be brought into awareness. The aggressive demanding husband in conflict with his dependent passive wife has to be seen in terms of the right unit – the total system constituted by their mutual interaction. The husband and wife may not contain the difficulties within their relationship and then we have to bring in other members of the family.

Organizational change

Reference to the task of trying to deal with tensions within family relationships brings me to the implications of trying to effect change within the systems established in small groups. If we remind ourselves that the characteristics of each system have been evolved to deal with the threatening tensions within it, then we will be prepared for the consequences of trying to change it. All of us are familiar with the anxieties aroused when we begin to alter our defense systems and it is inevitable that such alterations within the defensive patterns of a social system will also release anxiety and a degree of acting out. Social systems, like therapeutic groups, can create special difficulties during the change process, but it is also true that they offer considerable positive features in the support that members can give each other. When the group we are trying to help is part of a larger social system, then the effects of the larger organization on the group have also to be taken into account and vice versa.

New satisfactions have to be experienced and accepted before the old ways can be given up and during this process the role of a therapeutic person or group of persons has a close parallel with the role occupied by the therapist for the individual (see Menzies 1960, and Sofer 1961).

The small group in mental health programs

The recognition of the role of group membership as a requirement for personality functioning has stimulated much of our efforts to provide social settings for our patients to which they can either continue to belong or from which they can gain resources to participate in other groups. This topic does not need comment here but in developing more positive mental health programs two points may be noted.

First, because it has become part of our way of life to live in a rapidly changing environment – and in recent years the psychiatric consequences of dislocation have been a prominent feature in most parts of the world – we may ask if there are ideas which can help to forestall and to equip people to meet these changes. Much useful knowledge has been gained and I merely wish to draw attention here to the role of the family again. Many sociologists have commented on the way in which the family, and especially the marital relationship, is having to bear increasing stresses. The more the family is separated, the more it has to try to resolve by itself the inevitable powerful tensions within its relationships. Appropriate group memberships for the various members at the different stages of their development obviously relieve these stresses and bring increased resources to all. The healthy family itself is probably the best training ground to equip the individual to meet change because it is coping with constant growth and change in the role and status of all its members. We must therefore devote much more attention to the family as our most important unit of study and I have suggested that the object-relations concepts would seem to be most promising.

The second point concerns the role of the work group. Since participation in work groups plays such a large part in our lives, we have to learn much more about making these contribute to the enrichment of the person. The changing nature and role of "work" under the advances of automation will also demand much new thinking. Fortunately, progressive management is moving in the direction which we, as promoters of mental health in the widest sense, want to follow. We as psychotherapists have, however, also a duty to help by elucidating the phenomena of interaction and human needs. I have tried to indicate how the object-relations concepts are illuminating the dynamics of group process in ways that permit social and industrial administration working with the social psychologist to evolve methods of combining our production needs with small group structures that foster the individual's personal growth and well-being.

Summary

Much recent work in psychoanalysis and in sociology points to the value of the object-relations theory of the personality for understanding social interaction in the family and in small groups. This theory tries to account for the development of structures within the personality based on the central social relationships that have been experienced. These structures mediate a variety of needed personal relationships, both conscious and unconscious. The theory sheds light on the way in which the individual distributes these needed relationships in the groups to which he or she belongs and it therefore bridges the gap between personality theory and group process.

Chapter 5

Treatment in the postindustrial society

Editor's introduction

Technology-driven societies have lifted the burden of producing from human shoulders thus allowing for more leisure. Nevertheless, people are experiencing increased levels of stress resulting in alienation and violence. Sutherland thinks that this is due to the resulting increase in permissiveness, requiring the exercise of greater personal responsibility, a skill which has not been learned, and which therefore leads to personal unease. Furthermore, global communication means that differences in wealth and culture are more readily recognized and lead to intergroup tensions among postindustrial societies and also between them and less developed ones. These advanced postindustrial societies and the individuals who live in them have an increased need for psychological services – psychotropic medication and psychoanalysis. Borrowing from the work of Trist and Emory, Sutherland describes the features of the postindustrial age, and then gives a blueprint for how psychoanalysis can reach beyond the individual consulting room to extend understanding of society itself and its impact on individual lives.

Our changing society has become a byword, and the nature of the changes are such that sociologists view these as representing the emergence of a new social order. Because the most influential changes stem from our new technological resources, and especially because the energies of most people will cease to be absorbed in the processes of production, the new social order has been termed "the post-industrial society" (see Bell 1982). This changed order is only in the process of birth; but there can be no one who has been unaffected by what is already taking place. Striking are the changes in the existential quality of life for the individual. The traditional frameworks of control are being replaced by an enhanced permissiveness, a trend that evokes a rather widespread uneasiness because it outruns at times the complementary demands for increased responsibility on the part of everyone. Perhaps more disturbing are the new responses amongst whole sections of society, especially of violent protest and of a marked sense of alienation. Gaps between various groups, especially when these relate to the perception of privileged opportunities, are now felt much more provocatively – largely because of the rapid and vivid means of communication that television provides.

Psychoanalysis and the demand for psychotherapeutic services

Closer to ourselves as psychoanalysts are those changes for which we have been in large measure directly responsible. It has been said that the face of the world was changed when Freud published his first five case histories. Psychoanalytic knowledge has permeated almost every sphere in which development and functioning as a person is the major concern. As this knowledge increases, our understanding of the psychological disorders, their enormous incidence and range, has become more widely recognized. Moreover, the intimate relationship between culture and personality is reflected in new symptoms. Our art and literature, with their impact greatly intensified by the mass media, have made commonplace the vagaries of sexuality and the unbridled destructiveness which can be let loose. Our patients accordingly come less troubled by conflicts over instinctual impulses than by the bewilderment of a divided self. They present the schizoid futility of people alienated from those committed and responsible relationships to others, to themselves, and to their achievements, that give zest to living, and satisfaction and happiness at each phase of the life cycle.

Parallel with the increased awareness of the psychological disorders has been great rise in the demands for help from those under stress. In the last decade the surging movement to create widely available mental health services is indeed an arresting feature of the more advanced societies. The psychotropic drugs have enabled psychiatrists and doctors to make life more bearable for countless numbers – and to permit many who would formerly have been long-term inmates of our psychiatric hospitals to manage in the outside world. Nevertheless, the main endeavor in the mental health services has centered on the provision of more and more groups of professional and semiprofessional personnel, or less highly trained groups of counselors, who have developed experience and skill for helping persons in need towards a greater understanding of themselves and thereby, hopefully, increasing their well-being and effectiveness in the pursuit of their goals.

In this wide range of activity, psychoanalytic knowledge has been assimilated, often only in a very broad and general way, by the helping professions, and their skills have evolved in keeping with the extent to which they have been able to use this knowledge. Many of their leaders through their own personal analysis have raised the skill levels within their professions, have set new levels of expertise for others to emulate. These groups thus give help of a much more adequate nature than was previously available, usually in terms of support, advice, or exhortation. Amongst the social work professions, the evolution of skills has been conspicuously influenced by a further contribution from psychoanalysts, namely their involvement as consultants, often over long periods, in regular case seminars. Psychoanalytic knowledge differs from most other branches of knowledge in that its assimilation and use normally require some personal adjustment in the users. The collaboration of the analyst has permitted a substantial degree of working through of those restrictive attitudes, anxieties, and defensive traits that operate against the emotional freedom in the person necessary to transmute knowledge into personal skills; and it is only with such improved skills that these allied colleagues can gain sufficient trust from their clients for the latter to communicate more of their conflicts.

The stimulus of psychoanalytic understanding has not been confined to the kind of work just described. It has had a very great effect on the social sciences leading to a vast array of research into social behavior. Most relevant in our present considerations have been the advances in our knowledge of, and skills in handling, the dynamics of small groups and the interactional processes within the family – advances which have added whole new dimensions to our resources for alleviating the stunting or crippling effects of certain conflicts in personal development and functioning.

Some dangers

While psychoanalytic knowledge forms the core of much of this work, and although many analysts have played an active part in its furtherance, various dangers have inevitably been perceived (see Wallerstein 1968). We are now less troubled by the justifiable concern of analysts about the early overly facile transfer of their insights into "wild analysis"; yet it is useful to consider some of the present dangers as aspects of the community's responses which have to be faced.

The first danger concerns the nature of the help which can be given by others and in settings different from that in which the analyst works. It would be universally agreed that the kind of therapeutic work that a social caseworker or other professional helper can carry out appropriately does not attempt what the psychoanalyst does. This limitation need not be further considered because what is normally attempted by others has its own validity as well as being so often the only help available. It must, however, be admitted that the attitudes sometimes conveyed by psychoanalysts that this kind of work is a poor substitute for what more thoroughgoing analysis might achieve, is more a professional fantasy than an established fact. For many, psychological help, and particularly in crisis situations, is probably best given by the kind of relationship the good social or other professional worker can make – one in which the whole person with his own resources and those of his life space are kept firmly as the focus of concern. The main danger here is thus not in the nature of the new facilities provided by well-trained professional groups. It consists in their too rapid expansion in response to public demand – with a dilution of standards and attempts to assert that less help than is really needed constitutes adequate services.

A few other trends are also noteworthy. The question of responsibility, especially in relation to medical considerations, was a highly sensitive issue years ago when the developments described were starting. It has now receded as a major source of interprofessional contention, largely because settings have been created in which medical and nonmedical groups can work together with the interests of the individuals safeguarded. I should like to return later, however, to this question because it may well arise again as the personal welfare services expand on the scale foreshadowed by the present signs.

Another concern may be seen to emerge, somewhat paradoxically, from the influence of psychodynamic thought on the social sciences. We might perhaps put it as follows, albeit with rather gross oversimplification. Because personality development and functioning are closely interrelated to such social factors as family and group membership, and the culture in which the person grows and is maintained, there has arisen a widespread reaction against the slow and painstaking process that characterizes the psychotherapeutic model as a means of assisting the individual. The biological roots and the structuring of the personality then seem to get discarded in favor of what societal processes can do. There is no question that the social milieu can disrupt a person's effective functioning, whether it is active through pervasive features of the culture, or whether the noxious factors are confined to sections of the social environment, for example, the work situation. All research work on group functioning has demonstrated the constant need of the individual to have what we might term an adequate *psychosocial metabolism*. We know, too, that without such constant maintenance from the social milieu, highly developed, creative, effective persons can with surprising speed be degraded into almost unrecognizable, and even irreversible, remnants of what they were. The horrors of the concentration camps made this fact so painfully manifest that it is still difficult for us to assimilate.

The failure here is that of not separating two groups of conditions, namely, (a) developmental anomalies leading to maladaptive structuring of the personality; (b) deficiencies in the social environment causing functional disorder. These two are, of course, closely interrelated, for example, certain cultural patterns of child rearing may be more pathogenic than others; but it is necessary to separate them if remedial action is to be appropriate.

While this danger of assuming that social action by itself is sufficient to deal with psychological disorder may come mainly from the ameliorative concern of social planners and administrators, yet it also permeates the efforts of those in the helping professions. Thus in our mental hospitals, the valuable advances in creating a therapeutic community are often taken as sufficient in themselves to meet the need for psychotherapy. There is a fairly common assumption that getting patients into groups will of itself be adequately helpful to them. It does not apparently matter whether the professional leader has any psychodynamic training or not; all he has to do is to get people "communicating more freely" – one of the clichés of today, as fashionable as it is often devoid of articulate purpose. The support and reassurance, and often the changes in attitudes that patients can achieve from participating with others in a permissive setting, are manifestly of considerable benefit. But a psychotherapeutically trained observer of these situations cannot but be struck by the difficulties of patients which might be given more effective treatment if some of their less conscious origins could be exposed in a therapeutic way.

Psychoanalysts clearly have a fundamental contribution to make in the social movements today. They are already making a substantial one in many ways, particularly in the expansion of our welfare services. Indeed, that to be involved in this activity is "in the air" can be seen from the fact that close to 80 percent of the younger analysts in England have part-time posts in some kind of community mental health service – and this pattern is common in many countries.

In addition to participating in the development of community services, psychoanalysis has a long record of involvement with many areas affecting the development of the individual – above all, in child development. This whole theme is clearly much too large to receive other mention than to remind ourselves of its history and its present scale.

Implications of psychoanalysis

If we are to make our contribution more telling, I believe that we have to give much more thought to the whole theme of the relationship of psychoanalysis to society. We have, moreover, a moral obligation to do so. From the very beginning of its growth, psychoanalysis has never fostered a sect whose knowledge has been kept within its professional boundaries. We have constantly attempted to influence our society and some of the most profound changes in it can be laid at our door. It is with a view to improving our contribution that I am venturing some reflections on this dauntingly complex, yet urgently pressing theme. In doing so I propose to take three aspects: (1) the nature of the society into which we are moving and its implications for personal welfare services; (2) the contribution of the analyst to the personal welfare services; and (3) the contribution of the analyst to a central feature of this new society, namely, the concept of personal development with a capacity to meet change as distinct from what we have traditionally subsumed under the term, the welfare services.

The nature of the postindustrial society

In turning to the nature of the society we are entering, I mentioned at the outset that the social transition upon us is of a nature that warrants the conception of these changes as moving towards a new order. These changes are familiar to all of us; but their familiarity does not remove the need for us to try to make more specific their nature and hence to take more appropriate actions to manage constructively their effects. Change almost always evokes anxiety and one of the greatest contributions of psychoanalysis was to create the first setting in which the individual could change systematically, that is, with the possibility of the change process being understood both by the analyst as the person managing it, and the analysand as the individual achieving it. The changes made by the psychoanalytic method, however, have traditionally been within a relatively stable social environment. It may be that for this reason analytically induced changes have sometimes been rather pejoratively referred to as helping the individual to adjust to circumstances. The issue at stake today is what we have to offer, by contrast, to people experiencing movement and change as part of their milieu.

In making some observations about this task, I shall borrow extensively from the writings of two social scientists, Trist and Emery (Emery 1967, Emery and Trist 1965, Trist 1968). As these writers remark, although we are acquiring the knowledge with which the current social transition could be managed, the availability of such knowledge does not ensure its use. Clearly, however, the steps we take in regard to the welfare and development of people during the transition, that is, during the next few decades, will be critical.

The most noteworthy development in concepts about *personal welfare* lies in its being bracketed with programs related to *personal development*. It is not merely that these are related because they are both desirable values; it is the nature of the current social changes that puts them together as a necessity for adaptation and survival. Briefly, it is a new degree of interdependence of organizations in society that creates these new features. Such problems as poverty, water supply, and sickness or social deviance are now perceived by a community or society not as deriving from aggregates of subelements that can be dealt with piecemeal, but as integrated major problems requiring central planning. In this increased interrelatedness, the autoregulative mechanisms that were held to be adequate in our traditional industrial society (laissez faire) are no longer effective. This change, according to Trist (1968), affects the requirements of welfare and development in a new way.

a *Welfare* or *well-being*, to continue to function well, refers to states of a system under conditions which maintain the steady state. . . . This set of terms, therefore, is concerned with the "statics" of adaptation – with stability (not to be confused with stagnation which is a state of ill-fare) and with the regulation and maintenance of stability.

b *Development* or *progression*, to continue to advance, refers to processes by which a system reaches higher or steady states of a more adaptive nature. . . . This set of terms, therefore, is concerned with the "dynamics" of adaptation – with positive change leading to the establishment of widened and preferred orders. . . . Development involves discovery and innovation. It is concerned with the regulation of growth.

(pp. 10–11)

Trist then describes how in preindustrial societies welfare was maintained by the autoregulative processes operating through the kinship system. When these failed, development processes involved the taking of an active role by coercive methods, for example, autocratic regimes with armies. *Development here was thus a function of welfare.*

With industrial societies, the more dynamic environment created by technological change involved *welfare becoming a function of development.* Development was autoregulative, operating through the market process; but the welfare of more and more people required active or planned intervention because it was no longer autoregulative, being dependent on overall, economic developments.

With the society into which we are moving *welfare and development become interdependent functions.* The best welfare secures development and, conversely, adaptation of a society now depends on the ecological regulation of the interdependencies of the innumerable social subsystems that characterize large societies undergoing rapid but uneven change. If subsystems do not develop, they fall into states of ill-fare. But because of the interdependence, ill-fare in a few subsystems can produce widespread disruption. Thus the values and behavior of one section of young people can cause major damage to others. Autoregulative processes such as the remedial efforts of other local organizations can no longer cope adequately with welfare or development in these highly complex situations, and so an active role, that is, a centrally planned and integrative type of intervention, involving the society as a whole, becomes necessary as a rule. Two options are then possible according to Emery (1967). One, modeled on the physical sciences, moves towards an engineered society. The other, more related to the behavioral sciences, seeks a more organic society. It seeks a higher quality in *all* primary social units (as contrasted with this higher quality primarily in the control parts). To quote again from Trist:

At the higher level of complexity which characterizes the transition to post-industrialism a higher quality is required in *all* primary social units. By primary social units is meant the set of concrete social

> resources which exist in the life-space of the individual, i.e. the people and institutions with which he or she directly interacts: family, workplace, children's school, the particular community of residence, the services and amenities actually available: in sum, all those entities which compose the *primary social world.* The quality of those resources in each case determines the individual's "quality of life," on which welfare and development alike depend. The objective of taking the active role is to bring into being ecological systems able to maintain primary social worlds of high quality throughout a society. How to do this has now become the over-riding question as we move towards post-industrialism.
>
> (1968, pp. 17–18)

The concepts of welfare and development relate to social values and do not originate in science. They belong to what Trist groups as *ideo-existential phenomena.* These include: (1) such entities as ideals, philosophies, beliefs and values, and so forth, as make up the forces shaping the way in which the world is construed; (2) the activators of behavior – goals, aspirations, emotions, and so forth; (3) social practices and processes and social perceptions.

These phenomena are interdependent and, most important for the management of change are the gaps that develop from the slowness with which beliefs and values change compared with the emerging social realities. This characteristic lag on the *ideo* side makes for great difficulty in effecting changes in core values and in the basic shape of institutions for conscious and unconscious reasons. This lag also presents serious problems in regard to the achievement of the kinds of thinking required for the conceptions of welfare and development adaptive to the conditions of postindustrial society.

In the industrial phase of our development, the state took an increasing role in providing welfare services for the sick and the poor – though in connection with the latter there was a conflict between this aim and the Protestant ethic. Moreover, a variety of *preventive*, as distinct from remedial, measures had to be instituted to cope with infectious diseases. Other state measures included what can be termed *social defenses*, for example, to control the dangers of lawlessness or drunkenness. *Social security* measures were begun. A third welfare concept also emerged from the necessities of the ongoing changes, and one which began to relate welfare and development as interdependent. This was the concept of *improvement*, for example, by public utilities in the physical environment and on the personal side by education, better conditions of work, and so on.

The predominant values, however, created conflicts around these issues, especially the cost of the welfare function of the State.

In our current scene, these conflicts in values evidently persist. Yet, as stressed earlier, what the social scientists are establishing is that personal *development* as well as welfare is an inherent requirement besides being a desirable value if the new society is to survive. Actually there is already in the more affluent countries an impressive array of improvement activity especially in the field of higher education. Within these countries welfare rights are starting to be perceived also as development rights. Emphasis is no longer so much on minimum standards as on the realization of potential, both for the sake of the individual and for society – though the conflicts carrying over through our traditional ideas and values make for crises through very uneven acceptances of change, and the means with which to achieve the new goals.

Trist sets out some of the inevitable *changes in emphasis of social patterns* as follows:

Thus, *Cultural or Ideo-existential Values are changing*

From	To
Achievement	Self-actualization
Self-control	Self-expression
Independence	Interdependence
Endurance of distress	Capacity for joy

Organizational Philosophies

From	To
Mechanistic forms	Organic forms
Competitive relations	Collaborative relations
Separate objectives	Linked objectives
Own resources absolutely their own	Own resources as belonging to society

Ecological Strategies

From	To
Responsive to crisis	Anticipative of crisis
Specific measures	Comprehensive measures
Requiring consent	Requiring participation
Short planning horizon	Long planning horizon
Damping conflict	Confronting conflict
Detailed central control	Generalized central control
Small local government units	Enlarged units
Standardized administration	Innovative administration
Separate services	Coordinated services

Many of these considerations are not new. As I have said, however, a comprehensive grasp of all these changing features is necessary if the psychoanalytic contribution to their transition, a process now in being, is to be an effective one.

What is psychoanalysis to do?

If we assume that the changes in our society have the characteristics outlined, then we can reflect upon their implications for psychoanalysis. (I use this term as a convenience to cover the total activities and influence of psychoanalysis, that is, through the effects of its knowledge upon our society, the use of the psychoanalytic method itself, and all the ways in which analysts might facilitate the application of psychoanalytic principles by all those making practical use of them.)

The concept of welfare and development as interdependent, while representing a new aspect at the social level, has, in relation to the individual, characterized psychoanalysis from the start. The whole process of psychoanalysis was conceived as releasing individual patients from forces holding back their development. Treatment was judged to be successful in proportion as it enabled them to achieve full use of their resources. The intensely individual nature of psychoanalytic treatment has, however, been a major factor against the development of ecological strategies which could widen the use of psychoanalytic principles in the welfare services. Any therapeutic endeavor that can be used only for a privileged few is liable, in our current society, to evoke resentful turbulence when its existence is widely known. I believe it is this reaction that underlies such views as were recently expressed in an article in *Time* (March, 1969), when psychoanalysis was described as on its "way out" while all kinds of other methods were being acclaimed as answers to meet the clamorous need for more mental health services. We would all agree that the classical psychoanalytic method has never been "in" as a practical procedure in community services. If psychoanalytic views about people, their development, conflicts, and functioning have the validity we believe they have after these ninety years of constant and progressive work, in what sense can psychoanalysis be on the way out? We are, of course, accustomed to this kind of rejection of psychoanalysis. In the past we have relied on the autoregulative processes of a free market in the acceptance of ideas to deal with these "attacks." The social situation now presents another problem. Community mental health services are emerging as an ecological issue so that they will tend to be planned with a growing degree of integration and on a wide scale. It is in relation to this dynamic in the social field that psychoanalysis could be on the "way out."

We have to ask ourselves if we are really keeping psychoanalytic knowledge in step with the times. Our understanding of human behavior can be formulated at different levels of abstraction – from the personal to the more impersonal forces we postulate in our metapsychology to explain some of the problems at the personal level. There is a great deal in common amongst the various psychodynamic schools of thought as long as we remain at the personal level. It is differences in metapsychological theories that lead to what the intelligent outsider can only see as "religious" wars. And in regard to our own metapsychology, we really have to examine the degree to which it may now be anachronistic. We must ask ourselves whether or not it is out of line with modern behavioral science – and keep in mind that not all our critics have only resistances as the determinants of their thought process.

A lack of congruence with the current scientific world is fostered by the organizational forms of psychoanalysis. These consist almost entirely of training institutes, and even though several of these conduct research programs, the latter are frequently confined to the data obtained within the psychoanalytic situation. (Notable exceptions are child development studies.) Here I wish to emphasize that the basic task for psychoanalysts is, and remains, the improvement of their theory and practice, and to train practitioners to the highest level possible. The application of psychoanalytic knowledge to community problems is an additional role. Nevertheless, in so far as analysis takes this as a vital task, I believe the gains to its own fundamental work will be large.

Trist's three areas of emphasis, the cultural or ideo-existential, the organizational, and the ecological, provide a good framework for looking at this task of bringing psychoanalysis into an effective relationship with the needs of the community.

Psychoanalysis and current ideo-existential issues

The extent to which psychoanalytic views are accepted by the innovating sections of the public as relevant to the current ideo-existential problems will determine the use of these views in general measures for improving personal development, and in creating welfare services.

Taking the changing emphases for the individual, we see him or her as moving from an independent, self-controlled, achieving person who has to endure a good deal of restriction – both from outer and inner environments, with associated tensions and distress – to one who will be much more interdependent, more self-expressing and self-actualizing, and with much more freedom as a result to enjoy living. To me, the most noteworthy feature of Trist's aspects is the use of the word *self*.

It may be a reflection of the interrelatedness of what is going on in society that this is the area now recognized amongst psychoanalysts as the one in most need of study. The self is the term we use for the core of the personality that preserves continuity in change – its preservation is what makes change acceptable. If the integrity of the self is threatened, change is resisted – often violently, in keeping as it were, with the defense of our most precious possession. With so much change in the fabric of society, it seems highly likely that it is the threat to the self that is most closely related to the many manifestations of anxiety that we see around us.

The self as a central issue for psychoanalysis is familiar enough, but we need a great deal more specific knowledge of what creates a good core to the self and what are the social settings required to maintain it in such a way that the individual is constantly enriching it.

The formulation of a good account of the development and functioning of the self would be of major value in helping society to cope with some of its current ideo-existential problems. A whole area that is pressing for more clarification is the study of the dynamics of the ego-ideal. Our patients have perhaps led us, understandably enough, to be preoccupied with the ego, the superego, and the instincts. The ego-ideal is as it were at the interface between much of our self-feeling and the values in society which are congruent with it.

In the anxious striving for more understanding of the person, for knowledge of how positive attitudes are fostered as well as of the conditions which release a person's unique potential for losing his or her person-directed conduct and replacing this with sadistic and destructive behavior of a kind unknown in the animal world, the existentialist philosophers have offered an appealing approach. Although it is difficult to discern a conceptual framework in their writings that does justice to the dynamics of the biological processes underlying human behavior, they have with their phenomenological descriptions reinforced the view that psychoanalysis does not have at present an adequate psychoanalytic theory of the self. Here, however, we expose a paradox in the current psychoanalytic scene. As Weisman (1965) has put it, existentialists are concerned with the "hiatus between the *formulations* of psychoanalytic theory and the *problems* with which individual men are involved" (p. 10). The value of existentialist thought is to stress those subjective features that relate "to a unique responsible person from the *inside* of his experience, and which defy conventional categories and descriptions" (p. 11).

That the nature of the person has become a focus of psychoanalytic interest in the last twenty years is reflected in the widespread reference in our literature to such terms as the ego, identity, and the self. It must surely be important for us to devote more of our attention to the response to these ideas in various sections of the community. Allied professional groups can use our writings directly, and it behooves us, for instance, to ponder on the very wide assimilation amongst these groups of Erikson's studies on the problems of identity, so much so that the phrase "identity crisis" has become as popular as the "Oedipus complex" became a few decades ago.

Similarly, the object-relations theorists such as Fairbairn, Winnicott, and Guntrip have also made a very ready appeal to the mental health professions in Great Britain. Unlike those of the Culturalists, their views represent an evolution from classical psychoanalytic concepts. These writers retain the fundamental importance of the very early structuring of the personality in the mother–infant interaction, and hence the interest in their work cannot be said to be dominated by a rejection of the importance of infantile sexuality and aggression. Their appeal seems to lie in the more direct relationship to the problems of intrapersonal and interpersonal conflict than is apparent in much of our writing couched in traditional metapsychology.

The relevance of these theoretical developments to current ideo-existential concerns is intuitively grasped by our writers and dramatists – the main transmitters to society of any new insights. Writers do not propagate our conceptual views; but when deeply affected by the human problems they illumine, they create archetypal characters who embody the preoccupations of the age. The mass media, and above all television, have immensely expanded the scope and rapidity of their influence so that they stimulate a restless dynamic in the social field. Writers, too, can have a remarkable sensitivity in regard to appraising psychodynamic theory – they respond to what makes sense amongst the inarticulate gropings of most people.

Underlining these responses in various sections of the community emphasizes the dynamic properties of the social field. It is when we ignore the fact that the social field is itself changed by psychoanalytic ideas that we get such absurdities as the extrapolations that are made in relation to psychotherapeutic needs in the community. Thus one still hears the following kind of statement. One analyst can treat say 10 patients: there are x thousand potential patients in the community and so we need $x/10$ analysts – a statement made even when the size of $x/10$ is ridiculous. Such extrapolations really assume a view of society as composed of separate self-determining individuals.

The social dynamic aroused can be illustrated by various actions with sections of the community to give help to many whose troubles are either not met by current resources or who are not adequately relieved by them. To many of those involved in community mental health services, the disturbing issue recurs of how the growth of expertise in a therapeutic method tends to be accompanied by an increasing narrowing of its range of applicability. Movements such as Alcoholics Anonymous, the Samaritans, and so forth, come into being not only to fill a gap but also because the "experts" say so many people are unsuitable for their "treatment." These movements then tend to be ignored by the more highly trained psychotherapists – but may it not be that there are important aspects in the therapeutic relationships that these movements foster? At any rate, they are worthy of the psychoanalyst's interest.

We do not have to be the reformers of society. Our psychoanalytic model for the management of change is a unique one in relation to the ideo-existential problems of the age – for in our own work, our patients take their own destiny into their hands when we can assist them to learn more of themselves. It is a model that can be adapted by society in its own ways.

We may have to contemplate being more involved in creating opportunities for sections of the public to learn more about psychoanalytic knowledge – and the mass media make quite new possibilities in this respect. It is particularly important that psychoanalytic thought should permeate to a far greater extent than at present our views on education. Instead of being pejoratively linked in the public mind with neurosis, is it not timely for its "image" to be more identified with personal growth and development, that is, with education. This whole question, however, is so large that I cannot do other here than to bring the essential aspect before us, namely, that the nature of our relatedness to the social scene of today has a new dynamic and one on which we must reflect very purposefully.

The provision of psychotherapeutic services: organizational philosophies

In contrast with the as yet scarcely developed contribution that psychoanalysis might make to the ideo-existential problems, I believe that we are much clearer in regard to how we can assist with the expansion of facilities throughout the community for offering psychotherapeutic help (Sutherland 1966, 1968).

The situation in the field is one of widening awareness of the nature of psychological stress and one that is now prompting remedial action. We have also to keep in mind that increasing permissiveness will mean more need to seek professional guidance. Thus freer divorce measures will inevitably entail more responsible and constructive steps in relation to each partner in the marriage and to the welfare of children, that is, there will be a greater demand for good counseling services. Psychological disorders vary greatly in their severity and in the ways in which the underlying conflicts may be expressed. A large range of agencies can therefore be appropriate as the first ports of call for help, or the first place wherein an underlying psychological problem will be exposed, for example, the family doctor, social work agencies of all kinds, the courts, the clergy, and so on.

The uppermost need within these agencies is to increase understanding and skill. We have now had a good deal of experience in methods of doing this; Michael and Enid Balint, for instance, have written extensively on this subject (Balint 1957, Balint and Balint 1961). The essential step here is to have consultants meet in regular seminars with the various professional groups. Conducting these seminars is best done by consultants who combine psychotherapeutic expertise with experience of group work as the group reactions can often be used to give a direct experience of how emotional difficulties interfere with the tasks people have to do – in this case, learning.

Although different agencies may be created in the community, these cannot remain discrete. They inevitably have to become integrated parts of a *sociotherapeutic system* – along with the specialist psychotherapeutic and psychiatric center. In each agency, staff members are constantly testing the limits of their skills because it is in the nature of much psychological disorder that a presenting difficulty, once it is brought under scrutiny, reveals more complex issues. The staff of each agency has therefore to have free and welcomed access to the specialist center when they need further help. Again, a proportion of people using one agency as their first source may have to be transferred to another for a variety of reasons, for example, the other may be more appropriate for special problems uncovered. Such interrelatedness can only become effective in practice when the various units share a common core of understanding about human problems in addition to any special function each unit may have. Furthermore, the community has also got to share increasingly in this common understanding if the helping services are to be perceived as concerned with the welfare and development of its members. I believe the essentials of this common framework can be formulated in the vocabulary of everyday speech – or at least with very few technical terms.

With this kind of interrelated mental health service becoming available, we can see the position of the psychoanalytic/psychiatric center as a pivotal resource for the whole. The most disturbed individuals are its concern and the staff therefore acquires more comprehensive and deeper knowledge about psychological disorders. Inevitably the staff groups within the specialist center are looked to for helpful support and for the opportunities to increase understanding and skill.

The boundaries to what agencies can do will be pressed outwards all the time. This is in the nature of the work and the situation. The staffs in many of the field agencies, particularly the social work ones, will have to become increasingly responsible in the professional sense. They cannot develop unless they see themselves as creating independent professions fulfilling the criteria of being a professional body, that is: (1) building up their own body of knowledge with constant scientific scrutiny of their working principles; (2) formulating these principles for training; and (3) creating a code of professional behavior. The social work groups lean very heavily upon psychoanalytic knowledge, but they have their own specific tasks. The psychoanalysts within centers, however, can be invaluable sources of support to them in their professional growth – and, conversely, analysts can learn much from their work.

When the specialist centers take on this supportive and educative role, appropriate activities on their part are required. Psychoanalytic work has to retain its status within them as its detailed study of personal growth and functioning is our basic laboratory. In contrast with private practice, however, the psychoanalysts in a community-related center should try to make special studies of current social problems, for example, of drug addiction or some such problem prominent in their area. It is only in centers with a group of analysts that the optimal conditions for such studies are normally available, especially the opportunity to integrate the study of intrapsychic with social factors.

Additional to psychoanalytic work, the specialist center has also to use therapeutic methods akin to those usable in the field agencies. Thus it should develop considerable expertise in group psychotherapeutic methods, in marital and family therapies. With its resources of highly trained staff, it has to be able to offer consultative help to the other agencies in which these methods will play a prominent role. Moreover, within the specialist center, it is particularly useful when representatives of all the relevant professions are engaged in this work. Thus, it facilitates the growth of the social work professions when these groups can relate to a member of their own profession as well as, say, to the psychoanalyst in the specialist center.

I remarked earlier that these developments may raise again questions of professional boundaries, and such issues as when is someone "ill" (see Szasz 1961). In our field *illness* is a term that has originated more out of professional rather than scientific roots. It may well be that it is the meaning of "medical responsibility" that has to be reexamined. As I see it, what is specific to the doctor is those people in whom there is (a) a somatic manifestation that needs elucidation: (b) a degree of disturbance that can be made more manageable with the aid of psychotropic drugs; (c) a severity of disorder that needs special inpatient care. Naturally many people will present difficult decisions in regard to who is to take primary responsibility. Such decisions should become much easier to reach as the whole network of service agencies builds up active collaboration. Faced with the anxieties of changing professional roles, interprofessional tensions will be inevitable. It is salutary to keep firmly in mind that, if there is one field of work in which there will be no redundancy problems, it is ours – the field of mental health in which demands are going to grow all the more as services become available.

The relationship of the mental health services to the community: ecological strategy

A widespread network of therapeutic services will clearly be of the utmost significance in the community's striving for constant betterment. The people seeking help represent those who for a great variety of reasons are unable to function as they would wish in their community. The data available in all the therapeutic agencies must therefore be fed back to those in all key positions concerned with the improvement of our society. To do so involves much further work, for example, to elucidate some of the general processes underlying the very complex array of specific manifestations of disorder. The knowledge gained in the therapeutic center about the intrapsychic factors in "breakdowns" has to be subjected to the expertise that social scientists can bring so that the social forces affecting the community can be identified. This could be achieved by having the specialist therapeutic center as one unit in a complex – a group of units whose overall mission could be described as the study of human relations. The resources of this larger complex would be such that studies could be made of an appropriately comprehensive kind. This complex would, in addition to maintaining active internal scientific exchange, seek relationships with the relevant sections of the community, especially with those concerned with the planning for the main services affecting the social and physical environments.

Summary

I have tried to show what I perceive to be the forces coming into more prominence in our society, and which are impinging upon us with increasing urgency. Far from being on the way out, psychoanalytic knowledge could, and should, be more than ever on the way in. It is incumbent upon psychoanalysts, especially those in specialist centers, as many of us now are, to study the current scene as carefully as we can and to act constructively to the best of our ability. I believe that, if we do not innovate in regard to our own roles, our mental health centers will shrivel and hence the welfare and development movements will be impoverished.

Chapter 6

The self: a challenge to psychoanalysis

Editor's introduction

Sutherland begins with a case example of a woman who was alternately aggressive (like her mother who hated her) and withdrawn (like her passive father). She created a world full of hate to cover her longing for and fear of closeness. Sutherland uses this example to discuss the integrative pressure that therapy brings to bear on the non-cohesive self and its symptom-producing subselves. He goes on to discuss the self as an open, proactive system providing guiding images determined by good understanding of the self, its perceptions of the world, and how it is perceived.

The self constitutes such an overriding challenge to psychoanalysis that it must remain the ongoing central issue for the next phase in the development of the whole field. Clearly, when one raises such far-reaching questions as the concept of the self introduces, one can only – almost absurdly – oversimplify. However, I risk oversimplifying because the implications of the concept of the self are so important. For many years, the absence of the essential nature of the personal from Freud's metapsychology has imposed more and more strain on psychoanalysis, creating an increasing need for a psychological theory of the self. In my own experience, I (1980b) have been greatly influenced by my British colleagues, especially Balint (1968), Fairbairn (1954b), Guntrip (1969), and Winnicott (1971), all of whom have contributed to the understanding of the self by advancing the theory from where Freud left it. I have been impressed by how much their work now has in common with that of many American analysts, for example, Erikson (1959), Kernberg (1976), G. S. Klein (1976), Kohut (1971, 1977), Lichtenstein (1977), and Schafer (1968). The emergence of such agreement from independent sources is particularly important in psychoanalysis.

In this presentation, I shall first outline my work with a patient over several years to focus critical issues in a way that relates to your own clinical experience and so keep before us the data on which to frame the questions to be studied. Then I shall draw some general features of this patient's difficulties that seem to require a change in our theoretical standpoint. In a third section, I shall sketch how the self might be conceptualized in its development and maintenance. Lastly, I shall reflect on some implications these views of the self have for the future of psychoanalysis. Again, I wish to stress that I offer no tidy theory. I hope, however, that you will share my interest in working toward a better understanding of the person.

Case example: Lena

The patient, a middle-aged widow whom I shall call Lena, had had a difficult relationship with her mother from birth because of allergies, feeding difficulties, and fits for which she was in and out of the hospital much of her first year. From the time Lena can remember, she has believed that her mother hated her; her father just withdrew. Throughout her childhood and adolescence, her life was one long battle with her mother, and she also became more and more combative with the world.

Lena was bright intellectually and qualified to become a social worker. Soon afterward, she married a rather psychopathic man, who was killed in an automobile accident about two years later. Before he died, the husband was overseas most of the time, and so the marriage was hardly a relationship at all. Yet, in spite of the poor relationship, her husband's death intensified Lena's feelings that she was no good and there was no point in living. These feelings led to an attempted suicide and several months in a hospital. Lena was labeled depressive, although at times she experienced disordered thoughts with hallucinations, which suggested that she might be schizophrenic. She recovered sufficiently to manage her work for many years and sought help when she felt some of her lethargic, apathetic symptoms returning. She also became increasingly dependent on tranquilizers and alcohol.

Lena appeared constantly on the defensive against almost all close relationships, which she warded off either by withdrawing abruptly from people or by behaving aggressively toward them. Consequently, she became increasingly isolated. For example, her relationships with colleagues, the only people with whom she had much contact, were characterized by alternately thinking they were "not so bad" to more frequently thinking they were about to invade her. She achieved closeness with few co-workers, although she did establish responsive empathic relationships with her clients.

Lena believed that she had missed something in her childhood. Thus, she longed to get and to give affection, but she dared not express any lest she be "exploited." Her turbulent relationship with me brought out her destructive attitudes, not only as a defense but as a revenge – a quite prominent theme. For several years, Lena's treatment involved a struggle against her extremely tenacious clinging to an outer aggressive self, not only to avoid relationships but to ward off a greatly dreaded loss of herself such as had occurred during her breakdown. Her mistrust of finding a better world was almost total. It took her years to believe that I was concerned about her and thought she had good qualities to offer others. Moreover, she slowly realized that, by frequently attacking me, she was trying to destroy her treatment. Her treatment was made even more difficult to cope with because of her splitting off into a secret inner world a hidden self, with its rich fantasy world and its invulnerability and omnipotence.

The primitive nature of Lena's lack of a cohesive self behind her negative identity was evident during periods of particular stress. At these times, she became so disorganized that she would forget the meanings of familiar words – a serious handicap to her spare-time activity of writing freelance articles for the press. Words became just "sounds." Because of this loss of meaning, reading was impossible. Lena also believed that the words could jump out of the page as if to attack her.

Lena said that her body felt detached and strange, with little or no integration of either physical sensations or mental processes. She had difficulty speaking about the sense of self-loss because she feared that I would reject her for this "craziness." However, when she realized that I was trying to understand her experiences as repetitions of past terrifying experiences of being totally out of touch with any trusted figure, she was able to describe these feelings in spite of the intense anxiety and humiliation they aroused. Although she felt at her worst in this total chaos, she believed that she could regain an integrated self if someone thought she could do so and could convince her of that. At the same time, I sensed her confusion and understood that she was desperate to explode something out from inside herself, namely, the intensely hated persecutory world. Perhaps most striking was the way she created in the outer world a replica of her inner world, that is, a world full of hate. At best, she perceived the outer world as being unconcerned about her, leaving her omnipotent in her secret fortress and ensuring inner survival as a person with a self.

Central issues in the functioning of the person

Although some of these problems are specific to this individual, I believe they represent the central issues for most, if not all, patients. The following prominent features can be noted, leaving aside any claims to comprehensiveness or their relative importance.

1 Such patients are greatly preoccupied with insecurity about how other people accept and value them. Their powerful need for a positive response from others, frequently manifested in exhibitionistic components, may be hidden under extensive negativistic denials such as Lena employed. Even she, however, constantly hoped that people

would see behind her aggressive front a self wanting to be valued. Psychoanalysts must identify the nature of how their patients want to be valued by others and how these needs arise. They certainly concern a "whole," "the self," which cannot be broken down into components without disappearing. The nature and origin of this whole simply have to be understood as a gestalt.

2 Whether or not the self is a coherent unity in its earliest stages, it soon acquires divisions, or subselves, that are kept apart in their functioning by the incompatibility in the relationships each part seeks with the other parts. The splits clearly originate in the environmental mismatches. Nevertheless, the initial unity remains active in the awareness that the subselves are parts of the one self. However, there is a perpetual strain because of these divisions and because of the fluctuating struggle to integrate the splits. This strain, of course, is a powerful motive for seeking psychotherapy.

3 The subselves contain needs that press to be accepted as vital parts of the self, and, as such, these needs cannot be rejected; they are derivatives of the innate givens of the organism. But some of these needs are unacceptable to an infant's parents and therefore lead to painful consequences if expressed. Thus, the child has to cope with them away from the parents, for example, by fantasy activity or, later, by secret expression.

4 The integrative pressure brings out a basic feature of the self-system, namely, its active, initiating role with the environment. The self-system constantly strives to interact and establish compatible and reciprocal relationships with its surroundings. Underlying Lena's negativistic exterior was her almost intolerably painful feeling that everything she had ever given was rejected, and so she seldom offered herself to others.

5 One part of the self becomes dominant in the development of a *visible self*. The subselves are kept apart from this dominant one with varying degrees of splitting and repression; yet in many activities they are merged with the dominant self to achieve some expression, albeit unconsciously.

6 The activity of subselves creates symptoms, which may be relatively localized, as in perversions, or more general in their effects, as in Lena's lethargy and fears of disintegration. They cannot, however, be explained solely in terms of repressed impulses. They represent the solutions an original unitary self finds to express at a personal level its unmet or actively rejected needs.

7 From an early age, the self can be seen as a complex system that has internalized the important figures of the external world, divided according to their different aspects. The inherent social relatedness of the self as a whole is manifest from the start. The instincts do not have

their own internal templates to fashion the actual patterns of behavior that will satisfy them. These patterns come from the adaptive action of the self in its relationships with the real figures at hand, along with its inner-world figures and relationships, which can be manipulated with imaginative play.

8 I cannot go into all the intricacies of the numerous possibilities this inner world provides, for instance, by establishing relationships with objects that are fantasied as objects or by identifications with the objects, some with considerable stability, others with much more lability. These developments have been described in detail by Melanie Klein (1932), Fairbairn (1944), Winnicott (1971), Kohut (1971, 1977), and many others. A primary patterning of the self is established in the earliest relationships, in which the acceptance of the self as a person is intimately involved with bodily needs, and in which the self and its objects are still incompletely differentiated. This primal patterning of the ways the self behaves to gain security and acceptance remains a powerful determinant of future development, particularly in social relationships. In keeping with the incomplete self–object differentiation, relationships in these early states have a strongly compulsive character.

9 The primary patterns of the dominant self are elaborated by inner maturation and by increased experience of the world. In particular, the sexual instincts are fitted into these primary self-patterns in the evolution of the sexual identity, as originally described by Fairbairn (1954b).

10 Once a dominant self is fashioned and implemented, it forms what can be described as the individual's identity, that is, the self he makes visible because of its reality involvement and because others "identify" him by it. Thus, it is relevant to recall that Erikson (1959) at first chose the term *ego-identity*, an apt choice because it suggests the close connection of the visible self with reality relatedness. The concept of the ego as an independent entity, especially in motivation, seems unnecessary (G. S. Klein 1976). All the autonomous functions Hartmann (1958) described are employed by the self in action. Action, however, is controlled by the self-system, which is most active in relation to the environment. Lena's case is a striking example of how the self, especially in regard to its positive acceptance, can dramatically alter the individual's whole capacity to think and to hold on to meanings, that is, the structured layers of past experience. Her anxieties frequently prevented reality thinking because she had withdrawn from the real world. Confidence in the mother's love seems to provide the foundation for the capacity to keep experience – and hence thought and understanding – continuous.

11 When the dominant self is established as an identity, a person clings to that self with the utmost tenacity no matter how restricted or distorted it may be because the dominant self is not only the visible mode of

relating, it is also the cover for the whole invisible self in its closed world of secret inner relationships. As the individual's mode of surviving, the dominant self exhibits a profoundly aggressive attitude toward any attempt to take it away, even when the wish to alter that self brings the individual to treatment.

12 The ferocity with which the identity is defended calls attention to a puzzling phenomenon, namely, how this very structuring can be removed by a field change as opposed to a direct personal challenge. For instance, Lena's intense hate was aroused when she felt that I was forcing a different identity on her; yet she could lose her dominant self or identity when the external world felt empty of any source of reassurance to the self.

Some general comments about the self as an open system

Since Freud sought to keep psychoanalytic theory on a firm biological base, a few observations from this standpoint are helpful regarding one's perspective on any concept of the self. Freud's biological speculations, insofar as they impinge on clinical understanding, concerned mainly the origin and nature of the drives. It was inevitable that he should have reductionist science deeply rooted in him. Even when he had to give up the "Project for a Scientific Psychology" (1950) because of problems in dealing with the psychological, he remained wedded to his energy notions and to the second law of thermodynamics, which was then virtually the ultimate reality. However, advances in biology, cybernetics, and theories of open systems (such as living organisms, that is, those in which the system interacts incessantly and adaptively with an environment that in turn may show similar adaptive responses) enable analysts to establish a more appropriate basis for their views of both the psychological and the social and how their mutual relationships create the individual.

Apart from all the gains in psychoanalytic understanding, these developments liberate the thinking that is needed from the constant attack that psychoanalysis is outside "natural science." Prigogine (1976) and others (see Jantsch 1980) have now worked out the principles and associated mathematics of such open systems, in which there is the *necessity* for constant interactional developments, with structural changes to embody the "learning" that has taken place. Thus, predictability has a limited role in regard to open systems because unpredictable creativity in relation to unpredictable environmental change is the characteristic feature of these systems. Living systems survive by being negentropic, that is, they live outside the entropic principle inherent in closed systems. Death is not a running down of the machine but a "planned" event required by evolution. Concepts such as the death instinct must be appraised against the view that reactive aggressive behavior is required for survival. Within the evolutionary process, there is the thrust toward more and more freedom from environmental constraints. We are not the blind, passive victims of change and necessity Monod (1971) describes, for, as Jantsch (1980) puts it, "We are not the helpless subjects of evolution – we *are* evolution" (p. 8).

Evolution has taken us to our present place through our unique mental capacities, and in this development our simultaneous social evolution has been a necessity. The development of the individual with resources and adaptive capacities is clearly inseparable from the social milieu which evolves in parallel. It certainly sounds platitudinous to make that remark and yet, as we are all aware, until recently, psychoanalysis has not paid adequate attention to the dynamic way in which social and general environmental relationships are built into the person. These relationships structure eventual individual personal properties to create a system that cannot survive without appropriate responses from the environment which, in turn, has to change with developments in people. Our relatedness to our environment depends on our unique capacity to transcend it by making a reproduction of it inside our minds, where we then manipulate possibilities, from which stem our creative alterations of our reality. As a result of this evolutionary process, a remarkable freedom from the uncertainties of the physical environment has been achieved. It is generally agreed that corresponding adaptations in the social world have lagged far behind. One change that has emerged, however, is the entirely new importance attached to the self. The individual has acquired a new status in Western democratic social and political philosophies, one in which the full realization of his or her personal resources is a requirement (Emery and Trist 1973). On all fronts, then, the individual, self, and identity have become central concerns, and it is no accident that these concerns have developed in psychoanalysis. The self as the controller of perception and action has become the focal concept in relating the individual to the environment.

In studying development, it is useful to have in mind its outcome. How, then, do analysts view the optimal condition of the individual? I believe that the starting point must be "intentionality," the purposes, that is, the long-term relationships he or she wishes to make with the environment. Chein (1972) gives a useful description of this aspect when he states, "The essential psychological human quality is, thus, one of commitment to a developing and continuing set of unending, interacting, interdependent, and mutually modifying long-range enterprises" (p. 289). Love and work are central for the survival of these enterprises, but our expressive needs, especially art and religion, must also be considered. The dynamics of these needs do not stem from the instincts alone. With the capacity to transcend the environment, they seem to represent a need to give meaning and significance to life and to move toward what can only be described as "betterment" – perhaps an expression of the thrust of evolution in relation to environmental stresses. When such commitment is within a self whose main aims are adequately integrated with reality, there is the foundation for a creative, satisfying, and enjoyable mode of living.

How are the self, its development, and its functioning to be conceptualized? The patient I have sketched and others who are similar, as well as the writings of other researchers, suggest the following outline.

Just as anatomical growth with all its differentiation appears to be ordered by an organizing ground plan operating as an overall gestalt, so the development of the self must have a parallel gestalt integrating its interactions with reality. However coherent its unity may be at the start, the self-system rapidly acquires divisions or subselves resulting from the incompatible affects associated with experiences. Even with all the limitations of present knowledge, the self can at least be regarded as an overall system in which experiences are brought into cohesion. The gestalt appears to have a "desired" state of positively toned affect that accompanies the interactions between the organism and the environment, with each affect having its own specific quality according to the particular features of any relationship. Innate behavioral systems have their own affective expectancies so that when the infant "needs" something that matches the "shape" of this need, the appropriate object gives the self the feeling that things are "right." It is now known that these innate expectancies include, in addition to the bodily or appetitive ones, powerful independent needs to satisfy the impetus toward autonomous psychological development. Adult patients all too often express the feeling that "something is missing" in their self from very early times, when these needs were not met. In short, the inherent "form" or "shape" that the gestalt "needs" is to be a person. The crucial factor for an infant's optimal development is an input of enjoyment from the mother that reflects her love and care for the child as a spontaneously developing, autonomous person. This experience imparts to the embryonic self a feeling of being a sure and "right" part of a world which is represented by this welcome into it. The self-system needs to be "personalized" by being treated as an autonomous person by other persons. Children see and feel who they are by what is put into them by their particular mother and then by the other family figures. This process is a much more active one on the adult's part than is indicated by terms like "mirroring" or being a "container." This process needs all the shared experiences from encouraging stimulation and play that occur in everyday "tender loving care." In this mutuality, the child plays a decidedly active and evocative role toward the mother's responses.

Thus, the self-gestalt has to be viewed as becoming a proactive system, structured by an internal replica of its specific relationships with the outer world. The differentiation of the self and its objects in this inner world is a familiar process, and the inevitable incompatibilities between some of the infant's self-needs and the parents' responses to them create divisions within the self. As Lena's case illustrates, these divisions contain both the infant's unmet or rejected needs and parallel structures of the controlling, rejecting parents. These divisions remain permanently because they are parts of the whole, stemming from the innate makeup of the child. Within the overall system, these divisions establish a complex set of processes, such as providing fantasy objects with which fantasy relationships can be enacted as substitutes for reality failures. These divisions also provide a great range of different imagos with which the self may be identified to varying extents and with varying stability. Because they are unacceptable for open expression, these divisions remain undeveloped by experience with reality. They persistently seek relationships with the outer world because they need people, but because their aims have remained unadapted to the outer world, the latter has to be coerced to fit them. A dominant reality-related self, in keeping with the gestalt nature of the overall system of which it is a part, tries to manage the activity of these subselves by merging them with selected reality relationships – the process Waelder (1960) describes as the "multiple functions" of most behavior. Should there be a regression in the integration of the self – which can happen with various environmental stresses – then the primary qualities in these subself relationships (for example, the lability of self and object differentiation) show in compulsive relationships and in identifications with the different inner objects.

In the early states of the developing configuration of the self, the autonomous striving toward greater independence from the first symbiotic phase is characterized by labile fluctuations. On the one hand, there are regressions to the omnipotent and compulsive relationships and identifications of the undifferentiated phase, and, on the other hand, there are more mature patterns in which sharing with independent others for mutual gain replaces taking or wanting things for oneself. What might be termed a *primal self* is patterned in the early transitional states of object differentiation, when the child acquires a feeling of the "shape" of the self he or she is free to have. In these early stages the failure of the mothering and family relationships can create major distortions, either from deprivation of basic self-needs or from the not uncommon imposition of a parent's self-pattern onto the child. Early parental failures from accidental disturbances can often be overcome, at least in part, but all too often relationship failures are reinforced because of limitations in the parental personalities.

Lichtenstein (1977) suggests that this first personalization has a fixity in its patterns comparable with the early ethological concept of "imprinting." This first personalization certainly is extraordinarily persistent in the way it creates a scaffolding for future developments. Lichtenstein contrasts the development of the self in humans with the situation in animals. Self-development is necessary for us to relate to our environment, while in animals instinctual equipment gives an inner *Umwelt* with which they can readily adapt to the particular environment for which their equipment has been evolved. Living in our self-made environment we have to have our world internalized in a more complex and adaptive way.

An organization liberated from the stabilities of the instinctual systems has to pay a price for this freedom by losing the guaranteed, if inflexible, stability that instinctual systems provide. In the face of perpetual change, a sense of continuity is required for adaptive capacities. Also, with a structuring developed to cope with and anticipate the future in its own society, the affective tone of the self-system – its self-esteem – has to be maintained by affirmation. Lichtenstein (1977) suggests that, because the integration of the self is so important, an important inherited reinforcer of the self may have evolved in the form of nonprocreative sexuality. Such a function could explain the prominence of autoerotic activity for those selves that do not establish free relationships with reality, that is, most patients.

Affirmation normally comes from a range of social interactions. When reality freedom has been severely inhibited, the individual creates an inner world in which he compensates for this lack by omnipotent control of fantasied relationships. This inner world can become a serious maladaptive factor in the eventual self, for such a world is a distorted one with which to mediate relationships with reality. These relationships, instead of being established and enjoyed freely, become a safeguard of this inner world, where the individual protects his or her real self in a kind of fortress. Lena put up a hostile front to keep all possible intruders away from her secret world, where she felt at times an almost frightening omnipotence. Pure fantasy activity is seldom sufficient, and so the inner world has to coerce the outer to fit its requirements – a rather incompatible basis for adaptive relationships. This development is also the source of some of the most difficult negative therapeutic relationships. The analyst is perceived as a menacing intruder to be fought off at all costs, even though little or no satisfaction is gained from the restricted mode of living this situation permits.

Although he has not elaborated the point, Lichtenstein (1977) suggests that work seems to be a highly important area within the wide range of interactions that provide affirmation. The instinctive roots of work are manifold, for example, its relation to physical survival, to provision for the family, and to satisfactions that skills and achievements bring. Personal needs, however, are central. Thus, many studies of work (see Emery and Trist 1973) have shown that unless personal needs are satisfied, there is a disintegration of the self, which is manifested in poor performance, high absenteeism, and high sickness rates. Such manifestations are also characteristic of groups that have lost their social connectedness, for instance, displaced populations. When expressive or ideo-existential needs are not met, effects of such deprivation are seen in the loss of the self-system's effectiveness, as in widespread apathy or "depression" or in violence by protest groups that arises from the loss of a sense of significance or meaning to life. With much of this kind of stress, it is often not so much the absence of ideologies, religion, or values that deprives the self of a sense of meaning as it is the dissonance between the inner image of the person that is thought right for particular groups and the one that is proclaimed with intrusive force. Ideo-existential needs carry a considerable loading from the segregated subselves, and derivation in regard to these needs exerts a disintegrative effect, both by weakening the reinforcing affirmation the dominant self needs and by altering the status of the dominant self in managing the subselves.

When the self reaches adulthood, its relationships with the social environment have patterned its *identity* – the characteristic visible way in which the individual functions. When I suggested earlier that a primal self could be described that was fashioned in the phases of infantile dependence, I was distinguishing its form from that of its later *social identity*, in which various accretions have been assimilated; and because of its intimate links with social interaction, this later self in its social identity seems particularly dependent on a requisite social connectedness.

Thus, it is not difficult to recognize the fundamental role that the dynamics of perpetual relatedness with society play in maintaining the integrity of the self. This relationship of the individual to groups naturally attracted Freud's (1921) interest, and he advanced his theory of the ego by postulating the separate function of the ego-ideal in binding the individual to the leader. In characterizing the distinctive identity of a man outside the primitive or unorganized group, Freud described him as possessing "his own continuity, his self-consciousness, his traditions and customs, his own particular functions and position, and . . . [as keeping] apart from his rivals" (p. 86). Moreover, Freud noted that an individual would seek to preserve this identity against any negative impingement, with even a readiness to express hatred and aggressiveness, to which Freud ascribed the elementary character that he found in the death instinct. Since he believed that this identity was preserved by narcissistic libido, it is remarkable that he described the individual's distinctive identity on the basis of McDougall's (1920) conditions for the *organized group*: (1) the group should have a continuity of existence; (2) individuals within the group should know the nature, composition, functions, and capacities of the group; (3) the group should interact with other groups partly similar and partly different in many respects; (4) the group should possess traditions, customs, and habits, especially those that determine the relationships among members; and (5) the group should have a definite structure, exposed in the specialization and differentiation of the functions of its constituents (see also Freud 1921).

Bion's (1961) studies with actual unorganized groups show that, faced with a reality task the members cannot grasp, and given no help with this task by the leader, such a group rapidly regresses into what he called the "basic assumptions" of the group. He accounted for these states in terms of Melanie Klein's (1932) primitive mechanisms, yet the individuals showed a cohesion in regressing to their basic assumptions. Such behavior can be viewed as stemming from the loss of social identity and the emergence of the individuals' primal selves.

Implications for the future of psychoanalysis

These somewhat discursive comments are intended to emphasize that the self cannot be conceptualized except as an open system developing and maintaining its identity through the social relatedness essential to it from the start. It must be questioned whether or not the classical psychoanalytical theory of the person and his or her development and functioning does justice to this fact. Therapeutically, the analyst's task is to achieve greater integration in the self-system by reducing the separateness of the subselves. I have no doubt that what has been encountered as a negative or rather partial therapeutic reaction frequently derives from the way individual patients divide part of their self into a subself to be kept in virtually a secret fortress, with the rest of their relationships distorted to preserve this situation. This inner state, however, is entirely a product of their relationships within the family, and, even when they seem most cut off, the essential factors are the failed relationships and the terror of disintegration that remains. I have avoided using the term *narcissistic* because it has been connected for so long with the biologically oriented view that states of failed capacity to relate have their origin in the development of the libido rather than primarily because of failures of the social environment.

The implications of a comprehensive theory of the self and its personal (object) relations are, of course, much wider than the therapeutic problems. Although, as Freud (1926) pointed out, it is not the business of psychoanalysis to provide a weltanschauung or ideology, it is the concern of psychoanalysis to offer understanding of how the individual relates to reality and to him- or herself. The inexorable thrust of evolution keeps us constantly seeking to improve our situation in relation to our environment, and the image of us within a society has a profound influence on our behavior. The psychoanalytic image, I must stress, is not of where we should go. Rather, it is an image of the way our functioning as a creator of our guiding images is determined by the properties of our self and its perceptions of the world. This image of the person and the human race will be used by social philosophers. There is already evidence of what can happen when we humans are seen as being created by our drives and their satisfactions (Brown 1959).

By trying to belong to the "natural" sciences as they have been conceived following Descartes, psychoanalysts have alienated themselves in large measure from the humanities, and at the same time they have made even less impression on the "hard science" philosophy underlying medicine today. I do not believe that psychoanalysts have the right friends for making an effective contribution to the present climate of opinion. With a due importance attached to the self and its inner world as the mediator of social behavior, the works of the great writers and artists as well as developments in the social sciences should surely figure much more in psychoanalytic thinking. The human sciences badly need the kind of understanding of human relationships that psychoanalysis can contribute. Only in that way will the prevalent gap between psychoanalysts and other scientists be bridged. I also believe that the newer notions about evolution may well make it possible for psychoanalysts to be less dismissive of man's religious quests. Again, it is not a matter of saying "what should be," but of illuminating the nature and function of the great human expressive needs. When religion is seen as being rooted in our innate striving to understand ourselves in our environment, its origins cannot be reduced to infantile dependence. Nevertheless, the mode in which it is expressed may have to be freed from these early influences and matured to fit our expanding knowledge and understanding.

In a time of such turbulence as the present, with endless superficial remedies and treatments for personal problems, the psychoanalyst's task must be to get an account of the person that does justice to our full nature. This turbulence (Emery and Trist 1973) has resulted from the remarkable growth of the physical sciences with their technological advances, a growth that has reinforced the wish for "scientific" cures. In the view of many people for a long time, psychoanalysis has not been considered a science because of the failure to recognize that persons are complex, open, developing systems. I believe that this position is about to change radically throughout the scientific field, and that psychoanalysts must respond by putting people with all the subjectivity governing their actions to the front. I find it encouraging that in a recent book on ethology, Robert Hinde (1982), one of the leading scientists in that field (and incidentally, John Bowlby's guide in his ethological thinking), states that it would be wrong to pretend there is extensive common ground between ethology and psychiatry. For Hinde, the psychiatrist's proper concern is subjective experience. This view constrains what ethology can offer psychiatry, although its indirect contribution in conjunction with the other behavioral sciences is great. The self is surely the heart of the matter regarding the organization and functioning of subjective experience.

Chapter 7

The self and personal relations

Editor's introduction

Sutherland thinks that analysts should share their difficulties and failures so as to reach a more profound understanding and to contribute to the development of theory to help those who are suffering. This chapter offers a remarkable synthesis of the writings of those whose views he valued, applied to the task of addressing problems that have not responded to analysis. The chapter goes on to deal with the self as a dynamical matrix, an object for others, and an object in its own right. Dated February 1978, this precedes the better known "The Psychodynamic Image of Man" (1979) and "The Autonomous Self" (1980), all of which are preliminary to the full realization of Sutherland's views, which could not be completed before his death, and yet they offer a significant advance in thinking about the self.

Challenge to classical metapsychology

Psychoanalytic theory is manifestly in the melting pot. In Kuhn's (1962) terms, the paradigm of classical metapsychology was successfully challenged by Hartmann (1958) and his school, and though the changes in theory were initiated largely on general biological considerations of the problem of adaptation, they gave rise to a rich stream of clinical and developmental studies. Simultaneously, an independent challenge was emerging from the clinical work of a few British analysts with patients commonly regarded at that time as unsuited for psychoanalytical treatment. For many years the special social and political factors surrounding the development of psychoanalytical theory and practice kept these trends apart. The merging of them which is now taking place has inevitably widened the base from which theory is being appraised; and of particular importance have been changes outside of psychoanalysis, in the philosophy of science and in general biology. The new scene can be characterized by the rise of interest in such personalized concepts as "the self" or "identity," compared with the traditional theoretical issues couched in the language of nineteenth-century science; that is, in the impersonal terms of forces and energy transformations.

Clinically, a concept of "the self" has very real value in our understanding of certain fundamental aspects of personal functioning (see Khan 1974) especially when problems are presented as disturbances of total personal behavior. Having a concept of the self is essential for working with patients whose whole commitment to living is seriously impaired as indicated by such phrases as: "I go through the motions of living but I am not in it"; "I am not the self I feel I should be"; or "I do not feel I know who I really am." These, and similar descriptions are commonplace. What is striking is the emergence of these states of mind in persons who have previously had lengthy periods of analysis. British analysts who have either explicitly or implicitly made extensive use of concepts of "the self" have been much influenced by such cases, written about by Balint, Winnicott, Fairbairn, and Guntrip (see Chapter 3). The need for further treatment was not attributed to inadequate work on the part of the previous analysts – in fact they had mostly been treated by senior analysts – but was regarded as due to a pervasive disturbance at the core of the person which only became accessible some time after more superficial layers of defenses and conflicts, often in classical Oedipal terms, had been worked through. The nature of the self and its theoretical position therefore merit much more attention than has been given.

Ego and self

To what, then, does the concept of "the self" refer? There is most prominently the person's sense of self – his or her "I" – as a free agent in the creation of what is meaningful. What is it that is sensed? Chein (1972) in his examination of the question, "Who is the actor?" notes that although the self cannot be observed directly, seeing the self is not a requirement in the proof of its existence. The self can be present transcendentally as the intervening subject self which gives identity to past and future object selves. Chein states: "The most significant aspect of the self is the appearance of the object self as actor." All such observations, all referable to a continuing self-identity, make up a complex *self-concept* which embraces many constituents, such as the relation to one's body, the observation of the behavior that accompanies that relationship, and the attributions, explicit and implicit, made about one by others. Society contributes in a basic way to the development of the self-concept through the behavior it rewards. Nevertheless, although the self-concept construes the subject of the person's actions, *a concept cannot be the actor.*

Since he cannot readily find the real referents of the self, Chein appraises the ego as the actor. Within the ego system, many motives are concerned with doing things for "the self" and so the self as the object of these motives must be a structure which interacts with them. There are also motives that are not within the boundaries of the ego, but are subsumed under the terms superego and id. Chein has been found guilty of anthropomorphism in attributing to these subsystems humanoid characteristics, but he rejects the criticism. He maintains that the attribution is appropriate; for these systems function in action as human beings would. For Chein, then, there is a functional significance of the self in the ego structure, and that accounts for the interchangeability of the terms "self" and "ego." Psychotherapeutic work forces upon us the view that the ego has many structures with varying degrees of interrelatedness ranging from a relative unity in function to such extremes of disorganization as multiple personalities. Its organizing and controlling functions are concerned with maintaining adaptedness and anticipation, through the effectiveness of mapping the person's world. The ego is thus the system in which options are considered and decisions made.

Chein therefore concludes that the person or actor is an overall system constituted by the ego, super ego, and id, along with the self and the body. The first three combine to give a motivational system within which there are subsystems; and within the general system are the unfulfillable goals of seeking to anticipate the contingencies of an uncertain world. The essential psychological human quality is not one to be accounted for in energy terms; for it is one of commitment to a developing and continuing set of unending, interacting, interdependent, and mutually modifying long-range enterprises.

I have quoted Chein because his contribution to our topic from the standpoint of a sophisticated humanistic psychologist has so much of relevance to what we have to consider. It cannot be pretended, however, that the position of a self is unambiguous in Chein's views. A central integrative role appears to have been given to the self, not only in its transcendental function, but concretely. He observes:

> Self-preservative, self-enhancing, and self-determining motivation is directed to the self *per se* rather than to our concept or image of it . . . it is as if all the syntonic behaviors of the actor (that is, all the spontaneous directed activities in which he engages and with respect to which he at least subconsciously assents or accepts responsibility) emanate from it.

We are then surprised when we find decision-making located within the ego – one system, even if a highly complex one, that has not been allocated a supraordinate role. Further, in multiple personalities each one acts like a person encompassing at least part of the functions of all; the constituent systems of the person. Yet Chein takes these to be disruptions in the ego. Where are we then to place the origin of the splitting? Who or what splits whom or what?

The self as a supraordinate system

Are we not back in the same dilemma that confronts all attempts to build up the person in his wholeness from his parts, whether we are dealing with the organization of motives or even of behavioral systems as studied by the ethologists despite the hierarchical organization they allow on the basis of the components? A bold answer to this question has been provided by Saperstein and Gaines (1973) who insist that a psychological explanatory theory must rest on the personal phenomena of clinical data. Apart from Erikson's (1959) concept of identity, they conclude that most metapsychological approaches to the self, such as those of Hartmann (1958), Sandler and Joffe (1969), and Jacobson (1964), emerge with a presumably *scientific* description of the activities of the person resting on parts, and so avoiding the question of the self-as-agent. Saperstein and Gaines, as did Lichtenstein (1961), come back to the persistent influence of the Cartesian dualism of mind and body in which there is no place for such a self. Taking a stance on modern philosophical, biological, and psychological considerations, they view it as a necessity to conceptualize a supraordinate self-as-agent which can be explored as a natural phenomenon in any account of intentionality, purpose, and freedom of choice without resorting to entelechies. [Entelechy is the final perfection of a drive or principle of a system – Ed.] They then quote Langer (1967) on the dynamic whole of living organisms whose activities are integrated within a *matrix* which, though having various degrees of coherence and persistence, is a system that is "self-sustaining, and self-propagating, wherein every event is prepared by progressively changing conditions of the integral whole. Every distinguishable change arises out of the matrix, and emerges as an act of an agent; for such a vital matrix is an agent" (Saperstein and Gaines 1973, p. 421). Saperstein and Gaines take this vital matrix as a supraordinate self which is independent from and more than the sum of its parts though affected by them. In other words the matrix is the system at the highest level of the cybernetic hierarchy that the organism requires for the integration of its subsystems. Though similar to the biological organizing principles postulated by Spitz (1945) and by Sandler and Joffe (1969), there is here a clearer base for subsequent organization being developed by differentiation within an original supraordinate dynamic system concerned with the organism as a whole rather than having to find ways of bringing parts together. And all general systems theorists assume this kind of view.

Psychoanalysis increases the freedom of choice available to this self; and, though it is not knowable directly, its structure can be investigated through self-representations. It too is a hierarchically ordered system with its own structure so that its nature and functioning can only be understood by genetic reconstruction.

The views of Saperstein and Gaines have been stimulated by the gap between modern philosophy and biology on the one hand and the outmoded science available to Freud as much as by that between metapsychology and clinical work. It is all the more striking then that the explicit attempt to bridge this latter gap made by Fairbairn over thirty years ago, and hence without the help of the advances made in science and general biological theory during this period, should result in a theory of the self and its development so closely in agreement.

From pristine ego through object relationship to self

Fairbairn postulated the existence of a unified ego from birth. As Ernest Jones (1952), with quite exceptional perspicacity, stated in his preface to Fairbairn's (1952a) book, Fairbairn started at the center of the personality in contrast to Freud's working in from the periphery. Writing years before systems theory had become prominent, Fairbairn thus adopted a view of development as proceeding by differentiation within an overall dynamic integrative matrix, which is the carrier of the experience of the infant and within which structuring inevitably takes place according to the emerging patterns of experience.

The pristine ego he takes to be lacking in complexity because it is lacking in experience; but it is the active organizer of experience from the start and its experience in a state of total dependence is entirely centered on its interactions with the mother. At this stage there is no difficulty in substituting "self" for "ego." (Fairbairn's terminology does not do full justice to his position. He wanted to get theory on to a quite definite personal level because he considered that was the only level at which clinical phenomena could be discussed. At the same time, he had no wish to be thought of as setting up a new school; he regarded his work to be entirely a continuation of Freud's. The radical nature of his theories is therefore somewhat covered because of his using as far as possible a "classical" mode of expression, with terms such as "ego" for "self," and "object" for "personal" relations, so that the old and the new could be related. By the time Guntrip and Winnicott were writing, the word "self" raised few eyebrows!)

Like Hartmann, Fairbairn rejects the id as a separate area of the mind from which the ego is developed. Instinctive activity is merely one mode in which the self-matrix can be activated, this self-matrix being a highly dynamic system concerned in its earliest stages with making relations with the mother. These interactions bring satisfaction of bodily needs and provide a creative impetus towards growth constituted by the various maturational developments.

The innumerable subordinate functions and specific behavioral systems all serve as they mature to root the matrix in relationships in an extremely complex way. To simplify considerations, we can restrict ourselves to what Fairbairn conceived as the central self. We can ignore at this state the inevitable splitting in the self-system which arises from incompatible qualities and goals within the mother–child relationships. Within the system, the self pole differentiates from the object and, with ordinary good mothering as the necessary setting, the external world is mapped and created in the first instance internally. In this process, all the "ego-autonomous" functions play their part along with fantasy and the more specific behaviors. Winnicott (1971) stresses the appropriately responsive role of the mother in allowing the experience of the self as creating its objects, an experience which appears to be his way of describing the establishment of basic trust (Erikson 1950). He gives particularly sensitive accounts of the kind of relationship experience that permits the growth of a secure and *creative* self. For him the role of play is of the greatest importance in this development, and the capacity to play freely has to be founded on a quality of interaction with the mother that generates the enjoyment of play.

The formation of this mother imago is stressed by Sullivan (1953). For Klein (1935), working through the depressive position represents achieving an imago of the mother as a whole person who is reliably supportive. Within the ego-psychology tradition, Spitz (1945), Mahler (Mahler *et al.* 1975), Anna Freud (1946), and many others have confirmed this process of successful individuation resting on the good mother–child relationship, while the invaluably comprehensive studies by Bowlby (1969, 1973) have underpinned the relationship requirements definitively. Lichtenstein (1965) has commented on Erikson's concept of epigenetic phases as implying the continuity of a central developmental principle such as identity.

There is wide agreement that future development into adaptive and creative adulthood is governed by what happens in the interactive experiences of these earliest phases. The quality of the personal relationships at all subsequent stages through adolescence affects the form of the adult personality, yet deprivation of certain kinds and degrees at the first formative phase can be only partially compensated with later good experience. To put it in diagrammatic form, the first phase of interaction normally creates a self pole with a good mother imago which gives to the self-matrix a capacity to interact joyously with the world. The role of affect in such a relationship-seeking matrix is to monitor and reinforce the selection and organization of the activities that preserve good relationships.

When the good mother–child relationship is followed by experience with other family relationships of similar quality in which the child experiences mutual trust and a reliable and consistent concern for development of his independent creativity, the child passes through the phases that Erikson describes, and emerges as a young adult with an established identity. Identity is thus the pattern of relationships the self is able to make with others along with the patterns of creative activity in work and play. From an original interaction matrix structured when the self separates from the imago of the good mother, the course of development adds the content of the relationships with the father and other significant figures in fostering self-reliance.

Experience is expanded and new understandings and skills are acquired to give a range of competences. Adulthood merges what were originally the personalized imagos into the ideals and values that direct spontaneous creativity and sustained commitment to giving something back to life. For many, the life space in which their maturity is expressed may be a restricted one compared with that which richer talents and opportunities have given to others, yet the essential psychological processes are the same.

Living is about making relationships – loving, and contributing to the environment by working, as Freud said (1930, p. 80 fn.). The growth of the self towards achieving the capacity for love and work has been tracked in long-term studies of development. Bowlby (1969, 1973) summarizes a sample of these researches, which show the positive correlation between the future effectiveness of the personality and the quality of care within the family from the earliest phase through adolescence. Although Bowlby favors a theoretical position which builds the integration of the personality from separate behavioral systems – and he takes great pains to get the language for his approach – nevertheless the terms he uses in his discussion of the happy outcome to the child's development are interestingly "secure attachment" and "the growth of *self*-reliance"!

Clinical examples: sources of difficulty in love and work

The effects of early failures can be illustrated from some of the statements made by two analysands in the course of their analyses which had been sought following a feeling of virtual breakdown. The first had had a mother whose attitude, since ever she could remember, was a rejecting one. She never felt she could do anything right. Throughout her later years at home her emergence into womanhood was perpetually denigrated. Any attempt to show affection was regarded by her mother with a suspicious "what-are-you-up-to" attitude and any need to get it was repulsed with a "don't-be-silly" comment and emotional withdrawal. It took years of analytic work before affection towards me could be admitted. After one such admission following a period of anger and despair with me, she experienced a sense of relaxation in marked contrast to a state of anxious tension that had lasted for months. Accompanying this relaxation, there was also a change in attitude to work. Her work, which had been greatly blocked during this period of tension – her working capacity had always been unreliable – began to flourish, and she brought to it a new feeling of confidence and commitment. Because of her high abilities she had been able to achieve considerable success, though always there was a sense of never fulfilling her potential. She now had a feeling of greater freedom to work as well as to love – a markedly different feeling within herself.

The second, a man, had had consistent reliable mothering but from a mother who was a rather controlling, inhibited, religious person. He too had considerable difficulty in making close relations and his output of work varied. He felt that his mother had never accepted his spontaneous liveliness, and this aura of mistrust of vitality still enveloped him. Well on towards middle-age, he had a vivid sense that this feeling had been present at his core throughout his life. As with the woman patient, his high abilities had carried him along but the despair about his relationships and an increasingly variable work performance brought him to the point of suicide.

With both patients, it required a few years of treatment for trust in their analysts to grow to the point where they could feel less defended against making the close relationships they wished to achieve. What was striking was the general increase in freedom to work, to play, and to have enjoyable relationships with others, as they relieved some of the feelings belonging to the earliest relationship. Equally striking was the language they used to describe the improvement: "I feel better in myself."

These examples are, of course, commonplace. I quote them to emphasize the dominant theme amidst a variety of more specific complaints, a recurrent motif of the constriction of *the self as an overall system managing their lives*. And, as mentioned earlier, breakdown in the self-system as an overall manager is particularly striking in patients who have had lengthy analysis previously.

The sense of self

I have proceeded so far on a hypothetical "central," or even "unitary," self to simplify the discussion. What we have arrived at is the usefulness of postulating an overall integrative system that exists from the start to mediate the interaction of the person as a whole with his environment. Initially, its structuring is minimal in keeping with the prototaxic experience of the earliest phase, to use Sullivan's (1953) term. The main, the first, and the most critical development is the patterning of the system in terms of a self pole at one end of the dynamic relation-seeking system with an image of a mother at the other end. With optimal developmental conditions, this imago (later the ego-ideal) maintains in the system a positively toned affect and general attitude to the world that allows optimal maturational progress of innumerable behavioral systems. There seems to be no good reason for preferring the impersonal term ego to self for this system for which "self-feeling" or "self-esteem" are the terms that best describe its tone. What began presumably with the minimally structured feeling of being pleasurably or painfully real – and this quality of experience is obviously a product of processes in the nervous system – becomes differentially structured on the basis of these affective qualities. Affects would thus seem to be the "magnetic" force that coheres experience into patterns.

The sense of self stems from the whole matrix, and so it encompasses everything that goes on in it – from all the bodily sensations to the developing perceptual world, from outside the self to inner fantasy. Self-presentation and self-concepts become enriched rapidly, and, as has been stressed, are basically structured by the input from the early relations. This latter process has been described by various writers as the mirroring effect within the self of the image that the mother has of her child. The mother imparts through her responses, and especially through behavior affected by her unconscious attitudes, a pattern of how she wants the child to be and to respond to her. It is to this primary patterning of the person-relating self that Lichtenstein (1977) gives the term "identity theme." Lichtenstein rejects the term "self" because of its confusing links with "sense of self" and other dynamic connotations. He responded to pressure to avoid this vague term, which Hartmann had declared unsatisfactory since in the current state of knowledge it was not easy to distinguish it from the much more "scientific" ego. The identity theme (or self-system as I would call it), patterned by the way in which mother and child relate, is an essential achievement if the person is to function at all.

Lichtenstein (1965, 1977) regards the identity theme as virtually unchangeable, rather in the manner of the first structuring of response systems that the ethologists have called imprinting. He sees this theme in the development of the person as a motif in music, which is carried on in a series of variations. Identity is accordingly the social objectivation achieved through subsequent experience. This is virtually the same as the basic patterning of the self-matrix in a relations-making system. What was the relatively unstructured matrix thus becomes the structured system that governs the mode and mood of all subsequent relationships. It is the governing center required by any complex hierarchically ordered system. This does not imply a harmoniously effective control but it does mean that without an integrative supraordinate system the whole cannot survive. Subsystems can have ranges of autonomy in their functioning and can get out of balance to a disruptive extent. That kind of imbalance is a familiar occurrence at some time or other in all complex systems such as large businesses and organizations as well as in the individual. It merely emphasizes the point that the person needs a governing system, a system whose task is to plan, to make decisions, and to act for the whole. Consciousness and affect determine meanings and commitment, which are the essence of a self-system that is the actor.

The functions of the ego include the mapping of the environment socially and physically and the organizing of all the implications of action in response. The maintenance of the underlying commitment to action, however, seems to fall outwith what we usually refer to as the ego, even though the latter plays a major role in the later development of long-term goals. It is in this way that there is an advantage in referring the final determination of action to the self. It is difficult to see how a group of functions could acquire the directedness of a self-system. The ego is the organization of the transactions with the environment under the "direction" of the self-matrix. The ego, as Chein says, needs a self.

Splitting and the structure of the self

To revert now to the more ordinary circumstances in development, we have to look at the phenomena of splitting. Painful experience with the mother, when persistent enough, builds up a bad imago related to a self that also feels bad. Many different outcomes arise in the structuring of the self according to the degree and the quality of the frustration or mismatch between the needs of the infant and the input from the mother. The infant is so made that attachment to a mother is a necessity for survival, and since separation is the source of great anxiety – the view taken by the object-relations analysts – the need to attach is intensified, as Bowlby's evidence confirms. The imago of mother is thus installed even more dominantly when she provides less security. The child simply has to evolve ways of coming to terms with the particular patterns of the mother. Two main effects are encountered in clinical work. The child withdraws internally to lock up part of its response potential and so relates with an attenuated part of its resources. The metaphor of the self being locked behind fortress-like doors is a typical descriptor for the resulting schizoid personality. What then appears is a conforming or "false" self and a denuded, hidden personality.

A confusion from Fairbairn's terminology may arise here. What he describes as the central self normally forms in relation to a central core of the good mother which is normally more potent than other aspects. But this is not always the case. The mother may be experienced as over-exciting or rejecting of the child's needs for relationship, and the child is then deprived of the opportunity to take in a good mother experience at the core of the self. What the deprived child evolves is a self-system by which life under these circumstances is made possible. The child develops an *adapted* self, adapted to the mother's excessive influence whether this be from intensive over-control, or neglect, or unreliable, inconsistent responsiveness, rather than an *adaptive* self which good mothering fosters. (In passing we may ponder on whether the voices of criticism of psychotherapy as producing adaptedness rather than greater personal freedom may be loudest in those whose experience was largely one of an enforced adapted development.) When the patterning of early deprived relationships is reinforced in later years, especially during adolescence, then there is a high likelihood of failure to reach a viable living capacity.

The persistence of "life" in the withdrawn part of the self gives to the person the fantasy of what might have been; and experience outside the family helps to keep alive the hope for something better in his or her relationships. Even when the dominance of the "bad" mother is excessive, when hope is in danger of a complete replacement by despair, it is remarkable how such people retain sufficient hope to seek psychotherapeutic help, though the therapeutic task is then formidable. At the self pole there may be despair and hate of near overwhelming intensity. Then there is increasing danger of a move to identification with the hated mother to preserve the status quo lest a freer self lead to the terror of fresh abandonment or to unbearable humiliation and vulnerability if the withdrawn good self be rejected again.

It is not my purpose, however, to go into all the common patterns arising from splitting within the self. That could only be covered by a volume on psychopathology. My aim has been the limited one of advocating the replacement of the impersonal terms we have adopted and, in particular, to suggest that the self is a more useful concept than the ego as the actor and hence is the location of choice in regard to strategic decisions. Whatever the pattern of subsystems within the self, it is more appropriate to keep these in mind as modes of action of the self-system even though restricted or distorted. Schafer's (1976) plea for a language that locates responsibility is certainly one to be supported.

The self-matrix and its subsystems

The concept of relationships with internal objects has evoked surprising difficulty in some theorists. Conscious relationships with fantasy objects, however, have long been recognized, for instance, in the imaginary companions of childhood. Unconscious relationships have long been accepted in regard to the superego. The concept of an overall proactive matrix can readily include the functioning of a range of inner relationships as ways of dealing with "unsatisfactory" aspects of significant figures.

By placing subsystems within the self-matrix when they are in action, all subsystem action then involves the self as actor. And when we think of all subself relationships within the overall system we can readily understand repression arising from the pressure of a dominant relationship to keep an incompatible one out of action. Instinctive activity operates within the self-matrix even though it may be pressed largely into one subsystem, for instance, in repressed sexual fantasies.

It requires no great upheaval to adopt the notion of a supraordinate self-system within which the phenomena associated with what we have termed the ego, superego, and id can operate. It does offer the great advantage of bringing theory close to practice, and it may well help with our clinical understanding. Analysis has been very much under scrutiny in regard to its therapeutic results. As a treatment for conflict of certain depth, mainly involving the Oedipal conflicts, it brought great rewards. The status of the Oedipus complex, however, may well be a derivative of earlier splitting and structuring, as Fairbairn suggested, rather than a fundamental etiological situation. Most important, our whole conception of what is involved in diagnosis and treatment could be influenced by a better grasp of the part that deprivation plays in the earliest structuring of the self.

Analytical psychotherapy has appealed to many analysts who prefer a freer, more personalized setting. There is a tendency to regard this as a somewhat inferior procedure, despite the fact that, as the Blancks (1974) state, structural change can be greater in psychotherapy than in psychoanalysis because structure building is the very purpose of treatment when borderline and psychotic structures are the focus. The difficulty we so often encounter occurs when psychotic structures emerge from underneath the neurotic pictures that present initially.

Technical problems in the development of analytical psychotherapeutic practice are bound to occur if deprivation syndromes are to be met with a more personalized approach. The British object-relations analysts adopted a warmer, more spontaneous attitude in their treatment of severely schizoid patients than that of orthodox psychoanalysis. Schafer criticizes Guntrip for apparently advocating "kindly" theory as better than the orthodox concepts. These British analysts do not, however, revise theory or practice for *kindly* reasons. They are advocating a different view for *scientific* reasons, namely that the self system in these severely disturbed patients was crippled from the start because there had been a grossly inadequate experience of being loved for themselves. At this level of disorder, if an experience of personalized concern is needed, before progress can be made, then theory has to account for this; and, as I have mentioned already, many of the patients with whom they worked had already had long spells of analysis.

These problems can only be settled with more research. A difficulty in the evolution of psychotherapeutic theory and practice has always been the problem of appraising the state of a personality at one point in time in such a way that changes can be assessed. The more our theory fits practice, by using variables that can be related to practice, the better our chances of achieving more sensitive diagnostic instruments. By using a theory explicitly linked with the self and its subsystems it seemed to Gill and myself some years ago that language might be used to make such an instrument (Sutherland and Gill 1970). Our own efforts in this direction were little more than a first tentative attempt but, even so, they showed possibilities.

One possible implication for clinical work focusing on the self is a greater impact on the analyst. The existentialists stress the importance of the "encounter" for personal relations and development. Weisman (1965) emphasizes that analysis and analytical psychotherapy are essentially the study of encounters. As he puts it: "Being in analysis is the analysis of Being." Countertransference is an inevitable complication. Levin (1969) suggests that analysis of the self all the time may be too painful a task for the individual analyst and that groups of analysts might work together on problems of self–object differentiation. Publication of findings under the authorship of the psychoanalytic society to which the group belonged would protect the individual analyst from the consequences of revelations about his or her own self. We all have difficult cases, and we do not work together enough on those problem situations in which we have reached a block or a failure. If we could do so, we could capitalize on the opportunity to advance our understanding of the nature of the self and the problems in its functioning brought to our attention so vividly at the center of an analysis.

Conclusion

There is a growing body of opinion that the tripartite structural theory, id, ego, and superego, is not adequate as a theoretical framework for clinical work. Many theoreticians and most clinicians use the term "self" freely. Clinicians tend to use it as synonymous with the ego and, although theorists explicitly state that the self is a separate "concern," there is disagreement as to whether to refer to it as a structure. There is considerable reluctance to conceptualize it metapsychologically.

Existential considerations (as Weisman remarks, all analysts have an existential attitude though they may in no way share the views of existential philosophers) would certainly point to a foundation structure in the personality that establishes a pattern of relationships that mediates a commitment, or lack of commitment, to the social and physical environments. Thus Primary Anxiety would seem to be a prototype in itself for whatever causes the experience of self to become meaningless existence; it cannot be restricted to the image of a hungry or a frightened infant. Its antithesis is unconditional love or *agape*, and a similar antithesis is seen between hope and despair. Despair can put almost any or every psychic process and drive out of action, whether we prefer to think of these as located in the id, ego, or superego, and it is one of the most difficult problems to treat. This indicates that it has a specifically central origin and a pervasive role in the structuring of the despairing person.

I believe the notion of a dynamic matrix in which affect is located from the start of psychic life and which then embodies a dominant pattern of relationships to others is one well worthy of further study. It would seem that it is to the properties of this basic pattern that we refer when we try to appraise our therapeutic task. Thus an established pattern of self in relation to an imago of a good-enough mother as a differentiated object may be what makes psychoanalysis in the classical sense possible, for it is in this situation that the person has a stable enough core with sufficient autonomy and responsibility for his or her behavior. Kohut's (1971) work has brought out some of the complex ways in which the self-system can be stable and effective when the internal object within the self-system is not differentiated from the self pole, though with this narcissistic structure analysts have to be ready to modify their approach.

In view of these lines of thought, it would seem that all the differentiated conflicts of specific phases, especially Oedipal conflicts, may be the focus of much effective analytic work yet they may be only the prelude to more fundamental problems.

It will be readily seen that around this whole subject a number of viewpoints are converging. While Hartmann's autonomous functions of the ego introduced new factors to give a necessary independent complement to the role of the instincts from the beginning of psychic life, his theoretical views, as Schafer demonstrates so convincingly, got virtually aborted by his adherence to energy concepts. Melanie Klein (1935, 1946), as Guntrip (1969) has stressed so often, really introduced the notion of dynamic relationships within the psyche from the start, but she and her colleagues have not provided an adequate account of the "permanent" structuring of these relationships. Moreover, her view of development on the basis of part-objects is difficult to reconcile with Spitz's (1945) findings that adequate feeding in the absence of mothering is no guarantee of healthy development. What has been referred to as a self-system here, however, could be related to what happens when the "depressive position" is worked through.

Mahler's (Mahler *et al.* 1975) views on the emergence of the separate self in parallel with object constancy obviously overlaps, as do Erikson's (1950) phases of Basic Trust proceeding to Autonomy and Initiative. It is noteworthy, too, that Erikson later dropped the word "ego" from its early bracketing with "identity." Through the concept of epigenetic phases, identity implies a supraordinate core-system. These writers and many others appear to be moving in the same direction as the British object-relations theorists.

As Freud (1937) remarked in "Analysis Terminable and Interminable," the way through certain blocks to therapeutic success must rest on metapsychological speculation and theorizing. The clinical situations of therapeutic impasse, despair, and false-self functioning are now attracting considerable psychoanalytic attention. To meet these clinical challenges, our theories require substantial metapsychological revision. At the center of this task, is the study of the phenomena of "the self."

Chapter 8

The psychodynamic image of man

Editor's introduction

Sutherland defines psychodynamic as the descriptor of an approach to human conflict and motivation based in an understanding of unconscious processes in human behavior. He recognizes the importance of social factors and the need for social change, but he cautions that it is change at the individual level that enables social change to occur. The development of the individual is a value in Western society. Therefore, Sutherland focuses his remarks on professional care that fosters wholeness, personal autonomy, self realization, and well-being at the center of the self and which sees growth and development as a lifelong endeavor. He sees the self as a dynamic matrix in a state of constant relatedness. Society needs to provide caring services to individuals to maintain a healthy work-force and a good quality of life, to provide a matrix of caring in which the caring professions feel held, and to use feedback from the caring and educational professions to develop itself as an open, adaptable learning system capable of meeting the changing emotional needs of the people.

To be invited to give this first Malcolm Millar lecture is a great honor that I deeply appreciate. The psychodynamic approach of Malcolm Millar (Crombie-Ross Professor of Mental Health, University of Aberdeen, 1949–1976) inspired a practice and teaching that made a notable contribution to British psychiatry at a time when that approach was virtually denied scientific respectability. It is also a great personal pleasure as he and I shared a period of work together during the last war so that I got to know well his concern with providing care. It seemed appropriate, therefore, to choose a theme related to this concern.

A philosophy for the caring professions

"A Philosophy for the Caring Professions" is a large assignment so I shall select a few broad issues that I believe to be crucial for the future of our work. There is an infinite range of care-giving activities, most of which I shall take for granted. In the present context I want to focus on care devoted to the development and well-being of the person – to those factors that equip and maintain the individual in the business of living with a sense of wholeness and responsible autonomy; of feeling "somebody" and being "a somebody" to others; and of fulfillment in the use of his or her talents. I shall return to this question of what we mean by a person and also by caring at the personal level. At the risk of oversimplification, let me put it at this point that my interest is care related to what goes on at the center of people, where they are or should be as responsible free agents, rather than with what they might present at their individual boundaries.

A few remarks are also necessary on my use of the word *psychodynamic*. Most of the insights about the person that have proved useful to the caring professions have come from the psychoanalysts. This knowledge, however, has been expanded by many groups outwith the formal psychoanalytic organizations, so I have adopted the more general term to cover the broad approach based on an understanding of the person in psychological terms and which emphasizes the role of unconscious motives. Psychodynamic views have been widely disseminated and indeed are now part of our culture. In this process they inevitably get attenuated and distorted so that their full significance, and the way in which they are being developed, tends to get ignored. I shall thus try to emphasize what I see as important current trends.

Providing help for personal problems are several professions along with a great variety of counseling services. There are doctors and nurses, social workers, the clergy, and in recent years an increasing number of psychologists. To complicate matters, there is also a range of *therapists* practicing one or other of the many methods evolved to help with personal problems, that is, Gestalt therapy, transactional analysis, encounter groups. True, these methods are mostly used by the professions, but there has been a trend for people both within and outside the professions to take a "training" in the method and then to set up as practitioners without an adequate experience in dealing with psychological conflicts. I shall confine myself to the professions because I believe that they must constitute the vital core of our overall endeavor to provide articulated knowledge and responsible practice.

Professions imply a corpus of knowledge and skills shared by their members. When duly recognized, they give to society an assurance of competence and its responsible use; and they maintain a steady research and development endeavor to keep enlarging their competence. In providing help for personal stresses there are good reasons why professional resources should be supplemented by agencies in which the expertise is not as specialized. We could not possibly cope with the demands without them; and in respect of the quality of their work, the best of our voluntary services maintain close collaboration with relevant professional groups so that the interests of all parties are protected. There is also another reason why a large voluntary movement is desirable, namely, that society is thereby confronted with the scale of stress and so can initiate steps towards its alleviation. It is the professions, however, who have to take a lead in helping all the allied services to keep adding to their expertise.

When we survey all these activities, we cannot but be struck by their diversity in theory and practice. A rough continuum can be based on the degree to which the approach is manifestly personal in depth. At one end we can place the intensive analytical psychotherapies, the distinguishing feature of which is coping with unconscious motives. There would then be a range of methods involving personal interaction at a conscious level. The groups operating in this way are by far the largest as they include voluntary counseling services as well as the professions. Next might come the relatively recent behavior therapies in which the focus is on overt behavior rather than on the inner world of the person. Lastly would be the "physical methods," which attempt to alter the mental state by changing the underlying physiology as, for instance, by drugs or other methods.

The increased facilities for personal help reflect the great rise in demands for it. The origins of this situation are complex. Many believe that changes in society are precipitating the demands. On the other hand, the nature of psychological stress is more widely known. It is, therefore, difficult to ascertain whether there is a real increase in the incidence of stress or whether requests for help are more readily made. One thing certain is that the presenting complaints have changed towards a great rise in feelings of general personal malaise, for example, feelings of "depression" or futility, of loss of purpose, of not feeling sure of who or what one really is.

These features emphasize the point that we cannot consider the person apart from the society in which he or she has grown and is now functioning. There is no doubt at all that within the last few decades there have been very great changes in our social patterns and values with the result that appraisal of personal stress has become more complex. The assumed primacy of social factors led many young social workers some years ago to express vociferously the view that provisions for personal problems were useless – if not a bourgeois attempt to keep people adapted to society. What was needed was social change. There is no question that sections of the social environment can be unduly stressful and therefore every effort should be made to improve these. Nevertheless, there is no society in which individuals do not have problems of a primary personal nature. Personal conflicts are a product of the interaction of the social and the personal and we have to separate as best we can the contributions of each for remedial action. Also, we all have to keep in mind that society is not an entity as an agent of action. Changes in it come from individuals and our efforts must be to foster the kind of growth that increases their creativity.

The social and the personal

This theme of the social and the personal is so crucial that I want to enlarge on it to get a proper appreciation of the role of the caring professions. I believe important changes are occurring in this role in parallel with what is happening in society. For this purpose I shall draw upon the writings of two of my former colleagues, the social scientists Emery and Trist (1973). They describe the extraordinary technological advances of recent decades as having produced a profound change in the fabric of the social environment, especially in the modern Western nations. From a loosely knit laissez faire regulation of local and relatively autonomous social service and production units, our postindustrial society has changed this pattern to one of a tightly interwoven texture. This new interrelatedness gives a highly turbulent or unpredictable quality, because technological change can produce extremely rapid and extensive effects in large sections of our production system. Larger groupings result both in these systems and in the social services to create the necessary resources. The environment thus becomes more and more man-made with major problems not involving man versus nature so much as man versus man.

The survival of any society can rest on the maintenance of a steady state through established institutions and customs. Modern societies, because of external impingements and internal forces, are such that, unless they become adaptive learning systems, they perish. They must constantly develop, that is, meet challenge with creative changes in their internal structures. Such changes, on account of the high degree of interdependence amongst the component systems, have to be made increasingly by centralized planning for the society as a whole – and here we come to the greatly divergent philosophies of the modern world. Two options are available. One is the engineered society, modeled on the physical sciences, in which planning is done by a special section or elite group. This is the choice of the totalitarian countries. The other, the apparent choice of the Western democracies, rests more on the life sciences. It seeks to develop all members of society by a higher quality in all the primary social units, that is, the individual, the family, the work-place, schools, the community and the services and amenities it provides. Securing the highest quality of life has now become the overriding question as we move towards postindustrialism.

The trends in these directions are manifest in the changing concepts of welfare. In the industrial era the state had to take an increasing part in providing welfare services for the sick and in providing measures against disease in order to maintain the work-force. Gradually a new concept of welfare can be identified, namely, that the best welfare is secured by personal development, for example, by improvement in the physical environment and in personal resources through education, better conditions of work, and so forth. Today in the more affluent countries, emphasis is no longer on minimum standards for health and growth but on the realization of potential, both for the individual and society.

These concepts of welfare and development do not, of course, belong to the world of science. They are values or choices by which we shape our aspirations and goals, our social perceptions and practices. Our adaptive strategy is now increasingly towards the adoption of values that promote the optimal realization of individual potential. What is happening is far from a homogenous change since many of our old values persist even though detrimental to the newer ones. How then do we identify the adaptive values? This can be done by appraising the spontaneously emerging responses to what is sensed as inimical to development. Within organizations we have noted more collaborative groupings – changes from separate objectives to linked ones. In personal values, there is a very mixed array. Thus, as a reaction against the dehumanizing effects of common situations at work, there have been movements against some of the hallowed values of the Protestant ethic, for example, from achievement to self-actualization; from undue independence to interdependence; and from "grin and bear it" to a focus on joy. Contrasting with these ideas are changes that seem to have been initiated by the insidiously dehumanizing influences of technology. Toffler (1970), for example, has vividly portrayed in his book *Future Shock* how our attitudes to the expendability of consumer goods have spread to human relationships, a change that does not appear to be adaptive for personal growth and development.

Older men with their family responsibilities have naturally not been leaders in finding more self-expression. The counterculture impetus has come from young people with the consequent disadvantages of their inexperience. To want to "do one's own thing instead of someone else's" is eminently understandable, but it can be a disruptive social philosophy, especially when human nature is viewed in an alarmingly superficial way. Envy, hate, and destructiveness were what the establishment had, or did to you. The beautiful people would achieve love. But with no realistic commitment of one person to another, love soon became essentially pleasure seeking. Gratification and kicks became the goals as this "new narcissism" flourished. Although the excesses within these movements have abated, we have been left with a residue of belittlement of the person in some of his aspects. Thus at times sex therapy seems to get more emphasis than the need to improve personal relations. It is little wonder that a counter-reformation has appeared in the form of attacks on this cult of self-worship in books such as *Psychology as Religion* (Vitz 1977).

A seriously disturbing aspect of these trends was the backing taken from the writings of some of our prominent intellectuals such as Sartre (1943), Marcuse (1955), and Norman Brown (1959). The philosophies propounded, especially by Marcuse and Brown, were based on what they claimed, not without some justification, to be the essence of Freud's image of man, that is, the fundamental role of pleasure seeking from the satisfaction of the sexual instincts.

The role of care in the open society

Assuming that the development of each individual is our accepted social philosophy, the role of the caring services must then be directed to this end. At first sight this may not seem much of a change, but I believe it is. The traditional position of the carers has been very much one of ameliorating the lot of those extruded from the system, either temporarily or permanently, by picking them up in a net of charitable and philanthropic agencies. Beyond attempts to alter grossly harmful features of the environment, their main function was to keep those needing care out of the way until, hopefully, some could be returned to useful roles. Deviant behavior too difficult to manage was treated with more active defenses, for example, it had to be isolated or literally walled off. Such policies helped to preserve the status quo of existing institutions and their values, but only for a time.

True, we have now advanced a long way from that situation in regard to state provisions. I do not think, however, we have sufficiently considered the changed role of the caring services.

An open social system whose primary task is to develop all its members has to adopt a quite opposite attitude to disorders or deviance. The existence of everyone in trouble, whether ill-health, psychological disorder, or in a maladaptive group such as the poor, or in crime, now raises the question, how has this happened? What is going wrong in the system? From being largely a charitable endeavor with little expertise and almost no learning function built into it, caring is now at the center of the social system. It becomes a servo-mechanism whose feedback is critical in evaluating how much people are not in a state of developmental well-being. A caring system becomes an essential component in all the main institutions of our living and so a built-in requirement in all social planning. The fundamental concern with development also means that we cannot separate education from the caring system in our overall considerations. In the United States, the administrative triad of Health, Education, and Welfare is a political recognition that development is the best form of welfare.

The need for a developmental view of the person

The next question that arises is: do we have a concept of development of the person that can help us to realize our general philosophy? Our aim is not tied to a utopia nor to any specific ideological program. It is the essence of open system development that its ongoing spontaneous creativity will make for unpredictability – both in the individual and in society. We can thus aim only at making the adaptive capacities of both as effective as possible so that action can be planned in the light of maximum knowledge of what is happening in all sections of society and in the environment. And when growth and development are paramount values the future is always in mind. Gaining relevant knowledge does not guarantee that we shall use it, yet at least it can guide those who wish to promote optimal planning.

For a congruent educational and caring endeavor there must be a shared view of the nature of man or woman as a constantly developing person. We must have a framework that relates what happens at each phase to the next, and for matching what happens in the different sectors of the life space of the person. We cannot expect to foster responsible adults, for instance, if we treat people as such in one sector and at the same time deny responsible participation in another.

I believe a useful image of human nature is now being formulated amongst analytical psychotherapists, and following Chein (1972), I have preferred the term *image* to the word *model* with its mechanistic connotations and because the term *image* resonates with the unique feature of persons, namely their creative imagination.

The spontaneous trends that were noted all highlighted the importance of self-feelings: self-actualization, self-esteem, self-expression. It is striking that contemporaneously the self is also appearing as a focus of study in several sections of our professions. What we most need is an adequate conceptualization of the self. We have several incompatible claims here, for example, the Christian, the Marxist, the Behaviorist, and the Psychodynamic, and clearly we must examine and appraise their implications.

The psychodynamic image of man

Taking the psychodynamic first, the image of man left by Freud was of a titanic struggle between the powerful instincts of life and death and the need to control them. Personal development was governed by the vicissitudes of the instinctual drives, especially the sexual instinct with its progression through the zonal stages (Freud 1905). The core developmental achievement was the surmounting of the oedipal complex – the child's conflicts from his sexual fantasies about his parents. The personality was structured in terms of the instincts or the id, the ego or the system adapted to reality, and the superego or internal image of primitive parental figures controlling the id (Freud 1923). The general theory of man was thus couched in such scientific abstractions as energies, mechanisms, and functions together with a quite different level of functioning, namely, an internalized version of a relationship with "parents." There has been in recent years a growing dissatisfaction with his formulation and there have appeared attempts to bring the person into focus, notably those of Erikson (1950, 1959) with his concepts of *self* and *identity*. The word *self* has become more frequent in the titles of books and articles in psychodynamic journals, and the views of a number of British analysts have become specifically concerned with this topic, for instance, Balint (1968), Winnicott (1971), Fairbairn (1954b), Guntrip (1969, 1978). What they established from their work with persons having serious difficulties in coping with life was that in the very early development of the infant a basic psychological structuring takes place that determines the whole of its future development. They postulate that there is a unitary system from birth that is the potential self and that this system is personified, so to speak, into an "I" by the experience of a good fit between the personal care and love of the mother and the infant's needs. Instinctual satisfaction of bodily needs reinforces the development of this self-system but it is not the essential factor, which is the experience of being loved for itself. The self then acquires a feeling of being integrated with the outer world in a way that promotes positive interaction with it – an attitude of "belief in" that gives zest to living and to the rapidly developing exploratory interactions of learning about the world. Development takes place by differentiation of subsystems or subselves within the original unitary matrix. Painful emotions are unavoidable even in the best mother–infant relationships, and "good" and "bad" – or pleasant and unpleasant – experiences cohere into the first divisions within the self, namely, a "good" mother/world system and another "bad" one. Further development follows a double path. The good self occupies a central position that enables it to be enriched by all the learning experiences within the powerful impetus towards independence. Simultaneously, frustrations lead to the creation of an inner world in which the self relates to a range of figures representing aspects of the frustrating situations. Thus, some have a frightening persecuting quality while others are excitingly gratifying. These inner relationships are imaginative creations that are actively expressed in play and fantasy in childhood. When the foundation self is established with security and confidence, the inner world is progressively modified towards the real external one in the ongoing interactions of the ordinary good family in which father and other members play a more and more prominent part. In the early phases, intense love and hate, and magical omnipotence, characterize the inner relationships in keeping with the dominance of the intensity of the child's feelings. Infantile sexuality is assimilated into the self-systems with the establishment of a sexual identity – one which is finally consolidated after adolescence.

When relationships with parents continue to be unsatisfactory, then these relationships acquire distorted or compliant patterns – as if the manifest ones are maintained with an outer layer of the self while the inner relationships are intensified to provide satisfaction in fantasy, both loving and hating. And the most primitive violence belongs to this area of having to fight to maintain one's self in a state of adequate autonomy against what are felt to be the parents' destructive attitudes and lack of trust in the spontaneous expressions of the emergent self. The inner relations then operate in a maladaptive way by unconsciously dominating the relations with people in the outside world. The latter are responded to, not as they really are but as they are perceived through the patterns of the inner figures. Thus imagos of a frustrating "bad" mother that are too powerful may turn the later adult male away from women, or in marriage lead to his wife gradually being treated as this hated mother, so that she can do no right. Or his wife may find herself being progressively cast in the role of a mother who has to minister to the needs of a little boy. If father is built up internally as a persecutor we may later get the man who is afraid of all authority or who compulsively fights it. The permutations of these inner relationships are endless but it is their dominance over ordinary realistic relationships that gives rise to the infinite range of irrational attitudes and conflicts.

With normal good experience, the inner relationships are merged into patterns for relating to others as they really are, for enjoying the "otherness" of others. Such a person is not tortured with doubts about living but enjoys a spontaneous creativity in everyday activities. None of us are free from conflict arising from the inner cast of figures with whom we are identified but conflicts are ordinarily manageable. Normality means this capacity to give and take freely with others on a basis of realistic appraisals of oneself and others.

The self is thus seen as a dynamic matrix with a predominant central identity though liable in certain situations to change its center point to one or other of its inner figures – states we reflect in such simple remarks as "I was not myself then," "I was beside myself with rage," or "I was out of my mind." The self is established in relationships and preserves itself only by an ongoing *psychosocial metabolism*, so to speak, from constant relatedness. With growth, the relationship figures of early times become transmitted into wider and much less personalized goals so that we can describe or define a mature person, as Chein (1972) puts it, as, "one who has a commitment to a developing and continuing set of unending, interacting, interdependent and mutually modifying enterprises" (p. 289) – the latter, of course, referring to personal relationships as well as activities of other kinds. Cut off this relatedness and the whole person, mind and body, begins to fragment or deteriorate. Extreme manifestations of this state were made visible to us all in the tragic manifestations of the concentration camps and have now been studied more experimentally with periods of isolation and environmental deprivation. Less dramatic, but no less striking, is the fact that when people lose their main source of relatedness or significance, as with displaced people, or as happened in periods of chronic and despondent unemployment, the incidence of every kind of illness rises (Wolff 1960).

As the familiar words of Yeats put it:

> The falcon cannot hear the falconer:
> Things fall apart:
> The centre cannot hold:
> Mere anarchy is loosed upon the world.
>
> (W. B. Yeats, "The Second Coming", 1950)

The failure to establish a primary self-system of relatedness gives rise to the most serious consequences ranging from withdrawal from the external world to a great variety of tenuous adaptedness on the basis of a veneer of compliance. People who experience the reemergence of these earliest states feel as if "the power is switched off; nothing has any meaning"; a pervasive apathy supervenes, which removes even instinctual excitement. These states understandably pose the most serious therapeutic problems.

But while we encounter such states as a rule in people whose self-system has been severely crippled, we have to keep in mind that all the later structures of any self that mediate a satisfying and fruitful life can be overwhelmed if the social milieu does not support the maintenance of the vital core.

The psychodynamic image of the human being is thus one of the progressive organization of relatedness. The foundation layer of this system, the primal organizer that holds the developmental differentiation together, is established effectively only when the relatedness is one of love and care and, without a later input of that kind in mature patterns, it becomes difficult to maintain the system as a whole.

The psychodynamic image and care

In the light of this image of the person let me revert to the word *care*. *Care* is one of those primal words whose antithetical meanings aroused Freud's interest when he was struggling to understand the strange phenomena of dreams. It means both the burden that weighs on people and also relieving the person of this load. It also signifies the relationship that fosters growth and development. The caring relationship has thus a pattern of reparenting, which allows new growth. This suggestion as the prototype of care commonly arouses negative attitudes on the grounds that it implies infantilizing people, making them dependent. Further thought, however, shows this to be a quite unfounded view since the aim of good parenting is the very opposite, that is, to secure independence. What the caring professions have to appraise is whether or not their actions are appropriate to a philosophy that does justice to the human being's full nature as a person. If such an approach is shared, then they are, whatever their particular activity, part of a coherent endeavor. It is also one that can provide vital data on what society might be doing that is inimical to optimal development.

In being part of such an overall endeavor the carers also deal in substantial measure with what gives them care in coping with distress. The word *support* is frequently used in this connection yet we do not get its essence spelled out. To my mind what supports the carer is not encouragement in the conventional sense. Instead it is to be part of a learning system greater than himself. Anxiety from puzzlement, and often a degree of feeling overwhelmed by human problems, are best alleviated when we understand what is going on here, as elsewhere; "there is nothing so practical as a good theory," as Kurt Lewin remarked (personal communication, see also Lewin 1940). The opportunity to learn from discussion with others who take learning seriously is itself an experience of caring and being cared for – as in all good education.

The psychodynamic image of man thus puts care for the person as essential for growth and maintaining well-being. We are not dealing with a sentimental value. Care is a necessity in our philosophy and a necessity established on scientific evidence.

Some current images in relation to our philosophy

Our image may be only a sketch map at present but I believe it is even now good enough to keep us away from directions which can, at best, take us into a no-man's-land but which may lead us into areas in which man cannot survive as the free creative agent we value. Let me take a brief look at the different approaches to personal problems – an array that bewilders the outsider.

In practice, the various approaches seldom draw on a single philosophy. This makes difficult the task of disentangling what assumptions are being made, yet I think we can see the important issues clearly enough. With the great middle range of the rough continuum I suggested, that is, those therapies that use personal interaction in an empirical way and largely avoid deeper motivation, we have no great problem. They all have their contributions. Their serious drawback is that, without a conceptual framework about the full nature of the person, they can become "techniques" applied at times by professionals and others with little knowledge of what they are dealing with. They thus do relatively little or nothing to advance our basic knowledge, and the failure is reflected in the common fate of "techniques," that is, they gradually disappear because they are boring to both therapist and client.

At the other end of my continuum I placed the physical methods. Here again there is no question about these being useful when used with adequate discrimination. Although few would now advocate a position held by some extremists in the past, one still meets the assumption that these methods, by altering an abnormal functioning of the brain, are "scientific" in contrast with approaches that assume that what goes on in the mind is the important question in the vast majority of psychological disorders. It is from this view, whether held openly or covertly, that the recurrent fantasies arise of the drug that will really do the trick – the wonder breakthrough.

We are here involved in a basic issue about what is scientific knowledge in this whole field of phenomena at the personal level. The danger of this kind of belief is that instead of understanding and development, we can readily produce a massive societal addition certainly comparable with all the dangers of alcohol. The Office of Health Economics (1972) published a short report on *Medicine and Society* produced by a team of social scientists. Having shown the staggering rise during the previous decade of the use of drugs for psychological symptoms, they noted that much medical care was now concerned with symptoms that appeared to be of social or psychological origin. In many cases there was no scientific evidence that the prognosis could be improved. Devoting increasing economic resources to the application of medical technology in such cases could actually diminish rather than improve well-being. They concluded that it was not yet possible to define specifically the role of the health services in handling these new (social and psychological) problems.

I must emphasize that I do not put the sole responsibility for this situation on to doctors. Large sections of the community expect a magical solution for their problems and if not given one would merely move to the doctor who would prescribe, or worse perhaps, resort to available drugs such as alcohol. There is clearly a collusion going on which can only be altered by massive educational programs. Medical technology is no solution to the need for a personal growth-promoting care. Caring is far too deeply ingrained a human trait for us to believe that carers holding such beliefs do not care. It seems to be more a situation of people, possibly under the great pressure of too many demands, getting caught up in an unwitting drift towards substituting technology for care. Such trends must be watched.

This question of what is scientific knowledge in this whole field of behavior at the personal level is raised sharply by the behavior therapists. It is their contention that the analytical psychotherapeutic approach, as well as being ineffective, is also unscientific because in practice it is so subjective as to be incapable of offering testable hypotheses. Instead of starting from the exploration of all that might underlie a behavioral symptom such as a phobia, behaviorists focus on the external manifestations which they then try to modify by specifically designed procedures based on theories of behavior patterns as learned. There is thus a theoretical underpinning for what is attempted.

Again there is no question that useful changes in overt behavior can be achieved and, indeed, more effectively at times than with other methods. Experience has led many behavior therapists to become very interested in the characteristics of the personal relationship that develops between the client and therapist and so some of the initial simplistic notions are being modified. The issue is not so much the changes that can occur, for there are few approaches that do not produce some change, as what the implications of the underlying philosophy are for the individual and society. Many critics have dealt with the behaviorist standpoint and suffice it for me to refer to Barrett (1979), one of America's most distinguished philosophers. He has recently responded to its major implication, namely, that we can develop through such an approach a technology of behavior, as Skinner (1954) has described it, with which we can shape the future of man. The important belief here is that human beings would be much better developed, not through our ideal of the free and self-governing personality – for Skinner, that is a pernicious belief that has blocked progress – but through a really scientific program for their advancement. Such a program would, of course, be designed by the few who "know" what is best for the rest of us. Barrett remarked that when dictatorship acquires this kind of science then the revolution according to Marx had become the society according to Pavlov.

The pluralism in approaches thus reflects not so much a situation of stimulating differences within a healthy enterprise as one with serious and potentially dangerous contradictions. If the caring and educational endeavors are to take their proper place in a society whose primary value is the development of its people as creative responsible individuals, then we must resist philosophies founded on scientific reductionism, that is, on the belief that the complex processes at a higher level of the personal organization can be explained by the properties of lower order activity, that the whole does not have properties that cannot be accounted for with knowledge of the parts. Such beliefs lead us towards an image of man as a machine or a puppet programmed and controlled by an elite group or constantly searching for the magical drug that will remove human conflict.

The basic question we have to pose is how do we conceive of the person at the personal level. The Cartesian legacy, which separated the mental from the physical, still persists with extraordinary tenacity. The conceptualization of the person, or the self, is now thought by several philosophers to be their major task. If we regard the inner world as not belonging to the real world, that is, the world we can study objectively, then we inevitably adopt a reductionist position. We believe the real processes governing our lives even at the personal level to be those that are reducible to neurochemical processes, or as some concession to the reality of emergent phenomena to processes at the level of stimulus–response organization. The self or the person does not then require to be taken seriously, that is, as mediating emergent phenomena inexplicable by lower levels of organization.

In facing reductionist beliefs we must ask ourselves, "Is anything more real for us than our self as a free agent?" Nevertheless it is extraordinary how this reality of the self is ignored or denied. I have to emphasize here that I am not asserting the correctness of any particular psychodynamic theories. It is the legitimacy and the necessity of its approach that have to be accepted. Guntrip (1978) has argued this whole issue with great clarity. He points out that even if we accept Popper's (1935) criterion of falsifiability as a requirement for scientific theories, Popper's belief that because psychoanalytic theories are not falsifiable, they cannot be scientific is simply not true. Freud discarded his theories at various times when the evidence no longer supported them and this process has gone on constantly. What has to be appreciated is that the falsifying data in regard to a psychodynamic theory may take several decades to accumulate.

Research into the realities of the self cannot be studied by the experimental method. Bronowski (1965) recognized these realities but concluded they could only be studied in literature. Such study, however, is not a firsthand one of the psychic self at work, the phenomenal reality on the top of the hierarchy of existence! The self can be studied directly in action only within a therapeutic relationship. This most fundamental knowledge for man is thus the unique privilege of the caring professions. To quote Weisman (1965), another analyst,

> Psychoanalysis is not a delusion, practiced by the fanatical and perpetrated upon the gullible; nor is it a mere recital of psychodynamic litanies. Its basic fact is the *encounter*, which . . . is an effort to meet the patient as a unique being, with respect to himself, his world, and other people. . . . *The encounter is the fact of being in analysis for the purpose of the analysis of being.*
>
> (p. 105)

Therapeutic relationships are not scientific procedures, whether in general medicine or in psychotherapy. The scientific component resides in the kind of knowledge we use. We have to formulate our understanding of what happens in these encounters in the best way we can to do justice to the phenomena and to be open to constant checking against fresh findings.

As with the drift in medicine from care to technology, there can be a drift into reductionist standpoints without a full recognition of what is taking place amongst those helping with personal problems. Professions such as social workers and the clergy are much less prone to reductionism because they cannot use the "scientific" methods associated with it. They can, however, as can psychotherapists, become dominated by "techniques" and so lose the openness that should constantly develop practice and theory.

It is in our academic centers for psychiatry and psychology that there is the greatest need to have these issues examined because they are the prestige influences for our whole caring endeavor. Although most centers would deny an overall reductionist position, certain trends are ominous enough to warrant scrutiny. Thus, most students attending psychology courses in our universities are greatly disappointed by failure of these courses to give a framework for understanding the individual or the family at a personal level. And we have only to survey the research output of psychiatrists and psychologists to see that an incredibly small proportion of their effort goes to a study of the dynamic processes underlying human relationships – those processes that constitute the essence of the therapeutic encounter. It seems to matter little how much the data studied are "trivialized" so long as the methods of using them, usually statistical, are of the requisite sophistication. By "trivialization" I mean either the isolation of limited, or almost subpersonal, sections of behavior or else the choice of what one might term the superficial indices of the underlying dynamics. What can one really do in a therapeutic situation with measures of a hypothetical entity such as "aggression," or "masculinity–femininity," or a list of the roles family members commonly take in the "good" family? Is there not a concealed assumption that we have got "scientific" "data" or "facts" that we can "administer" to our clients or patients like a medical treatment, which should then lead them to alter their behavior?

The reductionism here is compounded by the transfer of the traditional medical model of doing something to the patient whereas with personal conflicts we can only provide a relationship that lets the individual recognize his or her own nature. When we deal with subsystems of the organism that can be isolated and defined, we naturally have much more control; and this model has given us marvelous therapeutic resources for many conditions. With problems at the personal level this cannot be done. To revert to our caring prototype, it is noteworthy that we do not hear much of techniques of parenting. When we do, it is usually from those whose experience of "parental technique" has created their situation as patients. What they almost invariably describe is the lack of being treated as a person. The pressure to do this so-called scientific research is arguably one of the greatest drawbacks at present to the development of the therapeutic understanding and skills that are so much needed. The commonly expressed claims in academic centers that we have got to be scientific are seldom accompanied by an appropriate consideration of the meaning of this word – and why the assumptions made in using it are either not exposed or are denied.

There is also the fact that therapy as a goal is not a part of science. It is an act of human concern. Its effectiveness, however, rests on the adequacy of our validated knowledge.

The practice of analytic psychotherapy, with the time it takes and the highly specialized training its adequate use requires, of course precludes it from being an available therapy. Its value is in the knowledge it gives, knowledge which is already being wisely used in a great range of more practicable ways. The concepts it has provided underlie much of such widely used approaches as group and family therapy, counseling, and the therapeutic community.

True, it may press people to face up to what are painful aspects of themselves, but it does so on the well-founded belief that when they do so they are thereby more mature and richer personalities. When used well, psychodynamic knowledge is assimilated into the personality of the carer who then *is* that knowledge in relationships: it is not a technique like a piece of gimmickry stuck on to the surface of the person.

In what I have said about the psychodynamic image, you may be thinking I have left out one of the great areas of experience, namely, religion. Obviously, I cannot embark on that theme here. Let me say, however, that Freud's views on religion as they were described over fifty years ago in "The Future of an Illusion" (1927) cannot be taken as representative of psychodynamic thought today. Freud at that time was greatly impressed by the role of infantile dependence in the creation of a God based on a needed father – a view reinforced by the images and metaphors of institutionalized religion. In recent years there has been much more detailed study of the development of the internal representation of God and the relationships, both mature and immature, with that inner figure.

As consciousness of our situation in the universe expands, modern people cannot readily accept the old modes of representation. Nevertheless, we retain our powerful need for non-visible but meaningful realities capable of containing our potential for imaginative expansion beyond the boundaries of the senses (Rizzuto 1979). In this sense, religion is no illusion. For many, the position of feeling the lack of appropriate expression fits with Einstein's view of himself as a deeply religious unbeliever (see Pruyser 1974). An adequate psychodynamic image can help to separate what are personal stresses that originate from conflicting processes of development from those that may arise in a mature self reflecting on our relationship with something beyond what science can deal with. That there is a need to get these personal stresses distinguished from religious questions is seen, I believe, in the confusion several young clergymen experience over whether they should become social workers rather than stay in the ministry.

The psychodynamic image is thus not an antireligious image of man, though it may support a search for expressions that are congruent with the rest of our consciousness in the modern world.

To summarize what I have said:

1. Our current social philosophy is that the best hope for humankind is to foster the optimal development of the individual. To further that aim we must have society functioning as an open adaptive learning system.
2. Such a system has to monitor constantly what is happening in its various sections and this is the vital function of our caring and educational endeavors.
3. To fulfill that function there must be a shared philosophy on the nature of the person.
4. I have suggested that the psychodynamic image of the person in relation to society is the best guide we have at present.

5 I have stressed that caring and educational procedures based on a reductionist view can foster dangerous dehumanizing trends and must be combated.
6 In this overall task of developing our image of the person in our society, and indeed of the human race, we need the caring professions, education, the Church, and all the other creative thought we can muster to realize the importance of their role and to fulfill it responsibly and assertively.

Our concern today must be less with "The Future of an Illusion" and more with "The Illusion of a Future."

Chapter 9

The autonomous self

Editor's introduction

Sutherland follows Fairbairn in believing that the infant is born with a distinct self equipped with a self-organizing capability. The infant is ready to relate, to be, and to do. Then development proceeds in relation to the responsive mother who gives meaning to the self and who provides interactions that are the stuff of psychic structure formation. Sutherland reviews theories of the formation of the self (Freud, Klein, Winnicott, Balint, Hartmann, Erikson, Lichtenstein, Mahler, Kernberg, and Kohut) and moves on from a materialist view of the self as an isolate to a view of the process-oriented self in the social environment continuing to develop and differentiate over time in the light of experience.

Early theories of the self

Several trends have contributed to the recent emergence of the self as a central issue within psychoanalysis. Common to all these trends has been the growing awareness that the fundamental assumptions of psychoanalysis did not do justice to new clinical findings. In contrast with the classical theories – which based development on the instincts and their vicissitudes, and from these, the tripartite structuring of the mind – more recent theories have increasingly seen psychopathological manifestations as being involved with the person as a whole, that is, the self. This self developed those disorders when it lost a core integration that had hitherto been referred to by such phrases as "an intact ego," or as a strength derived from a sufficient degree of cohesion in managing the instincts. Instead, the individual presented conflicts within the self or "identity." Divisions within the self caused doubts "about who one was" and other disturbing existential phenomena. Psychoanalysts were thus confronted with serious questions that exposed the inadequacy of current theory, which was considered to depersonalize individuals and especially their motivation. This belief was confirmed by what was happening in society, as poets and writers all too frequently expressed.

In Freud's first theorizing, he took for granted the personal level of conflict in the repression of painful ideas and feelings because of their incompatibility with the values of the central self. The "I," as Freud (1923) termed it, was clearly the self in all its subjective richness of meaning. A progressive depersonalization of this "Ich" seemed to begin when the instincts and their biological energies were conceived of as playing the dominant role in the unconscious psyche. This trend persisted for the next half century and was reinforced, as Bettelheim (1982) was driven to stress a few years ago, by the translation of the German "Ich" into English as the neutral word "ego" (p. 80); but its perpetuation almost certainly drew on the pervasive and tenacious influence of scientific materialism. Freud's genius, however, could not be wholly constrained by this limitation. In spite of holding on to this philosophy as part of his thinking until his death, he introduced into the self the personalized structures of the ego-ideal and the superego from his study of group behavior and the psychoses, while in the ego there was personification by identifications. When the tripartite theory emerged, there was thus a scheme of development starting from the drives of the impersonal biological instincts and proceeding with the formation of a person through interaction with the social reality of the family. This atomistic buildup of parts, however, fails to do justice to the uniqueness of the self as a functioning whole, especially in light of the growing awareness of existential issues that emphasize its central role. Nevertheless, as Franz Alexander (Alexander and French 1946) maintained when the tripartite theory was formulated, there was now "a psychology of the total person."

The new formulation proved to have enormous appeal as well as great heuristic value. A wider range of disorder was investigated in depth to an extent not thought possible, and Anna Freud (1946) and Wilhelm Reich (1949) advanced the understanding of ego and character formation. The most radical development came from the work of Melanie Klein (1932), who pursued the implications of Freud's views on the importance of early development by boldly and rigorously applying the psychoanalytic method to young children. The consequence was the rather startling finding of the rich content of children's inner worlds, worlds populated by a range of figures in fantasied loving and hating relationships with each other and with the ego. Because of the extreme violence and sadistic destructiveness in some of these relationships, Klein postulated that they were direct reflections of the instincts, and especially the death instinct. The destructive impulses aroused intense anxieties, which Klein related to a dread of disintegration of the ego, or to a loss of the cohering function of the internalized good mother. To lessen these inner terrors, the ego split into parts so that the dangerous impulses could be separated from the good figures. Impressed with the salient power of the instincts, Klein did not pursue the theoretical implications of her findings about the structuring of the self as vividly personalized in the inner relationships, except to assume that the ego must be a unity from the start. Thus she did not examine how perception and action were influenced by simultaneous dynamic effect from more than one of the internal objects. (At that time, the ego and the self were interchangeable terms, and they remained so until Hartmann separated them as a theoretical necessity.)

In contrast with the Viennese analysts, who gave Klein's ideas a hostile reception, the British analysts were divided in their response. A substantial group believed that her data warranted careful appraisal and assimilation. From this group, some became enthusiastic followers while others were stimulated to create their own lines of thought. Among these, the best known were Balint (1952, 1968), Fairbairn (1952a), and Winnicott (1965) (see Chapter 3). Each was a highly independent thinker, yet all shared the attribution of a fundamental role in shaping the personality to the actual earliest experiences of the infant in its personal interaction with the mother and the family. From this common emphasis, they became known as the object-relations theorists, and many analysts subsequently developed their views further. For our immediate purpose, the most significant feature of their initial work was that they arrived at the need to conceptualize the self. Only Winnicott took the step of adopting the term, although, like the others, he did not formulate a systematic conceptualization. Fairbairn acknowledged, in his later years, that although he would have preferred to use the term, he believed it was more appropriate to retain the common psychoanalytic vocabulary at the time of his writing.

Balint's virtual arrival at the concept of the self is evident in his description of patients who regressed during analysis to a state in which the interaction between them and the analyst was dominated by its preverbal quality. Verbal interpretations then had little effect; instead, the patients responded to the experience of being "recognized." By this statement, Balint clearly implied a reaction of the person as a whole, whose unique feelings were being emphatically understood and accepted by another person. The holistic quality of such an experience cohered in a relationship between two selves.

Winnicott concluded that many, if not all, patients to some degree had a split in the self and its sense of being that led to a separation of the "false" or compliant self from the "true" self. (This repressed or "hidden" self became a central focus for Winnicott's pupil, Masud Khan (1983), in his later clinical studies.) This split arose from a mismatch between the infant's needs and the mother's perception and reception of these needs, either through the mother's failure to recognize their nature by faulty empathy, or by an intrusive response based on her own conception of what the infant's needs should be. Whatever its origins, this division bedeviled the whole development of the individual; and it was extremely resistant to change because it had evolved as a defense against the dread of loss of the self, that is, of madness. Winnicott's work eventually had a growing impact on analysts because of the new way in which it illuminated many psychopathological manifestations.

Despite the genius quality in his work, Winnicott did not propose a revised metapsychology. Instead, he believed that Freud's libido theory and his own concepts could coexist as parts of the psychoanalytic understanding of the person. Greenberg and Mitchell (1983) found Winnicott's attitude toward his own theoretical contributions so bizarre that they devoted about five pages to its elaboration. They clearly found it difficult to understand his almost obsequious claim to be merely expanding some of Freud's ideas, while in fact he was emphasizing the crucial role of the earliest mother–infant relationship in shaping the structure of the personality. In their view, Winnicott's need to avoid challenging Freud's assumptions led him to concoct a viewpoint that differed from Freud's, and then to accept the simultaneous operation of two incompatible explanatory schemes. The Greenberg–Mitchell account of this anomaly is of special interest because of Winnicott's irrational attack on Fairbairn's confrontation of this issue. Instead of recognizing that Fairbairn was in fact spelling out, with remarkable conviction, evidence for what they were both advocating, Winnicott reacted as though Fairbairn had personally attacked Freud.

Fairbairn differed from most psychoanalytic theorists in having had philosophical training before he studied medicine and psychoanalysis. From his early years, he had shown a strong interest in identifying the basic principles underlying processes and making his own appraisal of these principles when applied to his own clinical findings. This attitude was reinforced by his geographical isolation from the other British analysts, which freed him from the pressures within the analytic movement toward strict conformity with Freud's writings. His thinking was thus individualistic, yet suffused with a disciplined critical approach, which led him to prospectively reject the views of others until he matched them against his experience. For Fairbairn, reaching conclusions that differed from others might be the greatest respect he could pay them, because it was from their work that he started.

After close study of a group of patients with schizoid personalities, Fairbairn summed up their psychopathology as resulting from failure by the mother to convey a feeling that she loved and valued them as persons in their own right. Fairbairn assumed an innate need in the infant that had to be met by the mother's emotional attitude toward her child. This need was thus unusual, as he conceived it, for it was a purely psychological holistic one arising in the self. It was not an appetitive bodily need to be gratified with pleasure as tensions terminated, as were the instincts in Freud's scheme, but rather a need for an ongoing personal relationship. The infant clamored for joyful, stimulating interchanges, as in playful baby talk and games, quite independently of the care ordinarily given in response to physical needs. For Fairbairn, the infant was thus "personalized" by being spontaneously responded to as a person right from the start, first by the mother, and later by the father and other family members. It was this welcome into the world of social relations that laid the foundation of the security essential for the development of potential personal resources through the resultant readiness to establish these relationships.

Because future personality structure was so closely determined by the quality of these early experiences, Fairbairn asserted that psychoanalysis would advance only by changing its underlying assumptions. Specifically, the crucial role attributed to the vicissitudes of instinctual energies and their satisfaction must be replaced by a theory of how the personality was structured as the consequence of its experiences, especially in the earliest stages of development. Fairbairn called this view an *object-relations theory*, a term that has stuck even though he later believed it would have been more appropriate to call it a *personal-relations theory. Object*, however, was the usual word for the aims of the instincts when these were conceived of largely as needs for which body parts might be the object.

Continuing evolution of the self

Despite the increasing inadequacy of the tenets of scientific materialism to explain the phenomena of living organisms, and even though the theory of open systems was developed to account for their properties, the grip of materialism has continued to exercise its influence. We have only to note the great reluctance to move away from concepts of drives as though they are biological energies pumped into the psychic apparatus and hence essential for any explanation of motivation. In the perspective of drive theory, the evolution of an ego is an organization of experience forced on the person to cope with the id and its perpetual pressure to action in the outer world. Moreover, because the instincts constitute the supply of energy, they drive the organism to homeostatic constancy and eventually to the state of maximum entropy (that is, death). Fairbairn, on the other hand, postulated a holistic ego right at the center, which was structured from experience. Such a notion was in no way a naïve separation of mind from body, but it employed the current biological concepts of holistic organizing principles. It also emphasized that new levels of organization invariably produce new properties that cannot be predicted from knowledge of the parts. No amount of knowledge about the hydrogen and oxygen atoms would let us predict that combining them results in a colorless liquid – water.

Fairbairn's line of thought, although starting from the clinical data provided by his schizoid patients, was also influenced by his antipathy to the atomistic approach that materialism engendered and by contemporary theories of embryology. The dominant concept was of a ground plan within the organism that controlled the emergence of its differentiated structures and maintained their interdependence. There was little understanding of how such an influence could be mediated, but Fairbairn's notion of a latent holistic force was supported by the growth of Gestalt psychology. During this period, the question of a holistic force independent of the instinctual drives was gripping the attention of other psychoanalysts. Hartmann (1958) made the first prominent contribution to this development. (Fairbairn and Hartmann were actually evolving their theories at the same time, but the outbreak of World War II prevented any mutual influence.)

The problem that Hartmann considered to be unsolvable, in terms of instinctual forces driving the individual to seek the pleasure of discharge, was how such motives alone could lead to the essential property of the ego – namely, the capacity to delay action by anticipating greater gains through knowledge and planning. For Hartmann, this capacity required an autonomous ego whose development had to be seen as that of a variable, independent of the instincts, with its own innate endowments governing its maturation. It also had to be distinguished from the whole person, which Hartmann held to be the self (that is, what was cathected in narcissism). In commenting on Hartmann's theoretical formulations, Lichtenstein (1977) noted that Hartmann saw the need for a radical rethinking of psychoanalytic theory if that theory were to rightfully claim the title of an evolutionary approach to human mental development. Hartmann, however, did not get beyond the concepts associated with ego functions, partly because of his adherence to mechanistic principles. Nevertheless, Lichtenstein followed up some of their implications. Thus, by assuming that "the whole person" was cathected by libido in narcissism, we have to ask whether this organizing principle is distinct in origin and function from a structure synthesized from the other psychic structures. What we observe of the "whole person" are the bodily and psychological transformations during the life cycle. The invariant self as a whole is the constant thread that gives the feeling of being the same person. Yet it cannot be derived from the parts. Thus we are aware of unrealized potential, of complex relationships, as in amnesias when the self-perception is changed, or when it is maintained in an unstable state against a feeling of not being the "true self." Lichtenstein believed that Hartmann's "third force," or independent variable, within the psyche must be invoked. As Masud Khan (1964) observed, "the discussion of ego-pathology has extended to the larger issues of identity formation . . . and the establishment of self" (p. 273).

The theme of identity is associated with Erikson (1959), who located the development of the ego within the social relatedness of the person. Throughout his thinking, he has always integrated the biological with the cultural, but his scheme, unlike the theory of libidinal development, covers the whole life cycle. The epigenetic phases he postulated in development, from infancy to old age, have now become a part of culture. What we must note is that an identity principle, a biological organizing principle, underlies these phases. Indeed, Lichtenstein asserted the establishment and maintenance of identity as the principle that defines the concept of living and the survival of life. In animals, as in humans, this principle commands absolute priority over any other need.

In the lower animals, identity is largely that of the genotype, which is fashioned to a high degree by the genic endowment within a predictable environment. High up on the evolutionary scale, the saurian's development takes place entirely under the impetus of the innate behavioral mechanisms. The human being, in marked contrast, has prolonged gestation followed by years of nurturance from adults, without which the infant cannot survive. Spitz (1965) showed that the infant dies if no one gives enough love and care to set up a self, or organizing principle, that wants to live. The evolutionary endowment in the infant and in the mother is thus of a completely different order from that of the lower animals, one presumably evolved to cope with human survival through membership in groups. Humans also pose the problem of the plasticity of the phenotype. The behavioral characteristics of the adult human being vary greatly from culture to culture, within the same culture, and, to some extent, within the single individual when required. Any organizational principle is therefore concerned with the emergence of identity from potential forms of characteristics that are shaped by the experience in upbringing.

What Erikson described as identity was the objectification of the self into a person with a sense of being a "somebody" aware of personal history and whose self had been organized into patterns laid down by peer social groups. The person recognized by others was the identity as objectified, while the inner sense of being this person reflected this identity, although the existential awareness was absolutely unique to the individual. This inner core, which was distinguished from the public identity, could be carried only by an ongoing structure that psychoanalysis had not specified, although, as Lichtenstein said, an adequate knowledge of who a person was could never be inferred from what the person was.

Lichtenstein, from his remarkably comprehensive and penetrating considerations of the problem of identity, was one of the first psychoanalysts to offer a metapsychology of the self. Starting by assuming the existence of an innate organizing principle, he did not agree that this principle can be derived from the other metapsychological constituents. Spitz assumed its independent status from the work of the embryologists. Spiegel (1959), however, accepted it on the psychological basis of its being the self. It acts from the beginning as a frame of reference against which experiences are judged. Sandler, although postulating an organizing activity that appears very early, saw it as a reflection of the synthetic function of the ego (Sandler and Joffe 1962, 1969). For Lichtenstein, however, this latter conceptualization is a rather advanced ego property that would operate only later.

The self as "organizing principle"

The confluence of psychoanalytic thought represented by these brief references reflects a rising dynamic toward the recognition of the self as an independent variable. Couched in the tentative expression of "organizing principle," this force nevertheless has the most fundamental role in the very survival of the person as the agent responsible for the integration of experience. The abstract term "principle" indicates that although it determines the development of the future person, the only formal characteristic that can be attributed to it is that of coordinating the experiences from the rapid developments in bodily resources, the maturation of the innate behavioral systems, and their interactions with the mother, the father, and the family. To give more form to this potential, Lichtenstein suggested that, at birth, the infant's experiences with the mother start a transformative structuring or patterning into what he called a primary identity. This conclusion is inevitable, and all clinical experience confirms it. For this reason, I believe we must regard this variable as the self.

The potentialities are clearly plastic in that they determine what might be analogous to the trunk of the tree from which all the future shape – with its infinite possibilities in regard to the branches, the foliage, and the flowering for procreation – will emerge from the specific features of the environment that nourished it. The process of becoming is that of development with all the unpredictable distortions that may be induced by an unpredictable environment – either in pathological structuring in place of the normal, or in reactive deformations in the whole, to make good the absence of what should have been an available environmental constituent.

In the formation of identity, Lichtenstein attributed much more innately structured action to the infant than is usual. This assumption receives support from the subsequent studies of infant development. (From his philosophical training, Lichtenstein suggested that the theoretical barriers to linking the inner subject with the outer world have been created by entrenched Cartesian dualism.) Thus, from von Uexküll's (1986) concept of an innate scheme in the embryo of the more primitive animals (wherein their drives have their object imprinted sufficiently for their behavior to be directed to it from the start), Lichtenstein suggested that the infant self innately expects to find the constellation of a mother responding to it, and it responds at once to the mother as the object that completes the arc of its inner tension. Correspondingly, the mother begins to personalize the infant. It is the particular model that comes from her own needs, conscious and unconscious, that gives identity to the child. This initial "shaping" of the self operates permanently as "an identity theme" that persists throughout life although modified by subsequent experience into many "variations."

Lichtenstein concluded that identity evolves into the structure through which the individual will perceive and interact with the world, and thus become responsible for survival as a human being. He further stressed that the identity must be constantly maintained against any tendency to regress, a task normally effected by membership in various groups to which the individual belongs. The two basic features of the self are thus brought to the fore – namely, its autonomy and its concurrent membership in a community. As a self-organizing, dynamic open system, the self places paramount emphasis on its autonomy, which is synonymous with survival. Nevertheless, as Angyal (1965) noted in his conceptualization of the person in terms of systems theory, the self must retain an *autonomy within a homonymy of relatedness*. Threats to the self evoke the defensive ferocity of the animal faced with a lethal predator.

In this connection, Freud (1921) discussed the libidinal ties among members of the group, noting the spontaneous intolerance to strangers that has to be overcome:

> This self-love works for the preservation of the individual, and behaves as though the occurrence of any divergence from his own particular lines of development involved a criticism of them and a demand for their alteration. We do not know why such sensitiveness should have been directed to just these details of differentiation; but it is unmistakable that in this whole connection men give evidence of a readiness for hatred, an aggressiveness, the source of which is unknown, and to which one is tempted to ascribe an elementary character.
>
> (p. 102)

In a footnote to this passage, Freud referred to his recent linking of the polarity of love and hate with the opposition between the instincts of life and death.

Lichtenstein's contributions thus clarified the position that the self should occupy in the basic assumptions of psychoanalytic theory. Although representing a radical change in theoretical principles, Lichtenstein's synthesis is a model for establishing the evolutionary status of the self from many trends in clinical thinking within psychoanalysis during the decades prior to his book, *The Dilemma of Human Identity*, in 1977. The importance of these principles is perhaps best indicated by Lichtenstein's (1977) comment concerning Hartmann's recognition that the "pressures of needs and drives appear as manifestations of personal will" (p. 235). Lichtenstein further reinforced this perspective by noting Hartmann's (1958) prediction "that the psychology of will-processes is destined to play a role in the psychoanalytic psychology of the future" (pp. 74–75).

The contributions of Lichtenstein and Erikson, because of their focus on the development of the self into an "identity," tend to be considered in isolation from their fundamental postulates regarding the development of the self. Both of these writers describe how the adult self is shaped by its identifications and internalizations. Erikson assumed the existence of the self as the central structured potential from which the eventual identity of the adult emerges. Lichtenstein suggested that this self-structure is so constructed that it "expects" from birth to be treated like a person. As he made clear, conceptualizing the self to be at birth a dynamic structure that will play a crucial role in development challenges all the assumptions of classical theory. Erikson had considered that the libidinal phases, as Freud described them, developed alongside the epigenetic states in the formation of identity. Such a view, however, cannot be sustained because the libidinal theory accounts for the development of object relations in terms of the phases of libidinal development.

Recent theories of the self

Within the past few decades, the self has become the explicit focus for several analysts whose writings have in turn made it an issue of widespread interest. Prominent contributions, much influenced by Hartmann, have come from Mahler (Mahler *et al.* 1975), Jacobson (1964), and later from Otto Kernberg (1976) who was influenced by them. Even though accepting the self as a structure separate from the id, ego, and superego, Mahler, Jacobson, and Kernberg nevertheless have held that their findings – thought by some to require an autonomous self of independent origin – can be accounted for in terms of classical theory.

Mahler's studies of young children, both observational and clinical, are now an integral part of the development of psychoanalytic theory. In contrast to Hartmann, who had left the self as a rather ill-defined entity, Mahler introduced a concept of the self as the whole person, which emerged as a coherent identity as the result of development through phases of differentiation from a symbiotic matrix. The experiences of the infant with its mother during the earliest phases had a crucial effect on the future personality. However, as Greenberg and Mitchell remarked, Mahler struggled to retain the role of drive theory in the face of evidence from later research strongly suggesting that the infant possessed independent resources and separateness from birth. Mahler did this by denying that what she had described was a metapsychological theory; it was essentially only a descriptive phenomenological account. It was the organizing function of the ego, as specified by Hartmann, that created the self through its representations within the ego becoming cathected by libido. Nevertheless, Mahler had moved away from the oedipal relationships as the foundation for "a totality of tenderness, security, and pleasure that is experienced in a full relationship with another person" (Greenberg and Mitchell 1983, p. 303).

Jacobson's (1964) seminal writings have demonstrated that she clearly saw some of the limitations of drive theory. Her intensive work with very disturbed patients forced her to recognize the need to include the consequences of early relationships in the formation of the self. In her first theorizing, she adopted Hartmann's position of regarding the ego as a system of functions and the self as existing within the ego through its representations. She nevertheless concluded that the self contributed an independent dynamic influence; for instance, she believed that the ego acquired a likeness to the love object only by introjecting aspects of it into the self. The desire to be like the object contributed to differentiation of the self. Jacobson's acceptance of the fundamental importance of relationships led her to broaden the classical concepts. Thus orality for her included what the mother is for the infant in all aspects, and it operated to organize the manifold experiences. Here, too, Jacobson viewed affects, not as deriving from discharges of tensions, but as including the quality of the experience (that is, the factor added to it by the specific relationship). Of course, this line of reasoning raises a key question about drive theory – namely, how the energies of the drives can account for the great spectrum of experiences. Jacobson believed that this is possible along the lines she suggested.

This issue is unavoidable for any theoretical scheme, and we see it again in Kernberg (1976, 1980). Prior to the impact of Mahler and Jacobson, he was greatly stimulated by Fairbairn, a debt he acknowledged after his views on borderline patients had become established. Although he explicitly adopted the stance of an object-relations theorist, he disowned Fairbairn's position insofar as the latter asserted it to be incompatible with drive theory. For Kernberg, it is from the drives that representations of the self and objects are developed into internalized relationships. Because of this aspect of Kernberg's theoretical work, Greenberg and Mitchell have classified him as belonging to the current trend of "theoretical accommodation" that attributes much of the structuring of the ego and the self to a social origin apart from the drives. They added, however, that those who have adopted these theories, yet who also hold to drive theory as essential for a metapsychological component in any psychoanalytical theory, fail to realize that in doing so they have constructed a theory that is quite different from Freud's.

Kernberg has postulated the internalization of dynamic systems with a self-image linked to an object. The introjection of the object, however, is not entirely at the behest of oral impulses. At the early stage, self and object are poorly separated and affects can be intense, especially violently negative feelings. With maturity, the relationships of similar affective tone build up into identifications and eventually form the ego identity. The drives thus play an initial part in providing the affects from which the subsequent organization of the person is built. The self remains essentially as a phenomenological term in the experience of relationships and their subsequent organization by the ego.

Kohut (1971, 1977) is by far the most prominent writer to advocate a radical view of the self as the active agent in the initiation and organization of behavior. He conceptualized the self at birth as largely a potential only – one that is required to merge with the mother to function in a progressively organized way and with a sense of constancy and spontaneity. The essential dynamic system is thus that of a self with a self-object, or undifferentiated mother, operating in the earliest stages as an ego. As separation proceeds with development, the self becomes more autonomous and effective; but a tie to others remains throughout life even when the self fully recognizes the separateness of others. The closeness of the self with the self-object is such that it is the subjectivity of this latter to which the self mainly responds. With ordinary good parenting, the self works through two critical phases for its effective development. First, the mother, as the main influence, has to respond empathically to the infant's presence and achievements. From this experience, the self gains a sense of omnipotence and grandiosity that, in due course, through interaction with others, is transformed into a reasonable sense of security, self-esteem, and achievement from abilities. As this earliest structuring of a grandiose self is taking place, a second structuring begins from the internalization of the admired parents as ideas. At first, the idealized parents exist as undifferentiated self-objects, and are then replaced by more separated ideal figures that function as the ego-ideal and superego. The behavior characterized in terms of the libidinal phases does not originate from fixations at the libidinal states, but from "oral, anal, or oedipal disorders" in the parents.

Kohut's theory replaces the drives with factors arising from the experience of relationships. The analytic process does not reside in the interpretation of drives and defenses, but in the intersubjective field constituted by the analysand and the analyst. In his first formulations, Kohut stressed that he was not replacing classical theory, but was instead advancing a view wherein the dynamic structuring of the self can be considered alongside the independent processes of the libidinal states and the drive theory. In keeping with this position, he regarded disorders of the self as separate from the neuroses, which are derived from conflicts between the drives that develop later. Some years later, Kohut concluded that the concept of "drive" was quite unsatisfactory, but he then decided to avoid breaking with tradition to preserve the sense of continuity of our science. Such an attitude from one purporting to make advances in a scientific theory cannot but remind one of Galileo recanting from fear of the Inquisition! It is the more extraordinary in that Kohut asserted, like Fairbairn, that the sexual and aggressive impulses, so prominent as symptoms, derive from disorders in the self and not from independent energies.

If we leave aside these "accommodations" as dictated by political rather than scientific considerations, Kohut certainly placed the conceptualization of the self in the forefront of psychoanalytic debate. His voluminous writings contain many valuable clinical observations. Nevertheless, he seems to present an oversimplified view that distortions in the bipolar structuring of the self, around the early grandiose needs and the attachment to idealized objects, explain all the major pathological developments of the self. He also underestimated, in the opinion of many analysts sympathetic to the object-relational focus, the ever-present manifestations of aggression aroused when the needs of the self are frustrated. But the essential limitation in Kohut's conceptual scheme is the lack of a convincing metapsychology, one that links the psychological to the biological factors that must be present for the evolution of a structure of such comprehensive responsibility for behavior.

Summarizing the progressive intrusion of the self into psychoanalytic theory over the past few decades, we note its growing prominence for theory and practice. The influence of ego psychology, so powerful among American analysts, has led to unresolved differences. The importance of conceptualizing identity formation emphasized the central role of early relationships and of subsequent relationships in the maintenance of identity. Only Lichtenstein, however, of those closest to ego psychology, favored the postulation of the self as an independent variable from which the identity is fashioned out of its relationships. Yet he stopped short of a theory of the origin of the self, even though he saw that the innately structured potential self must be the start of a metapsychology of the self. It is this problem of conceptualizing an adequate metapsychology of the self with biological roots that seems to have deterred most of those theorists inspired by Hartmann from moving from their acceptance of the essential role of early relationships in fashioning the personality on to a developmental origin independent of the biological instincts and the drive theory. It is this problem to which we must turn our attention.

I wish first, however, to refer to considerations from outside the clinical situation, because we seem to have created a major barrier by confining ourselves to it. Historically, Freud maintained that psychoanalysts should look to literature to learn what writers have to say about the psychological puzzles confronting us. As observers of the individual within society, writers are inevitably faced with the impact of various movements – intellectual, scientific, artistic, and sociopolitical – on the culture that in turn affects the individual. They can thus identify the features that bestow persistent personal characteristics.

Some extraanalytic conceptions of the self

Just as we can see Freud's discoveries about the unconscious as only one manifestation among many related turbulences in the cultural scene of the Western world a century ago, so with the recent interest in the conceptualization of the self. From this complexity, I believe that some aspects of the fields of literature, philosophy, the social sciences, and psychiatry have crucial significance for psychoanalysis because it has claimed, following Hartmann's work, to be the path to a general psychology of the person.

From the start of his psychoanalytic studies, Freud was greatly influenced by what the poets and writers said about the nature of human beings as an essential source of insight. Masud Khan, although regarded as Winnicott's principal disciple, has made particularly relevant contributions. His unusual combination of a literary cast of mind and psychoanalytic training has enabled him to offer acutely sensitive observations of the phenomena within the psychoanalytic encounter. His observations are also relatively free of the insidious theoretical prejudices that accompany the use of technical jargon. In the opening chapter of Khan's book of essays entitled *Hidden Selves* (1983), he quoted a passage from Trilling's Freud Anniversary Lecture of 1955 that goes right to the heart of our concern:

> The first thing that occurs to me to say about literature, as I consider it in the relation in which Freud stands to it, is that literature is dedicated to the conception of the self [Trilling 1955, p. 17]. . . . In almost every developed society, literature is able to conceive of the self, and the selfhood of others, far more intensely than the general culture ever can [1955, p. 19].
>
> (Khan 1983, p. 11)

And, we might add, more intensely than psychoanalysis does. Khan's initial theme in his essay is the emergence in European culture of modernism, a trend characterized as he said by "Man's decision to be his own sole witness and exclude God, more and more, from his private relation to himself and his personal relation with others" (p. 12). Put another way, modern individuals recognize a new degree of autonomy in their whole being.

Trilling (1955) saw Freud's mind to be different from the literary one in allowing intelligence to play a greater part. Freud was born when science and literature were perceived as cultural antagonists. He was, above all, a scientist and proud of it, yet he was one of the greatest humanistic minds. By drawing on both sides of himself, he made a creative leap that enabled him to suspend his disbelief in his patients' fantasies and so to study the unconscious areas of inner reality from which they originated. The understanding of motivation was thereafter permanently expanded. Trilling, however, indicated various features of the person that did not receive as much attention from psychoanalysts as from writers. Among the Romantic poets, for instance, Wordsworth (1888) extended the role of pleasure from almost exclusive links with instinctual gratification to a principle by which humanity feels, and lives, and moves, but also *knows*. When Keats (1919) said "beauty is truth," he was acknowledging this principle in the gaining of knowledge. Moreover, when he added "truth beauty," he affirmed the kind of pleasure the developed self derives from perceiving some of the painful facts within it. The ever-resounding echo of his aphorism throughout our literature for the past two centuries testifies to the profoundly aesthetic affirmation for the self from embracing the experiences of distress into its wholeness.

These deep integrative trends appear to stem from a creative dynamic more inherent in human nature than is conveyed by the somewhat tautological phrase, "the synthetic function of the ego." Trilling believed that writers conceive of love as a principle of order and even a civilizing power. Thus, when Blake (1965) called in a great voice for the armaments of libidinal desire, his purpose was to build Jerusalem in "England's green and pleasant land" (p. 95). There are here overtones of an outreaching impetus that may be more deeply rooted than the acquisition of the ego-ideal from the social environment – perhaps the open-endedness of humanity at the edge of evolution.

The two cultures

Freud was born when science and literature were becoming seen as two antagonistic cultures. A degree of conflict stayed with Freud, as he made plain in his uneasy ambivalence about the relationship between the individual and the culture. Today, when culture itself is as much the object of study as is the individual, there is a greater appreciation of the necessity for both to establish a mutually adaptive partnership.

The movement toward modernism shows various attempts to find substitutes for the relationship with an external destiny that the human self appeared to need if it was to retain its cohesion and keep alive a sense of well-being. The close interdependence of the personal self with the characteristics of its culture became increasingly manifest in literature throughout the century after Freud's birth. The separation from religious belief following the Enlightenment had been followed by the Romantic movement's attempt to substitute a reverence for nature, including as part of nature the development of the self from childhood experience: "The child is father to the man" (Hopkins 1918). What then ensued was a progressive inner-directedness, as though to find there some solution – for example, love or art – to what Robert Langbaum (1977) saw as a preoccupying concern in modern literature, namely, "the mysteries of identity."

Writers were too aware of the centrality of the self and its complexities to follow the scientific philosophy of humanity conceived of as a machine. For Coleridge (1991), the crucial factor in forming and maintaining the autonomy of the self is the imagination – the unique capacity of the mind. And these writers were reinforced by the surging impact of the philosophies expounded by the phenomenologists and then the existentialists. There could be no question of the fundamental role played by the sense of being, the awareness created from the concentration of all the organized commitments to the more or less coherent aims that constituted the business of living. These commitments embraced the urges of corporeality, the essential relatedness necessary to preserve with others, and the appraisals of the constraints and the opportunities in the external world, all of which seemed to express a constant intentionality with the judgements and decisions for action into the ever-present future.

Although the theory of evolution at first led to some lowering of humanity's self-image, there was no widespread acceptance of this image as being that of a machine. The image of the individual as a unique development in the evolutionary scale was firm enough to reject any philosophy that ignored specific features. What disturbed writers more, however, was the effects of the social changes brought about by rapid industrialization. Marx (1988) had confronted society with the alienating, dehumanizing results of uprooting masses of people from social environments in which they could feel a sense of selfhood from being embedded in extensive networks of significant relationships, and placing them instead where they not only lost this relatedness but also were stripped of the essential affirmation provided by meaningful work. When no means was found to replace the contribution of these nutriments, so vital for maintaining the well-being of the individual's identity (as Lichtenstein had postulated), the effects of society evoked strong reactions in our literature. Without the cultural environment that had evolved from the interaction of individuals and their social milieu, writers became concerned with a chilling trend to fragmentation of the individual. The brittle attachment to the illusory substitutes that emerged in the social "wasteland" now evoked, not the death of God, but a depressing concern lest the individual die because of the loss of identity and the consequent isolation, as in Samuel Beckett's (1954) *Waiting for Godot*. There was also a depressing impotence from the absence of effective remedial ideas. To evolve such measures has never been the function of our writers, nor should we expect it.

Again Trilling (1955) referred, even if not explicitly, to this situation – to a characteristic of the literary, in contrast to the scientific, mind. He perceived Freud as not really a literary mind because he always wrote about writers and poets as an external observer. The feeling of writers when they produced their work was something Freud never conveyed. Instead, Freud fused a partly literary mind with a scientific one, and it is the analytic objectivity of the latter that is required to work out the origins of phenomena as experienced by others. The infinitely complex interdependence of psychological, social, political, economic, and other factors could not be studied by the psychoanalysts. They might, however, have been more interested in the striking psychological phenomena that emerged, for these were clearly determined by a serious change in the psychic economy of the person. There were, for instance, the diminished commitments to essential relationships such as marriage and the family, and the substitution for these of sexual gratification separated from love in personal relationships – the cult of narcissism as it was styled – and a rising greedy demandingness of the welfare state.

Psychoanalysts were not indifferent to these developments. It seemed that the development of their work within the isolated privacy of the consulting room had reinforced an underlying lack in their theoretical account of the person as inseparably interwoven with the fabric of society. Their research could be restricted to people regarded as closed systems within the boundary of their skin. Put like that, such a view would be vehemently rejected, especially today when the focus of the analytic relationship is on what happens between the patient and the analyst. This change, in fact, underlies what is perhaps the missing component. For this change has now shifted the center of our concern from the way in which drives and their derivatives are defended against (that is, hidden from the self and others) to the nature of the self that has to contain these conflicts.

For Freud, a scientist in the tradition of the nineteenth century, the whole problem of the self was scarcely conceivable, although its reality could be recognized. Even today there is a powerful tendency among scientists to view the individual as a machine, or at best to recognize the unique properties of the mind and then consider its study as being outside the purview of science. The core problem is the age-long one of how an immaterial mind can be related to its material body. If we approach that problem head-on, we inevitably encounter insuperable blocks. What we can do, however – if we accept the central role of the self as the agent that embodies the organization of our experience and hence controls the effectiveness of our behavior – is to study its mode of developing and some of its functioning; and this we observe from within ourselves and through the inferences we make from observing others, including their accounts of their inner world.

Existentialism naturally highlighted the problem of the self in relation to changes in the culture, and its contribution greatly influenced literature. Its effect, however, seemed to be mainly to sharpen and emphasize the phenomenological descriptions. The impact on psychoanalysis was limited, perhaps because of the inadequate attention given to unconscious processes. Among psychodynamically oriented psychiatrists, especially in Europe, existentialism aroused a widespread interest in directing therapy to understanding the individual's existential conflicts. Laing (1960) combined his training in psychoanalysis with a profound and extensive knowledge of the phenomenologists and existentialists to brilliantly expose the deeper conflicts in the self. Nevertheless, although he was widely acclaimed by writers and psychiatrists, his impact on psychoanalysts has been limited. His original data came from the treatment of schizophrenic patients, and his etiological factors were held to be psychosocial forces within the family. Because of their entrenched views linking the deepest disturbances in the personality to the libido theory, the analysts may have felt uneasy with theories involving only the dynamics of psychosocial interaction, and thus separated from the powerful biological origins of the instincts. In other words, it seemed that the Cartesian tradition might still be holding sway. Perhaps it would be more accurate to suggest that even though the framework of classical metapsychology might need replacing, it nevertheless attempted to root the personal level in the biological in a way that had a deep appeal. Even though Laing pointed out the failure of psychotic patients to achieve an "embodied" self, there was no ready way by which the self could be given a specific biological foundation.

The self within society

When we put together these impressions from some extrapsychoanalytic sources, we are confronted with direct references in much of our literature to an autonomous self as a structured entity that exerts a central control over personal behavior. This self is fashioned from early experience into an identity – the unique grouping that each individual has of character, abilities, and social relationships into the individual cohesive organization that preserves a sense of continuity throughout the life cycle. This identity or self is a dynamic structure in constant interaction with the social environment and its culture. When the latter no longer provides the affirmation the self requires, then the self tends to disintegrate, with widespread disturbances in the sense of well-being and hence various pathological reactions.

An investigation by my former colleague, Eric Trist, and his associates contributed to an understanding of the nature of this deterioration in the maintenance of the well-being of the self (Trist and Banforth 1951). The study was carried out in response to a request to examine what was happening to coal miners who had been organized into work groups in which all the men had very restricted work tasks designed from a "time and motion" study of the job. Each group would take over from another group operating in one of three shifts into which the twenty-four-hour day was divided. Coming to the situation with a psychodynamic approach to the whole person, Trist and his co-workers found, in free exploratory discussions with the men, a universal feeling that the job gave rise to a great deal of irritation, boredom, and frustration. Sharing tasks created little cohesion in the work groups because supervision was focused on the contribution of each man and each group separately. No sense of responsibility or autonomy was fostered in the groups, so that friction was prevalent within and between groups, especially because no regard was paid to how a group could assist the next one when it left the coal face. By switching to an allocation of responsibility for each group, to an overall sharing of the task, and to an organization of work related to both the human needs and the technical constraints, there was a significant change in what can only be seen as responses of the men as whole people. Absenteeism and sick leave diminished significantly and production increased. In short, the workers as a whole functioned better when the quality of their self-feeling improved from a recognition of their autonomy.

Another study also suggests that an unstable environment has a negative effect on a person's overall organization. Wolff (1960), a physician concerned with community health, studied the health records of a large sample of people who had been displaced from their home countries and relocated. He found that the incidence of almost every kind of illness – physical as well as psychiatric – was higher than normal in the period following the change to the new country of residence.

Whether or not a specific biological foundation can be established for the self, these findings strongly support the conviction among the most discerning writers that when the self is not functioning well, whether because of pathological development or current environmental stress, then the consequences of what Balint termed "the basic fault" can be seen, probably over the whole psychobiological structure of the individual, involving both mind and body in varying degrees. How, then, is this structure, which is crucial to the person, to be conceived of if we are to do justice to its origin and nature? It is clearly an open system, that is, one whose organization is maintained only when its interactions with the environment are appropriate to the needs of the human being – physically, socially, and creatively. This is the question to which both clinical and other sources of evidence force our attention.

The nature of the human organism in the light of modern evolutionary biology

The basic assumptions of Freud's thinking were those of scientific materialism and its view of what is "real." It is from these that the "drives" are made essential to subsequent theoretical development. As Greenberg and Mitchell (1983) emphasized in their excellent account of the mainstream of theoretical thinking in psychoanalysis in the past few decades, there is a striking paradox in the fact that, increasingly, the theory is recognized as inadequate to account for the person in his or her most characteristic aspects – namely, the autonomy of the self. The self, as the central agent controlling personal behavior, develops from its experience in relationships and its indispensable role as a dynamic structure that constantly maintains a process of interaction from which transformations take place. Moreover, despite the perpetual changes resulting from experience, the continuity of the individual self is preserved. This concept requires a different scientific paradigm.

The science in which Freud was reared sought to reduce "the human world to the equilibrium perfection, structural unambiguity and permanence, hierarchical control, and predictability of machine-like structures"

(Jantsch 1976, p. 2). Freud never exclusively adopted all these beliefs, yet much of their spirit pervaded his thinking. The current biological paradigms offer some different lines of thought, but there is an overall change to a *process-oriented* understanding instead of one employing rigid system components and structures composed of them. In adopting what I find the most appropriate paradigm to fit the problems presented by the self, I have borrowed much from the views of Waddington and Prigogine, which in turn have inspired Jantsch to pursue their implications for the human sciences (Prigogine 1976, Waddington and Jantsch 1976). The new perspective is, above all, a direct result of assimilating the fundamental place of evolution in considering living organisms. All present forms of life have originated from earlier forms, and what we must account for are such characteristics as self-organization and self-regulation, with nonequilibrium and unpredictability of differentiation in the development of new structures from interaction with the environment. What is *real* in these continuous self-renewals and self-expressions is the self-bounding processes rather than the changing structures. Although evolution has led to many organic subsystems that maintain an equilibrium, this "homeostasis" does not obtain for the organism as a whole. There, equilibrium means death because it ends the never-ceasing processes of self-transformation and self-organization that constitute life. As said by Sir Julian Huxley (1953), our perspective must be *sub specie evolutionis* rather than *sub specie aeternitatis*.

Although the bodily structures have not changed much in humans since they acquired their distinguishing features, there have been relatively enormous developments in the human nervous system. The most significant feature of this development is that the brain structure of the saurians, the earliest animals in the most relevant level of the evolutionary scale, has proceeded to the later ones by the addition of two organizing structures. Each of these has mediated what we might term quantum leaps into a quite different level of flexibility in behavior from that of the previous level. The changes, of course, although resulting in enormous differences, are the end product of very long-term evolutionary processes. The result is that human behavior in its eventual mature form is influenced by these underlying earlier modes of responding to the world.

Clearly, we can refer to this evolutionary process in only the sketchiest diagrammatic way. But because the human position in the evolutionary scale is crucial in understanding human nature, even such a limited reference must be in our thinking. The first consideration, however, must be to note the characteristics of the living creatures associated with the quantum leaps into quite different modes of behavior compared with the earlier phases. The most relevant evolutionary stages for present purposes are those of (1) the land-dwelling reptiles, (2) the lower mammals up to the higher apes, and (3) homo sapiens. The crucial feature is the development of the brain achieved at these three stages.

Behavioral evolution of the self

Before considering brain development, the nature and organization of the behavior of the animals in each of these stages must be noted, because the behavioral changes evolve in parallel with structural additions to the brain that mediate the new behaviors. We assume, of course, that evolution is the means through which a given species increases its capacity to exploit the environment more flexibly and more creatively, so that its constraints are progressively overcome until the point is reached, with humans, where they largely determine the environment.

Evolutionary theory has changed in recent years from crude Darwinism, with its survival of the fittest (a distortion of what Darwin suggested in 1859), to the need to consider the population or communities from which genetic variations are selected. We then have to appreciate how the behavior of the phenotypes, or existing forms of the adult animal, as a factor independent of the particular genic inheritance, can decisively affect the latter. This view, as developed in various ways by the animals, can lead to changes in the transmitted genes and so bring experimental evidence to justify the widely held view that evolution could not rest on chance and necessity in the blind way it was once held to operate. According to this view also, the genic inheritance increasingly allows the environment to play a greater part as the evolutionary scale is ascended.

What we must keep in mind is that an unconscious primitive organization, or "self," appears to continue to exercise an influence on brain functioning and thus on our behavior when the later evolutionary modes are overwhelmed. As we move up the scale to humans, the enormous complexity of the brain is difficult to appreciate, yet we must do so if we are to comprehend the human self, the essential organizing principle, in an evolutionary perspective comprising the distinctly human acquisitions. Assuming that the brain has evolved to provide for their growth and development, we must list these acquisitions as accurately and as comprehensively as we can. The following six elements are a tentative attempt at such a list and are intended wholly as a basis toward elaborating an evolutionary perspective.

1 The unique property of the human mind is consciousness of "the self" and the capacity to transcend itself, to look at itself in its relationship with aspects of itself, with others, and with the physical environment.
2 The dimension of complexity refers to many different functions. Thus, compared with the nearest animals, the higher apes, the cognitive capacities permit an infinitely greater storage of information. There is also the unique degree to which humans evolve an "inner space" in which to create representations of themselves interacting with other figures and with things in their world. Also, these creations can be close to reality in form or completely changed to fit fantasy wishes.

3 While the "I" in these imagined relationships can have a representation to express its feelings in any particular relationship, there is ordinarily a continuity of feeling that it is the individual's own self within the changed character.
4 The self, or "I," is the agent responsible for all its varied motivations. This is the sense of autonomy of the self that is a normal characteristic. Although not in awareness most of the time, its perpetual immanent presence is at once revealed when it is threatened or ignored.
5 The autonomous self is the direct successor of the organizing principle in the embryo. After birth, however, it seems to act as we might imagine the reptilian brain mediating a sense of unity, that is, with peremptory action at the behest of the innate behavioral systems, only one of which (for example, hunger, sex, or attack) can assume a dominant position at any one time.
6 Although a primitive form of organizing principle may operate at early evolutionary stages, this principle is restricted by those genes that have been active up to that period. They have initiated the development of the behavioral systems required for the adult animal, which can then survive in the environment for which they have evolved.

Social evolution

When we reach humans, there is a *radically different situation*. Humans have evolved to become *social animals* who can survive only in small groups – at the Neanderthal stage, and thereafter only in communities that rely on a high degree of control of the environment virtually to the point of creating it. Paramount in this development are the means for keeping the community organized into a functional whole; for protecting it and its resources against attack, a danger coming almost exclusively from other communities; and for creativity in adding new ways – especially technological ways – of increasing resources and then of transmitting this acquired knowledge.

To fulfill these functions as well as others that arise with new situations, evolution has created *homo sapiens*, and for present purposes we can single out only some of the characteristics that would appear to be crucial in human development: (1) the essential nature that makes a *social* being and how it is developed and maintained; (2) how instrumental resources develop; and (3) how, with the capacity to see themselves as actors within the world, that is, to experience and reflect on the existential situation, humans cope with the new situation of pondering the "meaning" of all that they are now aware of.

Lower forms of life evolve highly elaborate and effectively organized communities on the basis of simple innate patterns, with individual members carrying out prescribed functions. The whole thrust of evolution, however, has been to foster the flexibility, resilience, and persistence of human groups by maximizing the potential resources within each individual rather than to confine communities to rigid hierarchical organizations.

By *social being*, we refer to the human consciousness of being a unique person aware of one's own identity and boundaries in relation to others. We have noted how gradually and reluctantly the concept of an autonomous holistic organization has been recognized as necessary to account for the experience and behavior of the person. We also must recognize that its structuring is an ongoing process. Our experiences are encoded, ordered, and used to build up and apply knowledge, a process that seems to be required in an active intentionality of the whole. The self is more than a computer, although many of the activities of the brain make great use of computational, sorting, and organizing processes. But the outer world is a vast array of possible data from which the mind of the person selects and organizes, and our clinical and observational studies all suggest that the basis for this creative selection resides at first in the powerful innate impetus to make "personal" relationships with the mother and then others. The experience with the ordinary good mother seems to be a basic requirement for the development of the active exploratory behavior that the infant is equipped to release. Above all, human relatedness rests on each person being governed by a self that can be created only by other selves.

This development has complex roots. The genic equipment prompts the groping toward objects in the outer world, but the effective behavior then has to be learned. Therein lies one of the great breakthroughs in our understanding of the nature/nurture controversies that gave rise to deep, bitterly defended schisms in the scientific world until a few decades ago. In mammals, the fertilized egg is kept inside the female, to be followed after birth by the closeness to and gradual separation from the adult to equip the child to fit in with the environment it will inhabit. Although humans lived in the ape-man stage as a social animal with resources for communication with others, the evolution of language made them capable of a very different interrelatedness. Language made selves known to other selves. Suckling the young also introduced a new factor into development, namely, the giving and receiving of tender loving care. Prior to this, attachments were made, but the complex feeling of "love" now appeared for the first time.

It may well be thought that I am recounting what is all too familiar. It is, and yet it seems so familiar, so much taken for granted, that its significance for the evolutionary perspective on the functions of the self is often overlooked. To account for the incredible resources that humans have acquired in controlling their environment, psychoanalysts have been satisfied with extraordinarily simple ideas, such as the ego developing to satisfy the instincts by an atomistic buildup from experiences. I believe all the evidence points to what appears to be a logical necessity – namely, a much more prepared foundation within human inherited endowment. We know that humans are now born, whatever their race or culture, with the vocalizations necessary for language, and that the particular language they learn will be that of their culture, transmitted by their caretakers and then their family and peers. The experience of nurturance "completes" the self by personalizing it. The self is then permanently related to others because others have been built into it, with the intense need for changing from infantile dependence to that dependence between autonomous adults. In this later feeling is the need to belong, to which is added the role of sexuality, which itself expands to the creation of the family.

Compared to the hunter-gatherer life where work was readily recognizable, the place of "work" in our society is difficult to specify because of the change in its character and function, especially with constant technological advances. The significance that work once brought has been disturbingly exposed, as technology removes its deeply felt role. What seems to be present among the effects of unemployment is much more than the loss of wages. With no prospects of work, people feel lost in a personal way, and the rise in explosions of violence seems to express a degree of frustrated rage, as though an attack or insult was being perpetrated on adult selfhood. It is perhaps noteworthy, too, that not only is a positive need denied satisfaction, but the autonomy of the person is also undermined by enforced dependence on the community. As well as apparently satisfying a need to be involved as a contributor to the community, work gives a great deal of expression to instrumental talents and skills.

Although these points are in no way meant to be a systematically ordered listing, I believe they are sufficiently indicative of the functions that the individual self has to fulfill if humans are to survive. The functions conspicuously characteristic of humans depend heavily on language. Social animals lower in the evolutionary scale use various sounds and signs for communication in specific situations, as in warnings of danger, in mating calls, or in shared contacts of limited scope. Language, however, represents what has already been described as a quantum leap in the capacity to share. In the first place, it is not learned by an atomistic buildup from sensory elements. It is assimilated from the communication of the subjective state of the mother with that of the child. Stern (1985) quoted Vygotsky as maintaining that the essential problem of understanding language acquisition is how meanings enter the child's mind through the process of mutual negotiation. This achievement follows the capacity to have representations of things by imagining them and so to use them as symbols. Imaginative play with symbolic objects and with words when these become the symbols permits enormously increased development in knowledge of the world and in the communication of subjective states and intentions. All these make possible the degree of sharing between minds that the constant close relationships of living in communities entail. The continuity of self-feeling must be maintained if this experience is to be preserved with a cohesion of vastly enriched organization. Only a unity could act as the agent employing all this knowledge in planning action; and with its consciousness, this gestalt is the self.

Early development of the self

The first preoccupying activity of the self is learning how to relate effectively with the mother. Feeding, of course, is dominant but not exclusively so. Sucking is mediated by a mother who, with the infant, fits the joint behavior into a successful pattern. The infant must be innately equipped to incorporate from the breast and to take in from the world, with a hunger originating from both sources, needs that can be recognized and responded to by the mother. At first, the self does not need to be conscious of itself in the manner of the adult. In an environment that is actively anticipating and providing for the needs of the self, the organization of experience can proceed by a sentience that monitors and distinguishes what feels "right" or "good" from what does not meet the tensions of need and so is effectively frustrating that is, "bad" or "wrong." The growth of self-awareness, however, must begin early to develop the capacity to be alert to the attitudes of others by recognizing their emotional states.

The clinical evidence from disorders in the self strongly suggests that effective development of the self rests on a joyful, empathic responsiveness from the mother. Various limited frustrations of particular behaviors can be readily tolerated if the overall feelings communicated by the mother, and later by the father, come from a genuine joy in the baby as he or she is. Such an attitude puts no pressure on the baby's spontaneous maturational achievements to match preconceived images the parents may be using as molds into which, often unconsciously, the baby is to be fitted.

Good-enough mothering gives the first "layering" in the structuring of the self as a person. At this stage (I do not think we can be too specific in terms of age), the main achievement is a self that can feel secure and ready to explore and incorporate the world as physical and psychological capacities and talents emerge. From the start, an immense amount of experience with the social and physical worlds is rapidly acquired. A "person" seems to be being established at first without much differentiation of gender, even though babies are responded to somewhat differently according to their sex. The next main structuring is for this person to become more specifically a male or female. It would seem from disorders of the self that the relationship with the father now becomes of critical importance. The growing assertiveness of the boy must be responded to as before by the mother's joyful acceptance, but the father's acceptance now needs to be available as well for both the girl and boy infant. I have also concluded that, for the eventual integration of the self, the relationship between the parents and their joint attitudes toward the child are almost as critically important as that of each parent separately.

In the earliest months – the traditional oral stage – there seems to be no question that orality represents a more general incorporative need for which the alimentary function is the prototype. The infant needs to incorporate the mother in a personal way, that is, as having the significance of a whole object and not one confined to the feeding activity. The affective qualities of the physical and psychological incorporations, however, seem closely linked at this initial phase, if we are to explain how greed for food or drink is so often substituted later for personal deprivation. In addition there is, of course, as the physiological result of the intake, the ensuing feeling of relaxation, of general loss of tension from frustrated social needs, and eventually of being in a state of some euphoria.

The question of how much the infant self is differentiated from the mother has tended to be regarded as settled by the assumption that there is a phase of nondifferentiation. This belief has been related to the phenomena of merging and identification, and also to the amount of differentiation or perception of a separate figure that would be possible with what is known of neurophysical development. Stern (1985) strongly advocates a recognized differentiation of the infant's own boundaries as present from birth, based partly on the grounds that it is difficult to see how two separate psyches could be undifferentiated, but mainly based on the findings from the infant–mother studies. From what we have stressed about the operation of an innate organizing principle, it would entail from the start in any organism a powerful assertion and maintenance of autonomy and of the integrity of its wholeness.

It is not at all fanciful to imagine such a powerful autonomy being present, yet covered over by the closeness of the attachment of the infant to the mother. When a self is postulated as the realization, from experience in relating to the mother, of a potential in the form of an innate gestalt that has the "shape" or "feel" of a person built into it, and that is strongly motivated to encounter this shape in the outer world, then a phase of undifferentiation is neither necessary nor conceivable. Such a gestalt would be activated not by energies external to it, but by its own nature to seek completion from the appropriate sources in the environment. This assumption implies nothing different in principle from the other innate behavioral systems, for example, seeking the breast and "knowing" when it is found. There is no doubt that the ordinary mother (and, indeed, adults in general) is highly and innately motivated to respond to the infant from the earliest stages as having this "potential person" quality.

We know, too, that sucking from the breast is not the action of a passive infant being supplied with all it needs. The infant shows a pronounced dynamic of its own to regulate the feeding process to match its own feelings, to train its mother, so to speak, in what is a relationship of mutual satisfaction. When things do not go well, there is marked disturbance in the infant's whole state. It is also well recognized that although various physical factors may cause difficulties, problems also commonly arise when the mother's attitude differs from that of the ordinarily spontaneously responding mother. Serious frustrations are then felt with great intensity, as witnessed in the infant's increasingly desperate signals that things should be put right. The self-feeling in these circumstances is undoubtedly one of disturbed security, with inhibitions in the readiness to relate to the external world socially and instrumental inhibitions of various kinds. We also need to note Spitz's (1965) finding that meeting the bodily needs for food does not necessarily keep the baby alive. There is a hunger for stimulating exchanges with the caretakers that must be satisfied to foster a vital dynamic to go on living.

We cannot deal with all the specific features of the rapidly changing situation of the infant with its mother. I simply wish to indicate that autonomous reactions – either positive, in which case the dynamic of the self is encouraged, or negative, when it meets with varying degrees of deprivation, from the less intense to violent expressions of aggressive behavior – all point to effective experience and responses that constitute an independently operating infant self. The infant's recognition of the boundaries of its own body at quite an early age also suggests that this differentiated self is present then (as in Stern's striking data on Siamese twins).

Intentionality

The existence of a subjective sense of the self and its conscious intentionality is strongly suggested by the observational data on infants approaching the end of their first year. The infant also "understands" the mother's subjective state about this time (for instance, see Stern on infant and mother "pointing," and the "visual cliff" data of 1985). By the end of the second year, the subjective sense of self, and of the self as agent in creating imagined relationships to gratify fantasied relationships, is clearly established. Stern's account of the emergence of the core self, the subjective self, of each of these with "the other," and finally the verbal self and the narrative self presents a convincing picture. What I believe to be one of its most fundamental implications is the role of holistic patterns from the start. Particularly important is the discovery of the innate organization of transmodal perceptions with integrated modes of response. We cannot conceive of such integrated holistic activity without assuming an integrated whole that mediates it. Although not so confidently established, it seems to me of great importance that Stern virtually accepts Trevarthen's belief in the existence of an innate capacity for the shared awareness of human subjectivity. Moreover, I find highly plausible Trevarthen's (1980) view that this developmental leap represents the differentiation of a coherent field of intentionality.

Intentionality has recently become very much a focus of philosophical concern. Its existence is much more difficult to conceive and to establish when we do not take into account the evolutionary development of the self; and, of course, for the physically minded theorists, it is thought to be a vitalistic notion. Thus, assuming the absolute necessity of the organism to maintain interchanges with the environment – an assumption so obvious when bodily processes are considered – a necessary condition for the survival of *homo sapiens*, the social animal *par excellence*, is the constant outreach to grapple with and overcome the limitations of the environment, both social and physical. The cognitive explorations required here would alone make for a perpetual intentionality, but the innate dynamic of the person at all stages, apart from the need to relate to others, has this need to keep realizing the self through the incessant urge to know more. That was what the Romantic poets sensed in their appraisal of the pleasure from knowledge and the deep identity of truth and beauty. What evolution has created so far is this innate organization that, out of its experiences, evolves the personalization of the organizing principle in a creative interplay between the child and its family, and subsequently between individuals and their culture. The subjectivity of the person is an incredibly sensitive monitor for regulating personal well-being, a sense of being, and with the further sensing that this feeling is only "right" or "complete" when it incorporates the innate need for "being" to be always "becoming." This truth is proverbial in almost all cultures, and I shall mention only this saying in the Gaelic culture of Celtic Scotland: "Joy of seeking, joy of never finding!"

It is from the interplay of the self with its culture that Erikson's epigenetic phases evolve. Characteristically, his phases are not tied to libidinal zones, but to changes in the quality of the dominant self-feeling in its relationships with its society. The patterns of relatedness thought to be derived from the libidinal zones are there. As Stern stressed, these patterns do not constitute a succession of stages, with each replacing the predecessor. What we now see to be covered by "orality" is the behavior determined by the intense incorporative needs to secure the appropriate intake from the environment, bodily and personally, for the developments urged by the genic inheritance. The resultant oral structuring is one that maintains a permanent process in the continuing of the self-process. Our clinical work demonstrates daily the labile balance of the appropriate give and take in social relations. With the good-enough mothering experience, this balance is maintained from everyday transactions. Where this experience has been lacking, we see greed and infantile dependence reemerging as the regression to more primitive modes of "taking in" to make good the deficiency. Early stages never disappear but remain as modes of relating that can be reactivated by various environmental factors.

Intersubjective sharing, as mentioned earlier, is the means through which individuals can relate with rapid appraisals of intentions and affects in others. This sharing develops from the simultaneous acquisition of self-awareness and the knowledge of the self-states of others. In short, the person is created from interchanges with other persons. Infant development research shows the progressive gains and their extraordinary rapidity from the latter part of the first year onward. The period of the most intense socialization has been described by Bowlby (1969) and his colleagues in terms of bonding and attachment theory. The attachment phenomena are very real, but I do not think these terms are adequate for the ongoing inner processes. The period of intense closeness that lays the foundation for attachment is used by Mahler as the one for the symbiotic relationship from which individuation evolves. For myself, I find it clinically much more useful to see the closeness as necessary behavior for the gestation of the self. Far from being undifferentiated, the self is being formed steadily, and any interference with this self-determined dynamic elicits intense aggression. Not unexpectedly, the embryonic-like state of the self needs the closest contact with the mother's "self" as well as her care.

The concept of an *innate dynamic gestalt* underlying the formation of the person resembles Lichtenstein's organizing principle, which constitutes the potential self that is then personalized by the earliest relationships with the mother. Moreover, this potential being personalized by this specific experience becomes the unique identity of the person. I have suggested that this potential be conceptualized as an inherited gestalt that seeks to become a person by finding the "expected" encounters. (Such a possibility is fairly readily conceivable today with the discovery of such holistic fields of force in the organism as are revealed in holograms.) The fitting of a particular gestalt with its environment is a process going on all the time. Postulating a central agent implies a view of development proceeding from this center by differentiation, with the creation of various subsystems.

References

Alexander, F. and French, T. M. (1946). *Psychoanalytic Theory: Principles and Application*. New York: Ronald Press.

Angyal, A. (1965). *Neurosis and Treatment*. New York: Wiley.

Averill, S. (1992). Epilogue. In *The Autonomous Self: The Work of John D. Sutherland*, ed. J. S. Scharff, p. 427. Northvale, NJ: Jason Aronson.

Bales, R. F. (1950). *Interaction Process Analysis: A Method for the Study of Small Groups*. Cambridge, MA: Addison-Wesley.

Balint, M. (1952). *Primary Love and Psycho-Analytic Technique*. London: Hogarth.

—— (1957). *The Doctor, His Patient and the Illness*, 2nd ed. London: Pitman, 1964.

—— (1968). *The Basic Fault: Therapeutic Aspects of Regression*. London: Tavistock.

Balint, M. and Balint, E. (1961). *Psychotherapeutic Techniques in Medicine*. London: Tavistock.

Barrett, W. (1979). *The Illusion of Technique*. London: William Kimber.

Beckett, S. (1954). *Waiting for Godot*. New York: Grove Press.

Bell, D. (1982). *Social Sciences Since the Second World War*. New Brunswick, NJ: Transaction Books.

Berne, E. (1963). *The Structure and Dynamics of Organizations and Groups*. Philadelphia, PA: Lippincott.

Bettelheim, B. (1982). Reflections: Freud and soul. *The New Yorker*, March 1st, pp. 59–93.

Bion, W. R. (1961). *Experiences in Groups*. London: Tavistock.

Blake, W. (1965). "And did those feet in ancient times." In *The Complete Poetry and Prose of William Blake*, ed. D. V. Erdman, p. 95. Berkeley: University of California Press.

Blanck, G. and Blanck, R. (1974). *Ego Psychology*. New York: Columbia University Press.

Bowlby, J. (1960). Grief and mourning in infancy and early childhood. *Psychoanalytic Study of the Child* 15: 9–52. New York: International Universities Press.

—— (1969). *Attachment and Loss, Vol. 1*. London: Hogarth.

—— (1973). *Separation Anxiety and Anger, Vol. 2*. London: Hogarth.

Brierley, M. (1951). *Trends in Psychoanalysis*. London: Hogarth.

Bronowski, J. (1965). *The Identity of the Man*. London: Pelican.

Brown, N. O. (1959). *Life Against Death: The Psychoanalytic Meaning of History*. Middletown, CT: Wesleyan University Press.

Buckley, W. (1967). *Sociology and Modern Systems Theory*. Englewood Cliffs, NJ: Prentice Hall.

Burrow, T. (1927). The group method of analysis. *The Psychoanalytic Review* 14: 268–280.

Cantril, H. (1955). Toward a humanistic psychology. *Review of General Semantics* 12(4): 278–298.

Casement, P. (1990). *On Learning from the Patient*. New York: Routledge.

Chein, I. (1972). *The Science of Behaviour and the Image of Man*. New York: Basic Books.

Colby, K. M. (1955). *Energy and Structure in Psychoanalysis*. New York: Ronald Press.

Coleridge, S. T. (1991). *Poems*, ed. J. Beer. New York: Alfred A. Knopf.

Darwin, C. (1859). *On the Origin of Species by Natural Selection*. London: John Murray.

Drever, J. (1917). *Instinct in Man*. London: Methuen.

Emery, F. E. (1967). The next thirty years: concepts, methods, and anticipation. *Human Relations* 20: 199–237.

Emery, F. E. and Trist, E. L. (1965). The causal texture of organizational environments. *Human Relations* 18: 21–32.

—— (1973). *Towards a Social Ecology: Contextual Appreciation of the Future in the Present*. New York: Plenum Press.

Erikson, E. H. (1950). *Childhood and Society*. New York: W. W. Norton & Co.

—— (1959). *Identity and the Lifecycle. Psychological Issues* 1(1): 1–171. New York: International Universities Press.

Eskelinen de Folch, T. (1988). Obstacles to analytic cure. In *On Freud's "Analysis Terminable and Interminable,"* ed. J. Sandler, pp. 93–105. New Haven, CT: Yale University Press.

Ezriel, H. (1950). A psycho-analytic approach to group treatment. *British Journal of Medical Psychology* 23: 59–74.

—— (1951). The psycho-analytic session as an experimental situation. *British Journal of Medical Psychology* 24: 30–34.

Fairbairn, W. R. D. (1944). Endopsychic structure considered in terms of object relationship. In *An Object Relations Theory of the Personality*, pp. 82–132. New York: Basic Books, 1954.

—— (1952a). *Psychoanalytic Studies of the Personality* 59–81. London: Routledge.

—— (1952b). Theoretical and experimental aspects of psycho-analysis. *British Journal of Medical Psychology* 25: 122–127.

—— (1954a). Observations on the nature of hysterical states. *British Journal of Medical Psychology* 27: 105–125.

—— (1954b). *An Object Relations Theory of the Personality*. New York: Basic Books.

—— (1963). Synopsis of an object-relations theory of the personality. *International Journal of Psycho-Analysis* 20: 275–286.

Ferenczi, S. (1955). Confusion of tongues between the adult and the child. In *Final Contributions to the Problems and the Methods of Psychoanalysis*, pp. 156–167. London: Hogarth.

Foulkes, S. H. (1964). *Therapeutic Group Analysis*. London: Allen and Unwin.

Freud, A. (1946). *The Ego and the Mechanisms of Defense*. New York: International Universities Press.

Freud, S. (1905). Three essays on the theory of sexuality. *Standard Edition* 7: 125.

—— (1921). Group psychology and the analysis of the ego. *Standard Edition* 18: 69–143.

—— (1923). The ego and the id. *Standard Edition* 19: 12–66.

—— (1926). Inhibitions, symptoms, and anxiety. *Standard Edition* 20: 87–172.

—— (1927). The future of an illusion. *Standard Edition* 21: 3–56.

—— (1930). Civilization and its discontents. *Standard Edition* 21: 64–145.

—— (1937). Analysis terminable and interminable. *Standard Edition* 23: 216–253.

—— (1937). An outline of psychoanalysis. *Standard Edition* 23: 139–207.

—— (1950). Project for a scientific psychology. *Standard Edition* 1: 295–343.

Gaddis, T. (1955). *Birdman of Alcatraz: The Story of Robert Stroud*. New York: Random House.

Green, A. (1987). Instincts in the late works of Freud. In *On Freud's 'Analysis Terminable on Interminable'*, ed. J. Sandler, pp. 149–170. International Psychoanalytical Association Educational Monographs, No. 1.

Greenberg, J. R. and Mitchell, S. A. (1983). *Object Relations in Psychoanalytic Theory*. Cambridge, MA: Harvard University Press.

Grinberg, L. (1962). On specific aspects of countertransference due to the patient's projective identification. *International Journal of Psycho-Analysis* 43: 436–440.

Guntrip, H. (1961). *Personality Structure and Human Interaction*. New York: International Universities Press.

—— (1969). *Schizoid Phenomena, Object Relations and the Self*. London: Hogarth.

—— (1975). My experience of analysis with Fairbairn and Winnicott. *International Review of Psycho-Analysis* 2: 145–156.

—— (1978). Psycho-analysis and some scientific and philosophical critics. *British Journal of Medical Psychology* 51: 207–224.

Harrow, A., Leishman, M., Macdonald, M., and Scott, D. (1994). Introduction. In *The Autonomous Self: The Work of John D. Sutherland*, ed. J. S. Scharff, pp. xv–xxv. Northvale, NJ: Jason Aronson.

Hartmann, H. (1958). *Ego Psychology and the Problem of Adaptation*. Original 1939, trans. D. Rapaport, 1958. New York: International Universities Press.

Hartmann, H., Kris, E. and Loewenstein, R. M. (1946). Comments on the formation of psychic structure. *The Psychoanalytic Study of the Child* 2: 11–38.

Heisenberg, W. (1930). *Physical Principles of the Quantum Theory*, trans. C. Eckart and F. C. Hoyt. Chicago, IL: University of Chicago Press.

Hinde, R. A. (1982). *Ethology: Its Nature and Relations with Other Science*. Oxford: Oxford University Press.

Hopkins, G. M. (1918). "The child is father to the man." *Poems of Gerard Manley Hopkins*, ed. R. Bridges, poem 68. London: Humphrey Melford.

Huxley, J. (1953). *Evolution in Action*. New York: Harper and Brothers.

Isaacs, S. (1948). The nature and function of phantasy. In *Developments in Psycho-Analysis*, ed. M. Klein, P. Heimann, S. Isaacs, and J. Riviere, pp. 67–121. London: Hogarth.

Jacobson, E. (1964). *The Self and the Object World*. New York: International Universities Press.

Jantsch, E. (1976). Introduction and summary. In *Evolution and Consciousness*, ed. C. H. Waddington and E. Jantsch, pp. 1–8. Reading, MA: Addison-Wesley.

—— (1980). *The Self-Organizing Universe: Scientific and Human Implications of the Emerging Paradigm of Evolution*. New York: Pergamon.

Jaques, E. (1955). Social systems as a defense against persecutory and depressive anxiety. In *New Directions in Psycho-Analysis*, ed. M. Klein, P. Heimann, and R. Money-Kyrle, pp. 478–498. London: Tavistock.

Jones, E. (1952). Preface. *Psychoanalytic Studies of the Personality*, p. v. London: Tavistock.

Keats, J. (1919). "Ode on a Grecian Urn." *Oxford Book of English Verse*, poem 625. Oxford: Clarendon.

Kernberg, O. (1976). *Object Relations Theory and Clinical Psychoanalysis*. New York: Jason Aronson.

—— (1980). *Internal Worlds and External Reality*. New York: Jason Aronson.

Khan, M. (1964). Ego distortion, cumulative trauma, and the role of reconstruction in the analytic situation. *International Journal of Psycho-Analysis* 45: 272–279.

—— (1974). *The Privacy of the Self*. London: Hogarth.

—— (1983). *Hidden Selves: Between Theory and Practice in Psychoanalysis*. New York: International Universities Press.

Kirkwood, C. (2005). Developing the Inheritance. Edinburgh Conversations, The Sutherland Trust, Edinburgh, Scotland, May 20.

Klein, G. S. (1976). *Psychoanalytic Theory: An Exploration of Essentials*. New York: International Universities Press.

Klein, M. (1932). *The Psycho-Analysis of Children*, trans. A. Strachey. London: Hogarth.

—— (1935). A contribution to the psychogenesis of manic-depressive states. In *Love, Guilt and Reparation and Other Works: 1921–1945*, pp. 262–289. London: Hogarth, 1975.

—— (1946). Notes on some schizoid mechanisms. In *Envy and Gratitude and Other Works: 1946–1963*, pp. 1–24. London: Hogarth, 1975.

Kohon, G. (1996). Review of *The Autonomous Self: The Work of John D. Sutherland*, ed. J. S. Scharff. *Journal of the American Psychoanalytic Association* 44(4): 1261–1262.

Kohut, H. (1971). *The Analysis of the Self. Psychoanalytic Study of the Child, Monograph 4*. New York: International Universities Press.

—— (1977). *The Restoration of the Self*. New York: International Universities Press.

—— (1979). The two analyses of Mr. Z. *International Journal of Psycho-Analysis* 60: 3–27.

Kuhn, T. (1962). *The Structure of Scientific Revolution*, 2nd ed. Chicago, IL: University of Chicago Press.

Laing, R. D. (1960). *The Divided Self*. London: Tavistock.

Langbaum, R. W. (1977). *The Mysteries of Identity: A Theme in Modern Literature*. London: Oxford University Press.

Langer, S. K. (1967). *Mind: An Essay on Human Feeling, Vol. 1*. Baltimore, MD: Johns Hopkins Press.

Levin, D. C. (1969). The self: a contribution to its place in theory and technique. *International Journal of Psycho-Analysis* 50: 41–51.

Lewin, K. (1940). *Field Theory in Social Science: Selected Theoretical Papers*, ed. D. Cartwright. New York: Harper & Row.

—— (1951). Formalization and progress in psychology. In *Field Theory in Social Science: Selected Theoretical Papers*, ed. D. Cartwright. New York: Harper & Row.

Lichtenstein, H. (1961). Identity and sexuality, a study of their interrelationship in man. *Journal of the American Psychoanalytic Association* 9: 179–260.

—— (1965). Towards a metapsychological definition of the self. *International Journal of Psycho-Analysis* 46: 117–128.

—— (1977). *The Dilemma of Human Identity*. New York: Jason Aronson.

Ludlam, M. (2005). Developing the Inheritance. Edinburgh Conversations, The Sutherland Trust, Edinburgh, Scotland, May 20.

McDougall, W. (1920). *The Group Mind*. New York: Putnam.

MacMurray, J. (1961). *Persons in Relation*. London: Faber.

Mahler, M., Pine, F., and Bergman, A. (1975). *The Psychological Birth of the Human Infant*. New York: Basic Books.

Malinowski, B. (1927). *Sex and Repression in Savage Society*. London and New York: International Library of Psychology, Philosophy and Scientific Method.

—— (1929). *The Sexual Life of Savages in North Western Melanesia*. New York: Harcourt, Brace, and World.

Marcuse, H. (1955). *Eros and Civilization: A Philosophical Inquiry into Freud*. Boston, MA: Beacon.

Marx, K. (1988). Alienated labor. In *Economic and Philosophical Manuscripts of 1844*. New York: Prometheus.

Mead, G. H. (1952). *Mind, Self and Society from the Standpoint of a Social Behaviorist*, intro. and ed. C. W. Morris. Chicago, IL: University of Chicago Press.

Menninger, K. (1958). *Theory of Psycho-analytic Technique*. London: Imago.

Menzies, I. E. P. (1960). A case-study in the functioning of social systems as a defense against anxiety. *Human Relations* 13: 95–122.

Middlemore, M. P. (1941). *The Nursing Couple*. London: Hamish Hamilton.

Mischel, T. (ed.) (1977). *The Self*. Oxford: Blackwell.

Modell, A. (1968). *Object Love and Reality*. New York: International Universities Press.

Monod, J. (1971). *Chance and Necessity: An Essay on the Natural Philosophy of Modern Biology*, trans. Austryn Wainhouse. New York: Alfred A. Knopf.

Moreno, J. L. (1956). *Sociometry and the Science of Man*. New York: Beacon House.

Morse, S. (1972). Structure and reconstruction. *International Journal of Psycho-Analysis* 53: 487–500.

Negroponte, N. (1995). *Being Digital*. New York: Random House.

Office of Health Economics (1972). *Medicine and Society*. Report No. 43. London.

Padel, J. (1995). Review of *The Autonomous Self: The Work of John D. Sutherland*, ed. J. S. Scharff. *International Journal of Psycho-Analysis* 76: 177–179.

Parsons, T. and Bales, F. (1955). *Family Socialization and Interaction Process*. Glencoe, IL: Free Press.

Peterfreund, E. (1971). *Information, Systems and Psychoanalysis. Psychological Issues, Monograph 255/26*. New York: International Universities Press.

Pincus, L. (ed.) (1960). *Marriage: Studies in Emotional Conflict and Growth*. London: Methuen.

Popper, K. (1935). *Logik der Forschung*. Verlag von Julius Springer. English translation: *The Logic of Scientific Discovery*. London: Hutchinson, 1959.

Prigogine, I. (1976). Order through fluctuation: self-organization and social system. In *Evolution and Consciousness: Human Systems in Transition*, ed. C. H. Waddington and E. Jantsch, pp. 93–126. Reading, MA: Addison-Wesley.

Pruyser, P. W. (1974). *Between Belief and Unbelief*. New York: Harper & Row.

Racker, H. (1957). The meanings and uses of countertransference. *Psychoanalytic Quarterly* 26: 303–357.

Rapaport, D. (1951). The conceptual model of psychoanalysis. In *Psycho-Analytic Psychiatry and Psychology*, ed. R. P. Knight and C. R. Friedman, pp. 221–247. New York: International Universities Press.

—— (1960). The structure of psycho-analytical theory. *Psychological Issues* 2(2): 7–158. Monograph 6. New York: International Universities Press.

Reich, W. (1949). *Character Analysis*. New York: Orgone Institute Press.

Rice, A. K. (1965). *Learning for Leadership*. London: Tavistock.

Rickman, J. (1957). *Selected Contributions to Psycho-Analysis*. London: Hogarth.

Rizzuto, A. M. (1979). *The Birth of the Living God*. Chicago, IL: University of Chicago Press.

Rosenblatt, A. D. and Thickstun, J. T. (1977). *Modern Psychoanalytic Concepts in General Psychology. Psychological Issues, Monograph 42/43*. New York: International Universities Press.

Sandler, J. and Joffe, W. G. (1962). The concept of the representational world. *Psychoanalytic Study of the Child* 17: 128–145.

—— (1969). Towards a basic psychoanalytic model. *International Journal of Psycho-Analysis* 50: 79–90.

Sandler, J. and Sandler, A.-M. (1984). The past unconscious, the present unconscious, and interpretation of the transference. *Psychoanalytic Inquiry* 4: 367–399.

Saperstein, J. L. and Gaines, J. (1973). Metapsychological considerations of the self. *International Journal of Psycho-Analysis* 54: 415–424.

Sartre, J.-P. (1943). *Being and Nothingness*. English translation, 1956. New York: Washington Square Press, 1992.

Savege, J. (1973). Psychodynamic understanding in community psychiatry. *Psychotherapy and Psychosomatics* 25: 272–278.

Schafer, R. A. (1968). *Aspects of Internalization*. New York: International Universities Press.

—— (1976). *A New Language for Psychoanalysis*. New Haven, CT: Yale University Press.

Scharff, J. S. (ed.) (1994). *The Autonomous Self: The Work of John D. Sutherland*. Northvale, NJ: Jason Aronson.

— (2005). The legacy of John D. Sutherland. In *The Legacy of Fairbairn and Sutherland*, ed. J. S. Scharff and D. E. Scharff, pp. 202–211. London: Routledge.

Scharff, J. S. and Scharff, D. (1998). *Object Relations Individual Therapy*. Northvale, NJ: Jason Aronson.

Schore, A. (1994). *Affect Regulation and the Origin of the Self: The Neurobiology of Emotional Development*. Hillsdale, NJ: Lawrence Erlbaum.

Skinner, B. F. (1954). A critique of psychoanalytic concepts and theories. *Scientific Monthly* 79: 300–305.
Sofer, C. (1961). *The Organization from Within*. London: Tavistock.
Spiegel, L. A. (1959). The self, the sense of self and perception. *Psychoanalytic Study of the Child* 14: 81–109.
Spitz, R. A. (1945). Hospitalism. *The Psychoanalytic Study of the Child* 1: 53–74.
—— (1965). *The First Year of Life*. New York: International Universities Press.
Stern, D. N. (1985). T*he Interpersonal World of the Infant*. New York: Basic Books.
Sullivan, H. S. (1953). *The Interpersonal Theory of Psychiatry*. New York: W. W. Norton & Co.
Sutherland, J. D. (1963). Object relations theory and the conceptual model of psychoanalysis. *British Journal of Medical Psychology* 36: 109–124.
—— (1966). The psychotherapeutic clinic and community psychiatry. *Bulletin of the Menninger Clinic* 30: 338–350.
—— (1968). The consultant psychotherapist in the National Health Service: his role and training. *British Journal of Psychiatry* 114: 509–515.
—— (1979). The psychodynamic image of man. In *The Autonomous Self: The Work of John D. Sutherland*, ed. J. S. Scharff, pp. 268–282. Northvale, NJ: Jason Aronson, 1994.
—— (1980a). The autonomous self. In *The Autonomous Self: The Work of John D. Sutherland*, ed. J. S. Scharff, pp. 303–330. Northvale, NJ: Jason Aronson, 1994. Based on an unpublished paper, "Hate and the autonomy of the self." Also published as: The autonomous self. *Bulletin of the Menninger Clinic* 57(1): 3–32 (1993).
—— (1980b). *The British Object Relations Theorists*. In *The Autonomous Self: The Work of John D. Sutherland*, ed. J. S. Scharff, pp. 25–44. Northvale, NJ: Jason Aronson, 1994.
—— (1989). *Fairbairn's Journey to the Interior*. London: Free Association Books.
—— (1994a). An object relations view of the great man. In *The Autonomous Self: The Work of John D. Sutherland*, ed. J. S. Scharff, pp. 350–371. Northvale, NJ: Jason Aronson.
—— (1994b). On being and becoming a person. Lecture at the Washington School of Psychiatry, 1993. In *The Autonomous Self: The Work of John D. Sutherland*, ed. J. S. Scharff, pp. 372–391. Northvale, NJ: Jason Aronson.
—— (1994c). Reminiscences. In *The Autonomous Self: The Work of John D. Sutherland*, ed. J. S. Scharff, pp. 392–423. Northvale, NJ: Jason Aronson.
Sutherland, J. D. and Gill, H. S. (1970). *Language and Psychodynamic Appraisal*. London: Karnac; Edinburgh: Scottish Institute of Human Relations.
Szasz, T. (1961). *The Myth of Mental Illness*. London: Secker & Warburg, 1962.
Toffler, A. (1970). *Future Shock*. New York: Random House.
Trevarthen, C. (1980). The foundations of inter-subjectivity: development of interpersonal and co-operative understanding in infants. In *The Social Foundations of Language and Thought: Essays in Honor of J. S. Bruner*, ed. D. Olson. New York: W. W. Norton.
—— (2005). Developing the Inheritance. Edinburgh Conversations, The Sutherland Trust, Edinburgh, Scotland, May 20.
Trilling, L. (1955). *Freud and the Crisis of our Culture*. Boston, MA: Beacon.
—— (1971). *Sincerity and Authenticity*. Cambridge, MA: Harvard University Press.

Trist, E. L. (1963). *Organizational Choice*. London: Tavistock.

—— (1968). The relation of welfare and development in the transition to post-industrialism. Los Angeles: Sociotechnical Systems Division, Western Management Science Institute, University of California.

Trist, E. L. and Banforth, K. W. (1951). Some social and psychological consequences of the long wall method of coal-getting. *Human Relations* 4: 3–38.

Turquet, P. (1975). Threats to identity in the large group. In *The Large Group: Dynamics and Therapy*, ed. L. Kreeger, pp. 87–144. London: Constable.

Tustin, F. (1972). *Autism and Childhood Psychosis*. London: Hogarth.

Uexküll, T. von (1986). Medicine and semiotics. *Semiotica* 61: 201–217.

Vitz, P. O. (1977). *Psychology as Religion: The Cult of Self Worship*. Grand Rapids, MI: Eerdmans.

Waddington, C. H. and Jantsch, E. (1976). *Evolution and Consciousness: Human Systems in Tranistion*. Reading, MA: Addison-Wesley.

Waelder, R. (1960). *Basic Theory of Psychoanalysis*. New York: International Universities Press.

Wallerstein, R. S. (1968). The challenge of the community mental health movement to psychoanalysis. *American Journal of Psychiatry* 124: 1049–1056.

—— (1969). Psychoanalysis and psychotherapy. *International Journal of Psycho-Analysis* 50: 117–126.

—— (1975). *Psychotherapy and Psychoanalysis: Theory Practice Research*. New York: International Universities Press.

—— (1988). One psychoanalysis or many? *International Journal of Psycho-Analysis* 69: 5–21.

Weisman, A. D. (1965). *The Existential Core of Psychoanalysis: Reality Sense and Responsibility*. Boston, MA: Little, Brown.

Winnicott, D. W. (1953). Transitional objects and transitional phenomena: a study of the first not-me possession. *International Journal of Psycho-Analysis* 34: 89–97.

—— (1958a). The capacity to be alone. In *The Maturational Processes and the Facilitating Environment: Studies in the Theory of Emotional Development*, pp. 140–152. New York: International Universities Press, 1965.

—— (1958b). *Collected Papers*. New York: Basic Books.

—— (1960). Ego distortion in terms of true and false self. In *The Maturational Processes and the Facilitating Environment: Studies in the Theory of Emotional Development*, pp. 37–55. New York: International Universities Press, 1965.

—— (1963). From dependence towards independence. In *Maturational Processes and the Facilitating Environment: Studies in the Theory of Emotional Development*, pp. 83–92. New York: International Universities Press.

—— (1965). *The Maturational Processes and the Facilitating Environment: Studies in the Theory of Emotional Development*. New York: International Universities Press.

—— (1971). *Playing and Reality*. London: Tavistock.

Winnicott, D. W. and Khan, M. J. (1953). Review of *Psychoanalytic Studies of the Personality*, by W. R. D. Fairbairn. *International Journal of Psycho-Analysis* 34: 329–333.

Wolff, H. G. (1960). Stressors as a cause of disease in man. In *Stress and Psychiatric Disorder: The Proceedings of the Second Oxford Conference of the Mental Health Research Fund*, ed. J. M. Tanner, pp. 17–33. Oxford: Blackwell, 1985.

Wordsworth, W. (1888). *The Complete Poetical Works of William Wordsworth.* London: Macmillan.

Yankelovich, D. and Barrett, W. (1970). *Ego and Instinct*. New York: Random House.

Yeats, W. B. (1950). "The second coming." *The Collected Poems of W. B. Yeats*, p. 158. Ware, Hertfordshire: Wordsworth Editions Ltd, 1994.

Zilboorg, G. (1941). *A History of Medical Psychology*. New York: W. W. Norton.

Index